# THE
# BARRY BROGAN
# STORY

# THE BARRY BROGAN STORY *in his own words*

Arthur Barker Limited   London
A subsidiary of Weidenfeld (Publishers) Limited

Copyright © Barry Brogan 1981

Published in Great Britain by
Arthur Barker Limited
91 Clapham High Street
London SW4 7TA

All rights reserved. No part of this publication may be
reproduced, stored in a retrieval system, or
transmitted, in any form or by any means, electronic,
mechanical, photocopying, recording or otherwise,
without the prior permission of the copyright owner.

ISBN 0 213 16745 X

Printed in Great Britain by
Butler & Tanner Ltd
Frome and London

# Contents

Introduction    *vii*

1. A Stolen Fiver Starts a Feud    *1*
2. Booze, Birds and Bedlam    *16*
3. A Riotous Start in England    *24*
4. The Soho Zulu    *33*
5. The First Big Bribe    *48*
6. Getting Rich Quick    *61*
7. Hitting the Bottle    *72*
8. The Wrath of Walwyn    *82*
9. Betting to Lose    *91*
10. Northern Jockeys in a Fix    *104*
11. Dr Hines and a Bitter Pill    *112*
12. Marriage is a Disaster    *125*
13. Cold Turkey    *133*
14. Crash Landing    *143*
15. A Tank with Banks    *156*
16. Going for the Wages    *168*
17. Bogus Bank Accounts    *177*
18. A Betting-Office Lunatic    *185*
19. Working with Pigs    *191*
20. Behind Bars    *199*

Barry Brogan: A Statistical Breakdown    *207*

# Introduction

THE FUGITIVE HAS STOPPED RUNNING. THE GRADUATE HAS GROWN up. At last all my wild and wasteful habits are becoming a blur in the past. A deep spiritual faith has taken over, a real desire to tell the truth, and an impelling urge to pay off my debts. Perhaps when I've achieved all these ambitions people will understand, for the first time, all the terrible agonies I've suffered over the past fifteen years.

I want to open up and let everyone judge why, where and how I went wrong. I want to talk of my enormous drinking and gambling problems, how they welded together and destroyed my riding career, wrecked my reputation, killed my spirit and brought shame on one of the best-known families in the United Kingdom.

Over the years umpteen kind and generous people have tried to prop me up, but I was so chronically sick in mind, body and soul I let them down. To be mesmerized by drink and gambling every minute of every day is like struggling through life on a ball and chain. In one ludicrous spell I turned over £250,000 while gambling. In twenty years, from 1957 to 1977, I lost the massive sum of £600,000. On holiday in Greece I consumed £700 of alcohol in a fortnight. On another occasion I collapsed in a drunken coma and was only found hours later by friends on a chance visit.

If I'd broken a leg I could have called in a doctor. But I had a disease called alcoholism and there was no one to understand my predicament. I was an outcast, lonely and confused.

Compulsive gambling is very much the same. I now live hour by hour, day by day, all the time resisting the tiniest temptation that might lure me back into the human jungle of waste and profligation. It's a constant fight, and there is no relief, like riding in the Grand National with enormous obstacles to leap every day of the week. Drink and gambling are a two-stone penalty and I shall be carrying them both for the rest of my life.

With the fellowship of Gamblers Anonymous and Alcoholics

Anonymous I'm determined to remain as I am: sober, rational and honest. There will be no sliding back. If I do it will be the end – literally. Now, when I'm sober, I can think clearly. I can get to grips with my conscience. At my worst, I was cunning and unreliable. Life-long friends cut me off overnight.

Deep inside, I was hurt. I want to straighten myself out. I was desperate to live a normal life with normal friends and normal social habits. But I kept going wrong, and this is the story of how it all came about.

J.B.B.

# 1
# A Stolen Fiver Starts a Feud

I REMEMBER I WAS JUST TEN WHEN I PROMISED MY MOTHER I'D NEVER smoke, never drink, never gamble and never mess about with women. Today I'm thirty-three, and in Gamblers Anonymous, Alcoholics Anonymous, divorced, and smoking like a trooper.

I made that promise to my mother at our family home in Gilliamstown Cottage, Rathfeigh, in Co. Meath, in 1957. My father, Jimmy, was farming its magnificent two hundred acres, but he dropped dead with a heart attack in February 1965, and my mother's been in charge ever since.

Before his death, my father rode and trained scores of winners on the flat and over jumps, and his early death at forty-four left a huge gap in my life which I've never been able to fill.

Born in Holler Street Hospital, Dublin, on 18 April 1947, I was the eldest of four children, followed by Ann, and Peter and Pamela, the twins.

Ann later rode several winners under rules as an amateur, and Peter rode as a professional in England and Ireland before retiring into market gardening with a thriving business in Dublin. Pamela also stayed close to animals and enjoys her job as a veterinary nurse while still living at home with my mother.

As children, we all loved horses, and I organized races on the lawn. I would type out tiny racecards, copying the names of horses from newspapers and form-books, and each of us would select one to race under.

I also worked out handicaps, always giving the girls a few yards start, but usually making sure I could beat them to the line! I was eight at the time, but already fascinated by the romantic world of horses and riding, and winning and losing.

I started to ride when I was ten. The late Captain Cyril B. Harty, father of Eddie and John, gave us a pony called Perkin and we all learned to ride on him. Later on, Captain Harty gave us a grey mare called Rossa. She won many top prizes at the

Royal Dublin Show, but I found her a handful and was scared of her.

On one occasion she refused with me in the schooling paddocks at the Royal Dublin and I was so frightened of her I jumped off and told my mother to find another rider. I was too young to die.

For six months after that incident I completely lost interest in ponies. Then my father rekindled the spark when he bought me a lovely chestnut called Trigger. He stood only 14.2 hands, but he was the pony that launched me and I owe everything to him. I rode him at shows and gymkhanas, and this led on to my riding in races.

Trigger was a tremendous hunter and I rode him when I was twelve with the Meath Foxhounds, the Tara Harriers and the Littlegrange Harriers, run by the effervescent and controversial Barbara Jennings.

Trigger gave me enormous confidence and we competed in all the top hunter trials, including the biggest at Castletown and Fairyhouse, and I ran out of room to hang my rosettes.

School life began in an infants' class in Skryne when I was five, and I stayed there fumbling with blocks and clay until I was seven. I liked school. I was always good at arithmetic – which later helped me with my gambling – and geography. I was absolutely useless at Gaelic.

From Skryne, I moved on to the Christian Brothers' Roman Catholic School in Drogheda, about ten miles from our home in Gilliamstown. I remained there five years, until my parents sent me to Mungret College, run by the Jesuits. Vincent O'Brien, the trainer, was one of its many notable Old Boys.

While at the Christian Brothers I ran up against a bully whom I used to buy off with cigarettes. He forced me to pinch them from my parents, and if I didn't produce them he would beat me up. So I took the easy way out and stole them. I used to worry terribly about taking the cigarettes. I didn't want to be caught, and I didn't want my parents to think I was smoking them.

Not that it was likely at that time: when I was twelve Anne and I took some cigarettes into the hen-house and tried to smoke them, almost coughing our lungs up!

To enter college I had to sit three entrance exams – Irish, English and mathematics. I achieved the full hundred marks in mathematics, ninety out of a hundred in English, and four out of a hundred in Irish! And I received those four for merely writing my name on the paper – Fionbarr O'Brogain. I never could grasp Irish.

Despite being unable to speak my native language I was accepted at Mungret College and left home to board there when I was thirteen.

We were a God-loving, religious family; I went to mass every Sunday and we said the rosary as a family once every week. Once a year, too, the parish priest would call at the house, say mass, and walk round the stable and bless the horses.

Because of my age, I went straight into the second-year class at Mungret. I hated leaving home and, at first, found it difficult to mix with the lads. They tended to take the mick out of me. I didn't know the facts of life. On my first night a boy called Finton Murphy came up and asked me whether I liked to masturbate, and I had no idea what he was talking about.

Sport soon became my strong point at college. I learnt to play rugby and was picked for the under-fourteens, -fifteens and -sixteens. I started in the second row, but I was so fast the masters switched me to blind-side forward and then open-side forward. I loved to nail the outside-half and through playing such a tough, physical game, I gradually felt my personality developing. In fact, my first school report said: 'This is an egotistical young man.' Well, at least I was finding my feet!

I also did well at athletics, starting off at the hundred yards and winning several cups and medals before acquiring enough stamina to run over 880 yards and eventually the mile.

My best friends at college were Bobby Barry and Tommy Stack. Bobby now breeds, buys and sells young horses in Bruff in Co. Limerick, and married Lady Sarah Stanhope, a former girlfriend of mine.

Tommy had special talents as a rugby player and was a splendid runner over a mile. I lined up against him once and gave myself no chance, but entering the last lap I was close on his heels, and finally raced past him and beat him to the tape. I considered that a special achievement. I was just fifteen and it was my first attempt at the mile.

I never worked hard at college and regret this immensely. I was more concerned with the racing pages and sport in general. I lived for the racing pages, and occasionally found ways of placing a half-crown each-way accumulator at Malachy Skelly's betting-office when allowed to enter Limerick city on our free day from school.

I also had an uncontrollable sweet tooth, and if I won any money from betting I would spend it on cream cakes and Sidona, my favourite non-alcoholic drink.

On one of my holidays at home, in December 1962, I remember a terrible incident cropping up. I arrived back from college without a penny to buy presents for Peter, Ann and Pamela. I felt rotten about it, and the action I took to put it right probably had a greater bearing on my adult life than anything else I can bring to mind.

I knew that my father prepared the staff wages every Friday morning. He would cash a cheque at McNamara's grocery shop in Drogheda and leave the money in the top left-hand drawer of his desk in the office. I knew the routine off by heart. So I plotted a way to steal the money to buy the presents.

There was a big tip going around for a horse called Flying Wild, running at Navan next day, 15 December, and my hero Tommy Carberry was riding it.

Making sure no one was in sight, I crept into my father's office and took £5 from the wages. I still don't know what came over me, but I was confident the horse would win and that I would make enough money to buy the presents; I would be able to put the fiver back and no one would know what had happened.

There were twelve runners, and Flying Wild started 2–1 favourite – and finished last! My so-called brainwave had backfired and I had nowhere to turn. Being just fifteen years old, and the son of Jimmy Brogan, there was no way I could borrow a fiver.

My father always paid the wages on Saturday night when he returned from the races, so when we came back from Navan he made a final check of the money and immediately found the fiver was missing. So a massive stewards' inquiry was launched and he went back to McNamara's, who were adamant that they hadn't made a mistake when cashing the cheque.

My mother became terribly agitated and made us all line up in the kitchen, grilling us one by one. Although it was playing on my conscience I strenuously denied taking the money.

But my mother couldn't be fooled easily. She was convinced I was the culprit and pestered me for up to three years about it. In the end I couldn't tolerate her harassing any longer, confessed to the theft and gladly handed back the £5. By this time my father had died and mother and I were drifting further and further apart.

I was ashamed of what I did and, as I've said, whenever I recall the incident am inclined to think that this was the wretched start of all the horrendous problems that were to engulf me over the next seventeen years. I had started on the road of telling lies and had virtually got away with it.

After I'd spent three mediocre years in college, and had reached sixteen, my parents thankfully accepted that I was in love with horses and allowed me to leave, and I started slogging fourteen hours a day in the yard. Up to that time there had been no cigarettes, no drinks and only Mickey Mouse girlfriends.

My father was already making a tremendous impression on me. I admired all his riding skills and the way he worked non-stop to build up the yard and attract new owners. He was always cool and level-headed, and rarely got stirred up. He was the same when riding on the track. Placid and fair, he had above-average talent, both as a flat and steeplechase jockey and later on as a trainer, with enormous patience and tact.

He enjoyed a great deal of success, but could never really decide whether training Gold Legend to win the 1958 Irish Grand National or Hopeful Colleen to win the Galway Plate gave him most satisfaction.

I studied him closely, particularly his placid temperament, and even then, in my teens, I wished I could grow up like him and be respected and admired by so many important people.

As things turned out, many good judges have told me that I inherited a lot of my father's riding skills, particularly his knack with young horses and awkward jumpers. Alas, I never matched his self-discipline, rational living and immaculate sobriety.

If he had a fault it was his mania for cigarettes. In later years he became hooked on the weed and smoked up to sixty a day – still I can't criticize him for that because I'm now doing exactly the same!

Yet he didn't drink. At least, not in excess. A glass of wine with his meal once or twice a week was his absolute limit.

It was during my second year at college that my father gave me my first ride on a racecourse. He put me up on a four-year-old called Felspar in a flat race for amateur riders at Leopardstown. My weight was as low as 8 st 10 lbs, but I finished unplaced.

My father must have spotted a spark of something in me, for he bravely persevered and I eventually rode my first winner on 18 May 1963 in a 'bumpers' race at Mullingar on a horse called High Priest – how about that for irony?

Obviously I felt ten feet tall, but inwardly I still had a ferocious urge to ride over hurdles, and my first opportunity came in a handicap race at Baldoyle on the super-safe Roman Folly.

He was a brilliant jumper, both over hurdles and fences, and I was always grateful to my father for the way he groomed me so meticulously for my debut. He was very sensible. He didn't put me on a novice but selected an experienced campaigner, and he knew the owner didn't care whether it won or lost.

Sadly for us all, it turned out a disaster. Going to the first hurdle I made a mess of everything and crashed to the ground. To this day I have no idea what precisely happened. All I can remember is hitting the floor on the take-off side rather than the landing side. The horse definitely didn't fall. I was entirely to blame.

A group of ambulance people came along and pulled me up and took me back to the weighing-room. I felt embarrassed and humiliated. Worse still, I felt I had humiliated my father.

For several days up to the time of the race the press had built me up as the eldest son of Jimmy Brogan having his first ride over hurdles in public. I was sure my father would blow a fuse and tear into me. Yet all he said was: 'Well, we'll have to get back to the schooling-ground, won't we?'

The relief gushed through my body. My father knew I needed to be encouraged, not slated, and this was his way of helping me. I understood and appreciated his common sense.

After much hard work at home, my first winner over hurdles was on Ballygowan at Leopardstown on 1 February 1964, and I later trained the horse to run in the 1965 Grand National at Aintree.

He was a problem horse. A nutcase. He'd run through wings of hurdles and bolt off the gallops and into the woods. Stable jockey Frankie Carroll tried to ride him, but he was dead scared of the horse.

I regarded it as a challenge to straighten him out, and in time I taught him to settle and showed him who was boss. My father was pleased with the work I did on Ballygowan and allowed me to ride him in a handicap hurdle at Powerstown Park. We finished third.

A week later my father saddled him at Mullingar, and we finished third again. Then he tried him in a chase at Navan, but we fell at the fourth. Yet every time I sat on him I was getting to know his quirks a little better, and I realized it was only a matter of weeks before we pulled off the win I wanted so much.

A few days after the Navan spill my father put me up on a frisky filly called Fur Coat in a hurdle race at Naas, and, complying with her name, she was a right madam.

At Naas, the runners jump off with their backs to the stands and this time they went away like the clappers. My father had told me to lie up with the leaders, but I was too scared. I was a bag of nerves and gave her a cowardly ride, so much so I finished last but one. Compared with the way she worked at home we knew Fur Coat was better than that.

For the first time my father lost his cool with me. He wasn't a man to make noises in public, but I knew by his abrupt manner that he was angry. A short while later, on the way home in the car, he left me in no doubt. He gave me a right rollicking. He said it was the end of me for a while, so I knew my chances of riding Ballygowan at Leopardstown were slipping away. My only hope was to talk my mother into persuading him to let me ride Ballygowan because it meant so much to me.

The tactics worked. On the day before the race my father relented. He told me I could ride Ballygowan, provided I did a better job on Fur Coat who was running in an earlier race at the same meeting. If I didn't show any improvement on my abysmal Naas performance, Ballygowan would go to another jockey.

So there was no messing about at Leopardstown, and I went out and gave Fur Coat the ride of my life. In fact, she ran too well – my father had wanted to keep her talents hidden so that she might be given a low weight later on by the handicapper! But he was thrilled by the way I rode her, although he was never a man to pat anyone on the back. You simply knew by his attitude whether he was pleased or disappointed.

Encouraged by my ride on Fur Coat, I felt in great form going out to partner Ballygowan. He was a lazy horse, and half-way down the far side I kept muttering, 'I won't give in, I mustn't give in,' and I pushed and shoved with all my might. Slowly and patiently we kept making up ground and in the very last strides we got up on the line to win by a neck.

During this time I had a dreadful habit of 'calling a cab' – taking one hand off the reins and throwing it high in the air as we jumped a fence. My father gave me some terrible rollickings for it.

On the schooling-ground I had often been too scared to start off, and it took me ages to regain my confidence. It was the same fear I had suffered with Rossa, the pony, and it took me another four years to conquer that fear completely.

Though I was never lucky enough to see my father ride in races, I saw his talents at work every day on the gallops and at the schooling-ground. Whenever a young rider couldn't cope with a difficult horse my father would drag him off and hop up in his place to show him how it was done.

The win on Ballygowan boosted my confidence immensely and I started to attract rides from 'outside' trainers. To convince my parents they were right to let me leave college, I set myself a rigorous stable routine. I worked like hell. I got up at four every morning and milked three cows and fed fifty calves. Then, at seven, I would feed the horses and muck out Ballygowan and 'do' him over, and when the lads arrived at 7.30 all the work would be done. I allowed myself ten minutes to gulp breakfast, then my father would come down for a chat and organize first and second lots.

At lunch-time I would feed all the horses again and grab half an hour for a snack. In mid-afternoon I'd bring the cows in and check over every horse, always running my hands down their legs to make sure they were cool and sound, and then scan their pots to see whether they had eaten their food. A tedious routine, but I revelled in it.

At six in the evening the lads would go home, and I would cross to the cowshed and milk the cows and feed the calves. I usually finished my daily chores at eight at night. A fifteen-and-a-half-hour day! The energy tank was always dry and I had no strength or zest to go out with friends. I was in bed by nine, and that was my life for two years. I worked like a slave, but I loved it.

I began to accept rides in point-to-points and gradually built up an abominable record. I failed to ride a point-to-point winner in a staggering 173 races! I remember riding one big horse, Brother J, and we were three fences clear and an absolute certainty when he fell at the second-last and I cracked all the ribs down my left side.

It was a quiet community life around our home, and the only parties we attended were given by Dan Moore's children, Arthur and Pamela. Peggy Nolan, another trainer, also knew how to put on a party and I loved going to them.

I developed a great interest in fishing in my teens, and Jack Doggett and I would go off for long hours searching for trout, pike and perch. My father would lend me the car on Sunday afternoons and Jack and I would go off with our tackle to the River Boyne in Slane.

I first fell in love with fishing when I was about eight. We had a little river running through our farm and it was rich with minnows and eels and the occasional trout. I would set lines at night and be up at six in the morning to see what I had caught. I was mad keen on fishing.

My first winner over fences came on a mare called Bland Lady at Down Royal on 16 May 1964. We finished on the far side, with the late Gerry Rooney, son of Willie Rooney, on the stands side, driving out the favourite, Quintin Bay. The finish was so close neither of us would go into the winner's enclosure. Thank God, my number came out first, and I felt I'd scaled a mountain.

As I've mentioned, one of my father's proudest moments was winning the Irish Grand National at Fairyhouse with Gold Legend in 1958. Johnny Lehane rode it. A sad case, Johnny. A few years later he committed suicide. Even more curious, the second horse, Knight Errant, was ridden by Cathal Finnegan, and poor Cathal also ended up taking his own life.

Quite frankly, Johnny wasn't the brightest person on earth. He was with us twelve years, and the Irish National victory went to his head. Johnny should have won the Galway Plate for us in the same year, but he split with my father after he didn't do his best on Hopeful Colleen at Mullingar. So Johnny rode Pharmaneuix II in the Galway Plate and Jimmy Mahoney rode Hopeful Colleen, winning at 20–1. I remember listening to a commentary on the race on the radio at my grandmother's public house in Celbridge.

We later heard that Johnny had taken the result badly and made a horrible scene outside the weighing-room. He couldn't accept defeat. He cried and shouted and it was shortly after this race that he left Ireland and joined Bill Marshall's stable in England.

I'm afraid Johnny had a terrible drink problem. It was painfully sad to see him slide, unchecked, right down the ladder. It's only now that I can fully understand how he suffered, and if I had gone through the same mental torture I could easily have ended up doing exactly what he did. Johnny drank a can of weed-killer and died an awful death.

Cathal Finnegan also occasionally rode for us. He was a cheerful, jovial chap but, like Johnny, became hooked on drink. Cathal was aware of his illness and tried desperately hard to control it, and even went to meetings run by Alcoholics Anonymous. Then one night he left his watch and a few valuables on the mantelpiece, drove to the River Boyne and threw himself off the bridge.

Those two appalling deaths shook me terribly, and, between them, yet another jockey, Johnny Rafferty, took an overdose of sleeping tablets and another life was thrown away.

Johnny was a lot senior to me and rode for a spell in England, mainly for Verly Bewicke. Then he returned to Ireland and became obsessed with drugs and drink. The late Willie O'Grady picked him out of the gutter three times, and I remember riding against Johnny in his very last race at Sligo in June 1965. By some weird coincidence the name of his last mount was No Good Johnny, and it finished last.

So, in a very short time, three jockeys I had known as colleagues and friends had taken their lives because they could not cope with the mental strain of daily living. I just prayed and prayed it would never happen to me.

Over the ensuing years, when I found myself ripped apart by drinking and gambling, I kept asking myself, will I end up like Johnny Lehane? Will I end up like Cathal Finnegan? Will I end up like Johnny Rafferty? It worried me awfully and many times I knew I was just a fraction away from taking my life, from throwing myself off a building or under a train, or filling myself with the bottles and bottles of tablets I was always taking. I could clearly imagine the next day's headlines saying 'Barry Brogan found drowned' or 'Barry Brogan found dead'.

I suppose, in a bizarre way, the deaths of Lehane, Finnegan and Rafferty helped to keep me alive. What they did in their very worst moments of mental torture acted as an alarm-bell to me. Thank God I always heard it, and I did the right thing every time.

Yet despite all I've been through, the saddest day of my life will always be 23 February 1965, the day I lost my father.

It was just after eleven o'clock when Frankie Carroll and I returned from working a couple of horses around the mile-and-a-quarter gallop. My father had watched the horses striding out, studying every movement in his own meticulous way, and we pulled up at his favourite vantage point on a ridge in the wide-open spaces, where he was waiting to speak to us.

It was a glorious morning. The sun shone, the air was crisp and pure, and the silence was golden. Then my father fumbled in his pocket for a cigarette, which he always loved to smoke while he discussed a gallop, went to light up, and collapsed right in front of us.

Frankie Carroll leapt off his horse and frantically rubbed my father's chest and breathed the kiss of life, working furiously to revive him. But it was to no avail. We had lost him.

I just stood and watched, stunned and helpless. He had never been ill, and had worked flat-out every day of his life. On the surface he seemed indestructible.

I tried to pull myself together, gave my horse to Ben Maguire, the man who supervised our gallops, and sprinted full pelt across the fields to telephone a priest and a doctor. I was terrified.

Right from the moment my father died I've lived with the haunting and irrepressible guilt that I might have caused it. My incessant rows with my mother disturbed him enormously. He hated family squabbles. I can't positively say what prompted all the trouble between my mother and me, but it probably went back to the time when I pinched that £5 note. She never forgave me.

Mother and I were always at loggerheads. It bothered my father because he was such a sensitive, compassionate man. On the night before he died he drove to Dublin to discuss me and my mother with two friends, Paddy and Moira Coldrick. That's how much it worried him. I never got to know what conclusions they came to; he wasn't spared the time to talk it over with me.

He was buried at Rathfeigh, and it seemed all Ireland took the day off to come along and pay their last respects. He was a great and popular man.

During that horrific week, the Turf Club granted me a licence to train and I immediately took over the family horses. My first runner was Clusium at Leopardstown, and he finished second to the mighty Flyingbolt. A meritorious start, I thought.

So I now had the responsibility of training the horses and selecting the races in which they should run, while my mother kept in touch with the owners. Our first winner came with Tartare in a maiden hurdle at Thurles on 8 April. He was a brave grey horse, and Tommy Carberry rode him; they won by four lengths at 4–5.

As the weeks rolled by I had to decide whether to continue training or look for a career in the saddle. It was a daily dilemma and haunted me until September 1965, when I finally decided to break with home and go my own way.

In my seven months' training with my mother I saddled nine winners, and proudly took three runners to the Grand National meeting at Aintree – Ballygowan (Tony Redmond up) in the National; Harry Lime (Timmy Hyde) in the Mildmay; and Liberty Truck (Lester Piggott) in the Liverpool Spring Cup.

Unfortunately Ballygowan refused at the twentieth, Harry Lime fell at the sixth, Timmy breaking his shoulder, and Liberty Truck coughed at the start and Lester withdrew him.

It was my first visit to England and I wrote myself into the record-books as the youngest trainer to saddle a horse in the Grand National. I was still just seventeen.

Besides training winners I was also riding them, and after the Galway meeting in August I decided I wanted to concentrate more effectively on the riding side of the sport. Then, out of the blue, I was offered the marvellous job of assistant trainer to the great and unforgettable Tom Dreaper.

It was a glorious opportunity for me. Suddenly I was riding exceptional horses like Arkle, Flyingbolt, Crown Prince, Muir, Stonehaven, Fort Lehey and Prince Tino. Dreaper had twenty-five top-class horses and trained for all the big owners, including the Duchess of Westminster and Sir John Thomson.

Tom Dreaper was bedridden and I used to visit his room at 7.30 every morning to see how he wanted the horses worked. Having been with my father I found the Dreaper methods most unorthodox. He never kept his horses out more than twenty minutes. The great Pat Taaffe would come down once a fortnight to school them, and there were other talented riders in the yard like Liam McLoughlin, Sean Barker and Paddy Woods, who is now training with increasing success. It was my job to partner all the horses we ran in races for amateur riders, to supervise the yard and to ride out two lots every day.

After work I would provide a detailed report for the Dreapers and stay for lunch at the house. I considered this a rare privilege and was proud of myself. I was doing well.

A week before I joined the Dreapers, on the last day of July in 1965, I had a fierce row with my mother and fled from home, full of anguish. I had £15 in the Post Office and I gave Ben Maguire my deposit book and he brought the cash to me. That's all I had to my name.

I took the money, ran across the gallops to the main Dublin-Derry road and hitched a lift to Dublin, spending the night in a guesthouse. Next morning I made my way to Tralee to ride Gambler's Choice for Gerald Hogan and we finished third.

When I left the weighing-room at Tralee, I was shocked to find a small family deputation waiting to put pressure on me to return home as though nothing had happened. My mother had brought my uncle with her and they drove me back to the farm. We talked into the early hours of next day, but I remained convinced there was no future for me there, and that I would be doing everyone a favour by packing my bags and saying goodbye to the place I once loved.

Now, alone in the vast, nasty world, I went back to Mrs Dreaper and she arranged for me to stay at the Ashbourne House Hotel in Ashbourne, just two miles from the Dreapers and four miles from my mother's home.

It was during this time I started visiting the dog track at Shelbourne Park in Dublin. I went on Mondays, Wednesdays and Saturdays, and to keep out of mischief I also went to the Harold's Cross track on Tuesdays, Thursdays, and Fridays. My gambling had now increased from a few shillings each way as a schoolboy to £20, £50 and even £100. I was earning £50 a week – equivalent to £200 today – and I pocketed a £10 bonus for every winner sent out from the stable and £25 for every winner I rode. I was swimming in money.

My insatiable enthusiasm for greyhounds undoubtedly prospered from my affection for Moira and Michael Reilly. Moira was my mother's eldest sister and she and Michael trained thirty greyhounds. When we were children, Ann, Peter, Pamela and I loved to visit them and take the dogs out and exercise them in long walks along the lanes.

Michael often took me with him to the tracks and I always put the money on for him, so that the snoopers wouldn't know what he was betting. I remember one hilarious occasion on our way to Harold's Cross for an evening meeting. Michael had prepared a greyhound especially for this one race, and he was certain it would win. To keep it keyed up in the car on the way to the track Michael asked a farmer to catch a hare for him, and he put it in a bag and left it with me on the back seat.

Hares can be vicious and will bite your fingers off at the slightest chance. Michael tied some twine around its legs and I gripped it tightly, occasionally allowing the dog a quick sniff.

About an hour before the race we stopped the car to give the dog some exercise, with me holding the hare. The dog got all worked-up and began leaping and yapping, and the hare tugged so hard to get free, that I lost my grip. It escaped and went sprinting off into the centre of Dublin.

I wanted to laugh, but Michael was furious. He was poised for the bet of his life and I had wrecked it all by losing the hare. Michael saw it as an unlucky omen and let the dog run without having a bet. It won, and he was even more irate.

Michael and Moira were exceptionally kind to me in my teens and I went to live with them at my grandmother's public house in Celbridge. My granny, Mrs Salmon, was a wonderful and dear lady and very generous, and she frequently came to my rescue with a pound note or two when I was running short. I was always her favourite, and I had a deep love and respect for her.

The Dreapers never knew what I did at night, and on one occasion I went to the Harold's Cross dog track and placed £500 on Fleur de Lys at even-money; it won by ten lengths in lashing rain and I was drenched to the skin. I was all alone, and chuffed to bits, convinced I was on the treasure-trail.

For a spell, after leaving Ashbourne House, I also stayed with Mick O'Donnell at Finglas. He was a quiet, home-loving bachelor, and I lived with him in his tiny flat above a cake shop he owned in a side-street. It was more the cakes than the company that kept me there. I love cream cakes, and it's not unusual, even now, for me to eat four or five doughnuts for dinner.

# 2
# Booze, Birds and Bedlam

WHILE AT FINGLAS WITH MICK IT WAS ALL DOGS AND HORSES for me. Particularly dogs. I was amazingly lucky with them. I was turning over a great deal of money and lived well; among other things I bought a brand-new Vauxhall Viva.

On reflection, I now realize that I had developed that fatal illusion that whatever I bet on was going to win. I was hopelessly addicted.

It was quite common for me to walk around with £3,000 stuffed in my pockets. I had no ambition to save the vast amounts of money I was earning and winning. I just wanted to spend, spend, spend.

Tom Dreaper was turning out a stream of winners and I was taking home a minimum of £80 to £90 a week in wages and perks. I was also lucky with presents. Anne, Duchess of Westminster, owner of Arkle and many other fine horses, was one of several generous owners who showered me with gifts and cash whenever their horses won.

My spell with the Dreapers lasted a lucrative nine months, from September 1965 to June 1966. In my last few weeks with them at Killsallaghan I accepted two rides for Matt Dempsey in a point-to-point event at Wexford. I travelled to the meeting with trainer Liam Brennan and two attractive sisters, daughters of a highly distinguished member of the community.

One of them – I shall call her Sandra – I fancied a lot. I had studied her closely at gymkhanas and she shaped up well. I was still young and naive, very much the 'green' lad from the country and still badly ignorant of the facts of life.

Sandra was older than me, and certainly well-educated on how to express the fundamental emotions of life. She was, in fact, pretty hot stuff!

While returning from the point-to-point, we pulled into the Fox Hotel at Naas, run by the convivial Frank Glynn, and I confronted alcohol for the very first time in two long glasses of delicious Gaelic coffee. Liam bought them for me, and little did I realize that they were to launch me on a raging river of alcohol for the next ten years of my life.

Sandra and her sister were taking stronger drinks, and I didn't want to be left out or laughed at. It was more bravado than a genuine wish to drink. I was immature, and easily led.

Actually, I had an inbuilt fear of alcohol because I had once seen an uncle of mine tight and it stuck in my mind. Moreover, as children we had been brought up on a strict rein. Drink was forbidden in all forms. Not even a taste at Christmas.

About three weeks after my coffees with Sandra, I conjured up enough courage to invite her out for a meal. She was a girl who had been around a bit. She had seen life, and I had not. She was a handicapper, I was a novice. But I loved a challenge. After our meal at an hotel she invited me back to her home in Kill, near Naas. I remember going to the house and feeling all shy and inferior. Her parents were on holiday and we had the run of the place.

Sandra and her sister got stuck into the Martini and a few friends called and soon a party was in full swing. Sandra kept pushing me to join in, but I didn't know what beverage to drink – until I spotted an uncorked bottle of Bristol Cream Sherry, sitting on a cabinet.

We often kept a bottle of sherry at home, and my father used to enjoy the occasional glass before dinner. Anyway, I didn't even pour it into a glass. I just grabbed the bottle by the neck and drank it straight down and it had a marvellous, invigorating effect on me. Looking back, I'm convinced I became an alcoholic that very second.

While lying back in their beautiful, soft, fire-side chair, and drifting into a mellow haze, I suddenly began to think, What have I been missing all these years?

The alcohol took over. I drank the whole bottle in an hour. For someone who had never tasted alcohol before – two Gaelic coffees excluded – it was an astonishing performance.

I didn't even get drunk, although I remember feeling sick and a little silly. The alcohol had a glowing effect on me. It helped me feel part of the party.

There was a beautiful swimming-pool outside and everyone at

the party stripped off and swam in the nude. Afterwards, Sandra took me to bed, but she didn't manage to seduce me. I think any normal lad would have coped, but I couldn't. I just dithered. We stayed in bed for just about three days, but nothing happened. I was a frustrated, brainless ram. She had a period on the third day, and there were specks of blood in the bed; I was so ignorant I thought she'd cut her finger.

The Dreapers marked me absent for three days, and this was the start of a succession of lies. I can't remember what bullshit I gave them, but I certainly concocted a load of ridiculous excuses.

I told Uncle Michael about my penchant for a drink, but he said it would do me no harm. He virtually encouraged me. So I started having a few drinks in the pub at night. I latched on to brandy and plunged into all sorts of trouble.

I began dating Sandra and going on the booze with her. It was at this time the blackouts began to hit me fiercely and left me in no doubt that I was speeding, flat-out, towards alcoholic addiction.

After a while, I found I couldn't match Sandra's immense capacity for drink; we had a terrible row and split up. But as Sandra went out, Tommy Carberry came in, and he introduced me to vodka, the drink that was really to ruin my life.

Our main rendezvous was the salubrious Royal Hibernian Hotel in Dublin. We congregated there every Saturday night. Tommy, Timmy Hyde and his sister, Mary, and several other jockey friends and their wives or girlfriends. They were pleasant, amusing sessions.

Poor Mary died a few years later in a road accident while returning from Naas races. Stan Murphy was with her and his injuries were so grave he never rode again.

We were all fairly big drinkers. We'd sink a few tonics at the Hibernian and then move to Alfredo's night-club, a lively den off O'Connell Street.

Carberry always had a girlfriend, and I was keen on Timmy's other sister, Carmel, a sweet, attractive brunette. Ian and Hugh Williams, Lord Petersham and Steve Stanhope also frequently tagged along. We were usually a gang of twelve and we drank wine all night, cracking jokes and enjoying a good giggle. It was all sane, civilized fun.

Tommy and I would always be left when the rest had gone home.

We would stumble from Alfredo's around five in the morning to early mass at Eden Quay, and the two of us would be found snoozing in a pew at the back of the church, pissed out of our minds.

After church, we would always collect two bottles of champagne and call on two girls who lived in a flat near the church. It was usually six in the morning, and we would wake them up and run around naked and pretend we were going to get into bed with them.

Tommy had a great tolerance for alcohol – I shall never understand why he didn't end up an alcoholic! Yet drink has never affected him, despite what the cynics like to say. He is riding as well today, at the time of writing, as he was fifteen years ago when number one for Dan Moore.

One of the girls, Neave O'Shea, would put me to bed at seven and let me sleep until one. I remember being half awake one morning and thinking I could hear water running in the room. I knew there was no wash-basin nearby, so I jumped up and there was Carberry standing in the corner having a pee on the carpet. He was well-jarred.

I remember saying, 'You dirty bastard!' But he didn't care a damn, and he walked across the room to pee in my ear. I couldn't stand that type of messing and ticked him off.

I drove Tommy to the Tipperary Hunt Ball one night and wrote off my Viva on the way home. Carmel Hyde, and an air stewardess, Patricia Rowe, who later became Timmy Hyde's wife, travelled down with us.

Shortly after midnight I left the ball with Tommy and Patricia. Carmel was still enjoying herself and decided to stay behind. I dropped Tommy at Dan Moore's and drove on with Patricia to Dublin.

The rain was lashing down and we had reached a lethal stretch of road between Naas and Newbridge when I started to feel drowsy. I struggled to stay awake, but I couldn't. The car struck a huge pool of water, and before I could come to my senses we were hurtling out of control into a wire-mesh fence at fifty miles an hour.

We stopped with a jolt and I looked across and saw Patricia slumped in her seat and unconscious. I was certain she was dead!

The windscreen was in smithereens and the car was a metal mess. I was terrified. A lorry-driver stopped and gave me a lift to a telephone-box; I rang Tommy and told him I thought Patricia was dead.

Joan Moore and Tommy rushed out to see me and Patricia was whisked off to Naas Hospital, still unconscious and, to my mind, never to be seen alive again.

Next day, my mother was told of the accident and all hell was let loose. I had fallen asleep at the wheel and that was that. I was sorry and shaken up, and I gave thanks to God that I was still in one piece.

Amazingly, Patricia survived and battled on with great courage in hospital. Hundreds of little glass splinters from the windscreen were buried in her face and ten years went by before they all completely disappeared.

That was the first of a dozen serious road crashes for me, and, quite incredibly, I escaped from them all without even a headache.

With my Viva towed off to the scrapyard, Uncle Michael generously bought me a black Morris Minor and I quickly smashed that one, too! I was driving to meet Tommy at the Hibernian when I reached a tricky, twisting stretch at Lucan where two pubs stand facing each other and the road narrows sharply. I was just sauntering along on a Sunday evening when suddenly there was a resounding bang on the bonnet, and a man came crashing through the windscreen.

I stopped the car, and the stunned, injured man slithered off the bonnet and dropped into a pool of blood on the road. I was petrified, and memories of that horrific scene followed me around for years.

When I saw him lying in the road, unconscious, in the blood, I was sure he was dead.

'Jesus!' I screamed. 'What have I done?'

And without thinking, absolutely terrified, I jumped back in the car, steered around the body and drove off and left him in the road.

Fortunately everyone in the pub had heard the commotion and trickled out to see what was happening.

Obviously I couldn't travel far before the law caught up with me; after five miles, bathed in a nervous sweat, I had just reached Chapelizod when a police car raced up behind me and gonged me to stop. Two strapping Garda policemen got out and gave me a right rollicking for running away.

They drove me back to the scene of the accident and then booked me for dangerous and careless driving. On reflection, I realize that running away was a stupid thing to do. But I panicked. I couldn't cope with the shock, and this became the story of my life. I found it easier to run away than face the music. I was banned for six months and fined £25, and deserved every penny.

On the happier side, the man recovered quickly and was back at work in less than six weeks.

By now my zest for alcohol was increasing daily, and I was developing a reputation for being the clown at a party. Undoubtedly my worst performance was thrust on a large, friendly gathering organized by Captain and Mrs Norah Wilson, mother of A.J. (Jim) Wilson, the polished English amateur rider. They put it on at their home in Moone, in Co. Kildare, and all the racing fraternity were invited; I got boozed out of my mind.

Yet, despite my condition, I behaved very sensibly until a few people started taking the mick out of quiet Billy McLernon, a splendid amateur rider who never touched a drink.

What they said to him riled me intensely, and I stormed out of the party and grabbed a handful of loose chippings in the drive and pelted them at the cars lined up all around me. I was in a terrible temper, and a rush of tinkling glass made a mess of the evening silence. Drink had taken over again.

After flinging the chippings at the cars, I charged off to the haybarn, somehow climbed twenty feet to the top and then threatened to throw myself down. Everyone rushed out of the house and tried to coax me down. I howled at them to get out of my way, that I intended to jump; but before I could take off two men scrambled up and grabbed me, lowering me to safety.

I was too drunk to go home, so I shared a bed with a girl we called 'Chunky' – why, I don't know. It was a head-and-toes job. I slept down one side and she was down the other.

Still dazed, I staggered out at six next morning to ride work for the Dreapers and ran into some disquieting glances from Mrs

Dreaper, who eventually took me aside and said Sandra's mother had been on the telephone looking for her daughter.

I told Mrs Dreaper I had no idea where Sandra might be, but she was still very cross with me. She had also heard I was drinking a lot, and getting into trouble. She warned me that if my conduct didn't improve she would have no alternative but to sack me. And she did!

Besides riding regularly for the Dreapers I was frequently put up by Tony Riddle-Martin and other trainers, and I got so many mounts in a season as an amateur that the professional jockeys started to complain I was pinching their bread and butter. Bobby Coonan was probably the biggest moaner.

The protest was so big that the Irish Turf Club introduced a rule restricting all amateur riders to a maximum of ten mounts in professional races a year. I had introduced myself to the officials for the first time, and James Barry Brogan was a name they and their English counterparts were going to hear a great deal more of.

It was at this stage that I landed a rich chase at Punchestown and encountered the queerest owner in the game, though on the surface he was a likeable, respectable businessman from Belfast with a grown-up family.

After greeting me excitedly in the winner's enclosure he wasted no time in luring me to his lair, where he planned to celebrate his success with a night under the bedclothes.

Before setting off for his lavish mansion he treated me to a sumptuous meal at a top hotel and promised me £1,000 in cash as a gift for riding his winner.

He looked perfectly normal and safe. There was no hint of what his devious little mind was scheming up for me. In the circumstances, there was no reason why I should not go with him, particularly as I was eager to lay my hands on the £1,000.

After our meal, he poured drink after drink into my glass, and by midnight I found myself wobbling all the way to his car. We reached his home around one o'clock. It was dark and empty. He told me he had despatched his family to Limerick for the weekend.

I was dizzy and tired, and I vaguely remember he put his hand under my arm and practically dragged me to a room at the end of the corridor. A large double-bed took up most of the space, and he pulled back the sheets and eased me down in my clothes, as I was. I fell asleep instantly.

Even up to this stage, I had no cause to doubt his motives for taking me to the house. He had been the perfect, generous host. Soon my illusions were shattered. I had been asleep just a short while when I felt a strange movement at my side . . . and then a hand on my knee!

I leaped up and looked across, and there he was, in bed alongside me. I jumped out, terrified. I shouted at him, but he pleaded with me that he had to share my bed because the six others in the house were stacked away while the painters were at work!

'Bullshit!' I screamed, and raced downstairs and out into the night, in the meantime shouting over my shoulder that he could stuff the £1,000 where the monkeys store their nuts.

I wanted none of his cash. How could I risk that he wouldn't spread the word around that it was payment for services provided? He sent shivers down my spine.

Obviously I never rode for him again. Unsuspecting top Irish jockeys certainly did, though they never mentioned any lewd suggestions going their way.

I hope I scared the pants off him, though not literally, of course!

# 3
# A Riotous Start in England

IN LATER YEARS, I MET UP WITH JOCKEYS LIKE JEFF KING AND Jimmy Bourke who dreaded riding winners for Dorothy Squires, an indefatigable entertainer and tremendous supporter of steeplechasing.

Whenever one of Dorothy's horses wins, she gets so worked up she rushes down from the stands, grabs her jockey and hugs and kisses him in public like a long-lost brother.

When she's finally finished with him, the poor jockey is gasping for oxygen and his cheeks are glowing a bright red with large lipstick smears, Dorothy's unmistakable print of approval.

Jeff King himself was a riot. Besides being a rider of supreme skill and courage, he was very much the Max Miller of the weighing-room. His bawdy banter proved a Godsend to countless keyed-up jockeys before they took part in an important race.

He'd stand on the table, commanding his audience, and the rest of the jockeys would sit around transfixed, latching on to every inspired word.

As you'd expect of Jeff, most of his jokes had a fair sprinkling of sex and physical anatomy, but he had a clever knack of telling them which made them funny rather than crude or offensive.

I'm sure many young and nervous riders have benefited more from a session of Jeff's humour before a race than any amount of last-minute advice from well-meaning trainers. He took away the tension and I loved to have him around.

And he wasn't slow to mix his gags with a little crackle about the lads. Phil Blacker and Richard Denning came in for some terrible leg-pulling. Phil and Richard had the biggest choppers in the weighing-room and Jeff wouldn't let them – or anyone else for that matter – forget it. I remember one occasion when Jeff suggested that Phil should paint 'it' green and lay it on a vegetable stall and wait for some old dear to pick it up as a cucumber. Yes, Jeff was an inspiration in the weighing-room and, despite his brusque, no-nonsense honesty with owners about their scrubby horses, he didn't have an enemy in the game.

If Jeff rode a bad horse, he made no secret of it when he returned to unsaddle. He wasn't tactful or platitudinous. He had no compunction about going straight in and telling the owner, 'It's useless. Wouldn't pass a funeral. It's dog meat. Put it in a tin!'

Jeff spoke from the shoulder, and I admired him for it. He was a true professional's professional.

Throughout my teens in Ireland, I continued to keep in touch with my best friend Tommy Stack. On leaving college, Tommy went to work for the Royal Insurance Company in Dublin and on most weekends would drive down on his Norton 250 cc motor-bike to visit me.

The end of our avenue led out on to a T junction and Tommy and I enjoyed testing our skill on the bike to see who could take the bend the faster. Obviously I had to do better than Stacky!

So, on my very last attempt one morning, I opened the throttle full out, roared down the lane, failed to negotiate the corner and ended up in a field across the road. Tommy's bike was a miserable wreck, and I didn't have the £40 to put it right. That little escapade remained a sore point between us for a long time.

Tommy also drove a bubble-car and on one ludicrous occasion in Dublin he literally ended up under a double-decker bus, but miraculously escaped unhurt.

Over the years, Tommy offered me a lot of advice and I respected him enormously. He is two and a half years older than me, and he's always cool and steady and never drinks. But, above all, he was a tremendous horseman. Strong and skilful and totally fearless. He possessed every ingredient you'd expect of a champion. He captured the title twice in 1974–5 and 1976–7, without any element of luck. Tommy was a true and noble champion. A great ambassador for the sport of steeplechasing.

We strengthened our bond the weekend I travelled to Aintree with my three horses. I had sacked my head lad and Tommy took a week's holiday from his insurance job to help me out.

He supervised the horses, kept an eye on the staff and paid the wages. He enjoyed it so much he resigned from the Royal Insurance and settled for a career in racing. Wise man.

Tommy's first major step came in the summer of 1965 when he wrote to twelve English trainers seeking a job and only Bobby Renton had the courtesy to reply. Bobby flew to Ireland and Tommy and I met him at the Shelbourne Hotel in Dublin.

Bobby went away promising to write, but when Tommy hadn't heard from him after three weeks he booked a seat on a plane from Dublin to Leeds and virtually told Bobby, 'I'm on my way, meet me at the airport.' Such a move required courage, but Tommy clearly had more than the average guy.

A year later, I was following him. Having been sacked by the Dreapers, I decided to turn professional and I rang Tommy and begged him to find an opening for me. Again Bobby Renton came to a young man's rescue.

He approached Hawick trainer Ken Oliver about taking me on as second jockey to George Milburn, and I flew into Edinburgh on Sunday, 10 August 1966, with, once again, just £15 in my pocket.

Ken and Rhona Oliver met me off the aeroplane, and within a few hours had introduced me comprehensively to all the riotous, drink-and-be-merry habits that were to be my life for the next ten years.

En route from the airport, we stepped straight into a boisterous Highland party put on by Tommy Dunn. I said I didn't drink. I felt the Olivers would keel over if they saw my capacity. Two hours later, I was soaked in vodka. Tommy's persuasion was too much for me. I didn't have the strength to refuse.

The Olivers fixed digs for me in a cottage close to the stables at Hassadean Bank. I arrived in my room at two o'clock in the morning – stoned!

On my first day at the Olivers, I chummed up with Eric 'Zeke' Boyle, the stable's third jockey, and in the evening, after work, he drove me in his old banger – the 'passion wagon' – to the Cross Keys pub in Denholm. We went straight into the brandy, and I spent £15 and couldn't remember walking out. I had been with the Olivers twenty-four hours and ended up drunk twice. It was a senseless beginning for a new stable jockey.

Like all the other lads I had three horses to look after, but when six weeks had passed I swopped my amateur licence for a professional one, and in my first season I stacked up 153 mounts and 28 winners, finishing fifth in the Northern Championship. I was chuffed to bits.

Mrs Oliver made me feel at home from the start. She even lent me her Mini or Land-Rover to attend midday mass at Hawick every Sunday. They became absurd occasions. I would leave church, cross the road and eat a meal at the Chinese restaurant and wash it all down with a whole bottle of champagne. I was due back at one o'clock, but it soon extended to as late as half-past three, and I'd be steamed out of my mind.

Mrs Oliver took it well at first, but after a while she started dropping hints like, 'Church went on a bit late today, Barry.'

One Sunday, I left the Chinese restaurant after polishing off a bottle of bubbly, nipped into the Tower Hotel for a few vodkas and then drove (if that's the word) to the Cross Keys for a few more.

Pulling up alongside the pub, I was in no state to notice that the local council had dumped a huge pile of loose chippings for road repairs, and I blindly drove the Land-Rover right on top of the lot. I parked, switched off the engine and stepped out – and slithered to the bottom on my backside.

A crowd left the pub and stared up at the vehicle. They blinked in disbelief as they struggled to work out how I managed to park up there.

By now, the money was pouring in from riding fees and winning percentages. I was doing so well I was able to buy another brand-new car, a red Vauxhall Viva. It had all the accessories: radio, cigar-lighter, a mass of mirrors, and a super Colonel Bogey horn with five melodious trumpets.

I had the car with me on the night I drank myself into a blackout at the Thornwood Hotel in Hawick. At closing time I somehow managed to crawl behind the wheel and zig-zag my way five miles through the night to Denholm. On reaching the corner outside the Co-op I couldn't go a yard farther. I stopped the car, slumped forward and fell asleep.

I was so shattered I left the ignition on, and my right hand fell on the Colonel Bogey horn and stayed there. Imagine the din! It was three o'clock in the morning, and Denholm was black and silent ... I was just three hundred yards from the village police station.

The horn blared away, but I continued to sleep. Bedroom lights flickered on, and the curious pulled back their curtains and craned out of windows to see what was happening.

Luckily for me, a good friend called Scott Elliott, a carpenter, was among the first to stir and he jumped out of bed, raced down the street in his dressing-gown and lifted me off the wheel.

Seconds later I heard the unmistakable drone of a police constable at the door. I vaguely remember him asking me to leave the car and stand up. I couldn't sit up, let alone stand up. I was completely blotto.

He took out his little black book and asked me my name. I told him, 'Donald Duck, sir,' which didn't help.

Scott Elliott knew the policeman well and assured him he would take care of me and put me to bed. He dropped me at my digs and took the car home with him.

I was up late next morning, and as I was eating breakfast at the Olivers' the cook bustled in and told us that Denholm had been rocked in the night by 'a brass band passing through'. The lads believed her, but I turned away, hand over my mouth, longing to laugh.

With breakfast over, I dashed down to see Scott Elliott, who advised me to call on the constable. I went along straight away to the police station, and was ticked off. The constable told me all Denholm was talking about the 'brass band', and I thanked him for being so understanding. Several months later I went back and expressed my gratitude in a tangible way, with two bottles of his favourite Scotch, and the police constable and I became good friends.

Before I bought the Viva, I travelled most nights by bus from Denholm to the Tower Hotel at Hawick. I would start in the lounge and always end up in the public bar. I would begin with brandy-and-Americans and work my night to a fine art.

As the cash got lower, I would leave the lounge for cheaper drinks in less expensive bars, and I would always sign off with a shandy. It cost 8d a half-pint, and it would always take my last coin.

I would spend every single penny on booze, and when I walked out into the street I was absolutely skint, with only the bus ticket to get me home.

During this time, I had developed a fancy for Barbara Fairbairn, daughter of Bobby, the ebullient Selkirk trainer. She liked going out for a drink, so we toured the pubs and dance halls and I usually ended up paralytically drunk.

After seeing her home at two o'clock one morning I failed to negotiate a bend in torrential rain and drove straight down a black, unlit lane. I was certain that if I kept driving I would eventually rejoin the road further along. But the farther I travelled the slower the car became. Frantically I rolled down the window and practically collapsed when I saw I was stuck in a bog.

I managed to open the door and fell out and sunk up to my knees in mud. I tried to pushed the car free, but it wouldn't budge. The rain was still teeming down and I was boozed out of my mind, but it was imperative that I should drag the car out of the mire and get it back to the Olivers.

Drenched to the skin, I walked all of two miles before I found a telephone box at Lilliesleaf and rang Bill Hughes, a smashing fellow, and farm manager for the Olivers. I asked him to put on a raincoat and bring the tractor to pull me out. We had a hell of a job!

It was five o'clock before we dragged it free, so I had two hours to sort myself out before the lads arrived. The car was smothered in muck and I drove it straight to the bottom yard and washed it furiously until it sparkled. Then I nonchalantly parked it outside the Olivers' kitchen window and no one could have guessed it had been wallowing in a bog. There was no time to go to bed and, despite being shattered, I rode out at seven as though nothing had happened.

During the summer of 1967 I fancied a holiday in Italy and didn't relish going off on my own because I had never ventured outside the British Isles. At first, Stacky didn't want to go, but when I offered to pay his fare, he practically leaped at the chance.

We stayed at an hotel in Visirba, on the beautiful Mediterranean coast. I got badly boozed on the aeroplane going over, but Stacky didn't touch a drop.

In the first week I drank morning, noon and night, and I fell in love with every girl I met. Then, after a while, I didn't drink at all.

I was sick of drink. I hated falling out of bed every morning, feeling rough and gripping a sore head.

Then Stacky fell in love with a Swedish girl. He deliberately avoided Italians because he'd been told he'd have to take the whole family with him, mother and father and all.

On returning, we continued the holiday with Tommy's wonderful parents in Newtownsands in Co. Kerry. They were dead against drink, and I knew this would present problems from the start.

Tommy had a brother, Steve, and a sister, Helen, and I got his brother-in-law, Paddy Roche, into trouble on the first night I was there. I left him to stagger home hopelessly drunk and unable to keep his feet. I did it for fun more than anything else.

Paddy Roche, Steve Stack, Tommy and I would meet every night in the huge Ballybunion dance hall in Kerry. About two thousand people would cram in all at once. I always took a dozen bottles of lager in a bag because the pubs closed after twelve o'clock and I couldn't buy a drink.

Mrs Stack didn't know I liked a drink and Tommy was determined she shouldn't find out. He would bundle me into bed and open the windows for the alcoholic fumes to drift out. Then he'd climb in beside me.

Unfortunately our plan went astray one night when we went our separate ways. I returned with a dozen lagers and Tommy was already in bed.

I didn't feel tired, so I sat in the kitchen, drinking my lager. There were bottles and tops lying everywhere. Eventually I fell asleep, and when Mrs Stack came down in the morning she found me snoozing in a chair with a ring of empties all around me. The secret was out, and it was an embarrassment to both of us.

After leaving Tommy Stack's family I was back in Scotland only three weeks before the start of the 1967–8 season, when Ken Oliver told me that owner Jimmy McNair wanted me to ride the stable star, Arctic Sunset.

This was tremendous news, although I felt genuinely sorry for George Milburn who had won on the horse many times and had deliberately delayed his retirement to continue the association.

As soon as George heard he had been dropped, he telephoned Ken Oliver and tendered his resignation. So I not only had Arctic

Sunset for myself, but I was now officially first jockey for one of the most formidable jumping stables in the country. I had really broken through.

During those early days at Hassendean Bank I lived in digs with a couple called Nancy and Jimmy Young. Not the popular disc-jockey, I hasten to add. I used to call her 'Mrs' – 'Yes, Mrs! No, Mrs! Three bags full, Mrs!'

While lodging with Mrs Young I always kept a couple of cases of the best champagne tucked under my bed. I had champagne on tap! Looking back at it now, I accept that it must have seriously precipitated my appalling alcoholic progression.

Many nights when I couldn't sleep at Mrs Young's I would suffer frightening bouts of anxiety panics. They scared the life out of me. I'd wake up in a cold sweat, shaking from head to toe. I'd toss around and go short of breath. I'd be convinced I was about to suffocate.

I had a terrible fear of death which has bothered me all my life; I'm surprised it's never put me in a mental institution. It's been a personal hell, but for years I told no one about it. Not even friends, jockeys, owners or trainers. I suffered in silence.

When I couldn't sleep, and the panics grabbed me, I'd take a bottle of champagne from under the bed, go downstairs and sit in the lounge and drink the lot to sedate myself. It was the only treatment I knew, but, ironically, every drop that passed my lips was contributing to my downfall.

When I returned from a wild booze-up, I always had a ravenous appetite and would raid her larder. Next morning, she would be up early, pointing her finger at me and nattering, 'I see you drank too much again last night. And had a feast ...' I was forever nipping out to the village store for biscuits, bacon or sausages to put back what I had taken the night before.

One night I was so drunk I suffered a blackout and didn't know what I was doing. I got to bed by remote control. Next morning, I sensed something was terribly wrong because 'Mrs' had left a cup of tea for me on the table, closed the kitchen door and was nowhere to be seen.

Puzzled, I went to look for her, and she snapped at me: 'I've had enough of you! I'm going straight to Mrs Oliver.'

She was furious, but I still didn't know what had riled her.

'What's wrong, Mrs?' I asked.

'Come into the kitchen, and I'll show you.'

Mrs Young had a large electric cooker, and she pointed to it and stormed, 'Look at those four rings!'

I couldn't believe my eyes. All four rings had been torn from their sockets and were twisting to the ceiling. Even worse, the cooker was full on, and the rings were glowing a bright red.

There could be only one explanation. I had yanked them out in my drunken stupor, switched on the cooker, and blithely gone to bed.

So I promised to buy her a new set of rings. A new cooker. Anything not to tell Mrs Oliver. But she had suffered enough, and she called at the Olivers and reported me.

Bearing no malice, I bought her four new rings, and I packed my bags and went to live with Alan MacTaggart and his wife Marty on an eight hundred acre farm at West Nisbert near Jedburgh. Alan had a permit to train and he owned some good horses, like Cherry Bank and Ted Broon. Many times after riding work at the Olivers I would help him to exercise his horses and feed the pigs.

I stayed with Alan and Marty for two years, and I've lost count of the all-night parties we went to. Alan and I would frequently get so boozed up we couldn't drive; we'd have to send an SOS to Marty at three in the morning and she'd have to come out and take us home.

# 4
# The Soho Zulu

WITH ALL THIS PREPOSTEROUS DRINKING, MY WEIGHT REACHED new heights. I was shaped more like a wrestler than a jump jockey and to fight the flab I roasted myself in the plush Warrender Turkish Baths in Edinburgh every Tuesday and Thursday before and after racing, and in the city's Portobello Baths every Wednesday and Friday.

A tiny masseur called Jimmy ran the Warrender Baths and I got him sozzled every time I called. I always went there with a bottle of champagne and a quart bottle of brandy. The champagne helped me sweat, and the brandy was for Jimmy. I would get him so utterly drunk that he couldn't stand on his feet, and I would laugh myself silly just watching him swaying and swerving, then falling flat across the naked customers he was supposed to be massaging. Jimmy's performances certainly made the baths a lot more tolerable for me.

Newcastle's busy Turkish bath was another sweltering prison. It was there I first met John Banks. The flamboyant bookmaker had just divorced his first wife and was courting his present wife, Anne-Marie. I met John by accident, and he summed me up quickly. He knew I was ambitious, and that I enjoyed a bet. He handled thousands and thousands of pounds for me over the next ten years and we exchanged vital 'grapevine' information to our mutual advantage.

Although touring the baths, my weight was still soaring to absurd levels. Instead of bacon for breakfast I was gulping Lasix pills by the handful. They made me urinate and sent me scurrying to the loo every ten minutes. They left me limp and weak, and I had to follow up with bottles and bottles of potassium tablets to restore the salt balance.

Most Mondays my weight would be up to 11st 10lbs, nearly always the legacy of wild weekend parties. I'd be close on two stones above the average riding weight for a steeplechase jockey, and to bring it back to near-normal I wouldn't eat a crumb for up to five days. Dehydration was a constant worry, and the palpitations grew worse by the week.

One of my biggest ambitions was to see the night-life of London. I had heard so much about casinos, clubs and Soho. In December 1967, my wish was granted. The English racing season was halted by a raging outbreak of foot-and-mouth and I was invited to appear on a television programme on a Saturday afternoon.

The BBC ingeniously wheeled a computer into the studio to 'run' the abandoned Massey-Ferguson Chase, usually staged at Cheltenham at Christmas-time, and I was down to ride Ken Oliver's brilliant jumper Arctic Sunset.

The BBC kindly agreed to pay all my travelling and hotel expenses for two days and two nights. I knew absolutely nothing about London hotels, and the first I saw was the Hilton. As far as I knew it was just an ordinary hotel, with ordinary rooms and ordinary prices.

I booked in on the Friday night with my friend Brian Lenehan, and I arranged to be at the studio for rehearsals at eleven o'clock next morning.

I took a taxi to Shepherd's Bush and was introduced to Julian Wilson, who was presenting the programme. Jockeys Stan Mellor and Willie Robinson were also there.

The computer was a fantastic judge of form. It whirred and ticked away smoothly, and finally coughed out me and Arctic Sunset as the clear winners.

With the programme and the ballyhoo over, we drifted backstage for the free drinks and celebrations. It was then that Julian Wilson suddenly walked up and asked me where I was staying.

Innocently, I said, 'Oh, it's a place called the Hilton.'

He winced and wobbled and put his glass down.

'Where?' he asked.

'The Hilton.'

'In all fairness,' he grunted, 'the BBC can afford to put you up, but not at the Hilton for two days!'

The bill came to a staggering £153. A little fortune in the late 1960s. Actually it was Lenehan who recommended the place to me and shared my suite, and he left me, muggins, to pay the lot.

Lenehan knew London well and I asked him to show me Soho and a prostitute at work. So he took me to a flat in Hertford Street. Lenehan tapped on the door and we walked into the sitting-room. It was very plush with expensive furniture and large, attractive paintings. It obviously wasn't going to be one of those £2 flash jobs. Lenehan marched in and I shuffled nervously behind him, the naive boy up from the country. Then suddenly this gigantic black woman, Simone, burst upon us from behind a red curtain, like a Zulu warrior.

Lenehan spoke to her and explained that I was a new lad in the city and that I wanted to learn a bit about the seedy life. He then went off and left me with her. It was about half-past four, and Lenehan and I had arranged to meet at a party in Knightsbridge at seven o'clock.

I shall never forget Simone. She dropped back into a chair wearing only a short, pink, see-through negligée. I kept staring at her – terrified! Then she lifted the negligée high up her body. She could see I was shocked, and leaned across and told me not to be afraid.

'I'm not going to eat you, boy,' she croaked in a deep, husky voice.

But I wasn't convinced. She told me to strip off and then proceeded to wash me all over and wash herself as well. Then she let me lie in the bath, and I had a vast erection. She grabbed hold of my 'old man' and said, 'Son, you've been done before.' But I hadn't.

Then she continued with the execution. It was horrible. I didn't enjoy a moment of it. In five minutes it was all over, and it put me off sex for ages. I was physically upset by the smell of her body and the crude act. Callous love-making. It was hideous and debasing, and I was disgusted with myself.

When it came to pay, she demanded £25 from me. But I didn't have this amount of money. I expected to get away with a fiver at the most. It was ridiculous.

So she started harassing me and I became scared. I have always hated violence. I was wearing an Omega gold watch at the time and I took it off and told her to keep it as security until I returned with the money.

I went straight to the cocktail party and protested to Lenehan, who stormed, 'Oh God, you haven't given her that gold watch!'

So he rushed off in a taxi, recovered the watch and I didn't have to pay a penny. Later that night, Lenehan decided to introduce me to casino life and we entered the Casanova Club, run by Pauline Wallis, who also owned that fine greyhound, Yellow Printer, and knew most of my Irish friends.

I was fascinated at seeing so many wealthy people investing such huge sums of money on the gaming tables and I joined in and played roulette. Nothing complicated; I just played black or red, and quickly found it painful. Before I had time to light a Havana I had lost £100.

In those days I didn't carry a cheque-book, but Pauline handed me a form on which to write the address of my bank, so that I could continue to play on credit.

I explained to Pauline that I was low on cash in my pocket and she readily gave me £200 in credit, although I knew I only had £400 in my bank at Hawick. So I risked £200 ... and then another £200 ... and in five minutes I'd lost the lot.

By now I was captivated with casino life, and in a short time was losing an astronomical £1,900. Pauline was pale with worry, and she came to me and pleaded, 'Now ease up, Barry, you've lost a lot of money.'

But I still couldn't resist, and I kept on coaxing her for more credit and she eventually let me have a further £200; my luck changed dramatically. At this stage, I was gambling an even £50 on red, and in thirty minutes I won back every penny of the £1,900, and ended up walking out with £180 in profit. From that night on I was well and truly hooked on casinos.

On my last night at the Hilton I met an old girlfriend called Mary Maguire and we toured the clubs and pubs, gambling and boozing. We were quite drunk when we arrived back at my room.

I remember ordering breakfast in advance and asking for kippers and steak, and plenty of champagne to be brought up at seven o'clock in the morning. All sorts of silly things. Then I fell asleep.

The Hilton staff took me seriously, and at seven the next morning I was disturbed by the clackety-clack of silver trays rattling into the room on squeaky wheels. I had a sore head and my eyes ached and I couldn't look at the food, so I waved my arms and told the waitress to take it away. It was a stupid waste of money.

During that wild weekend I also went to the Sporting Club in Knightsbridge and promptly lost the £150 I had received from the BBC for winning the computer race. I had kept back £200 to pay the Hilton bill, but that went as well. I lost a further £1,500 playing roulette, which I haven't settled to this day, despite a stack of threatening letters. This was my first senseless escapade into the magnetic world of gaming clubs, and I've lived to regret it.

Later on, I played regularly at the Sportsman's Club in Tottenham Court Road, the Sixty-Nine Club in Newcastle, the big clubs in Edinburgh and Southport, and in the resplendent Dragonara Palace in Malta.

Usually I would enter a club with no more than £150 in my pocket, and after I had lost the lot would go to the cash desk and acquire extensive credit facilities. Amazingly, I was never turned down. They were the halcyon days when I had no overdrafts, vices or bouncing cheques.

Fellow-jockey Macer Gifford often came with me, but he was sensible. If he lost £20, he was livid with himself and went stomping out.

In one scintillating session in Malta I walked away with £1,000. I had been looking for a gold watch and I picked out a Rolex Oyster Perpetua, an 18-carat day-and-date beauty which I eventually bought for £475.

From the £525 I had left, I bought two more watches, including one for Bill Smith, the royal jockey. I remember coming back through Heathrow and I put the three watches in my underpants and passed through Customs undetected.

On another occasion I wasn't so lucky coming back from Sweden. The customs people made me strip off and looked in every bag. Whenever I went to Scandinavia I would always bring back a pile of pornographic books for the stable-lads, and duty-free vodka and cigars to give away. On that day when they searched me they detained me for up to four hours and confiscated everything – cigars, booze, magazines, the lot – and fined me £100!

I first began to bet in large sums in the 1967–8 season when I became very friendly with Harry Beeby, a director of Doncaster Bloodstock Sales. Harry loved a bet and his offices were in the same building as my guv'nor Ken Oliver at Hawick. He liked to hear about the Oliver horses and I was able to tell him everything he wanted to know.

My very first investment was £20 to win on Drumikill at Perth on 28 September 1967. I rode the horse and we won by six lengths at 10–1. Drumikill was a brilliant hurdler and he went on to win four other races that season.

I always left my money with Harry and in the first season of serious betting I accumulated £6,000 with him, almost entirely from backing horses which I rode.

I was betting sensibly at that stage. Besides winning on the Oliver horses I was enjoying a lot of success for trainers Denys Smith and Tommy Robson. One of my favourite horses was Sixty-Nine, trained by Denys Smith and owned by the generous Joe Lisle, who also owned the popular Sixty-Nine Club in Newcastle. It became a regular resting place for me when desperate for a drink on my return from race-meetings at Newcastle, Nottingham or Wetherby.

Joe was just a gambler, but he never failed to pass me a substantial present whenever I rode a winner for him. My biggest success on Sixty-Nine was landing the TWW Champion Novices Chase at Chepstow in February 1967. Joe had a ferocious gamble that day and the horse's price plunged from 100–8 to 6–1 in some frantic betting before the 'off'.

Thanks to all my betting exploits, handsome presents and a constant stream of riding fees and winning percentages, I became quite affluent and found I could go out and buy a Rover 2,000. I also dressed well, ate well, was always seen in the right places, and smoked boxes and boxes of the best Havana cigars. My standard of living was sky-high and I always stayed at the finest five-star hotels.

At this time I had also become interested in diamonds and began buying them as an investment from Jim Ingles, a jeweller at Hawick. I successfully traded in diamonds for up to three years and clinched several lucrative deals.

It was during 1967 that Ken Oliver organized a riotous party that staggered on for three nights. He appointed me barman.

Oliver split the party into three. The first night was exclusively for his owners, the second for friends in the Borders, and the third for friends in the auctioneering business.

For seventy-two hours all I did was pour drinks – and drink almost as much as I poured! I didn't see bed for four days.

It was at the first of these parties that I fancied one of the girls; she was a few years older than me and with plenty of experience. She had travelled the world. Though on the plump side, she was attractive. She was also a lively, spirited girl and obviously enjoyed starring as the life and soul of the party.

On the second night she managed to lure me upstairs for a little horseplay while the others got sozzled in the lounge. I was soon stripped off and skipping around the table-tennis room with nothing on. We could hear the music blaring away and never imagined that someone would notice that we were missing and come sneaking up and find us. But Ken Oliver, the super-sleuth, did!

Suddenly the door swung open and there he was, horror and rage filling his face. I stood in front of him, completely naked, and he bawled at me, 'Brogan, you're sacked! Fired! Get out!'

I took little notice of him and the next night I was back again as barman and behaving as though nothing had happened. After the third night, and seventy-two hours on my feet, I was shattered, and I slept – alone – right round the clock.

From the start of the 1967–8 season I took on the extra job of helping Mrs Oliver with the entries. Together we worked out the weights and the handicaps and decided where the horses should run. All this technical work was left to us; Ken just trained. He rode out with one lot every morning and then disappeared to his office for the rest of the day.

I became deeply involved in this aspect of the training and felt an important part of the team. It was a successful system that continued throughout the three seasons I was there.

Because we worked so closely Mrs Oliver and I became quite friendly and there were several occasions when we met off duty for a quiet drink and a chat. We were very good friends. I was still the innocent country boy, comparatively inexperienced but always showing a ready and eager willingness to learn. Older women seemed to be interested in me a great deal, and I couldn't work out why. I was flattered, and did nothing to keep them away.

Ken used to pass remarks like, 'You want to be careful, Rhona, or you'll be ending up with a little Brogan...!'

It has always been an established routine in racing that before a jockey mounts in the paddock, the trainer, or his representative, provides precise, last-minute instructions on the best way to ride the horse in the race. Such information is often important and, occasionally, essential, particularly if the horse has any peculiar habits, or the jockey hasn't ridden it before.

No jockey – not even Lester Piggott – is above a word of advice if he is about to partner a horse that has to be ridden in a specific manner to obtain the best results.

In a career spanning three thousand mounts I've been bombarded with every conceivable type of instruction – some amusing, some absurd, some ingenious, and some quite deliberately villainous. Trainers have whispered words like, 'Don't be too hard on him today, lad. I've got him all lined up for a tickle at Towcester next week.' Or, 'The owner's in Barbados, but will be back for Doncaster, and he likes a bet. Try *not* to be in the first three if you can, but don't get yourself into trouble.' Or, 'Shout like hell at him going down the back straight and he'll stop in ten yards.'

Fortunately, not all trainers are bent on making a career out of conning the public, and the soundest advice a rider is likely to hear is, 'Don't go to the front too soon. He's a bit of a rogue, so wait until after the last.' Or, 'Don't hit him on any account, or he'll pull himself up.'

Instructions vary enormously, but the most thorough and time-consuming I ever received came from the copious pen of Wantage trainer David Gandolfo, racing's answer to William Shakespeare. He wasn't able to attend the meeting at Market Rasen, so he sent his instructions on twelve pages of notepaper, all neatly folded in a large white envelope and left for me in the weighing-room, along with my colours.

Gandolfo had booked me for Dragoman in the Lincolnshire Long-Distance Novice Hurdle on Saturday, 2 March 1968, and it turned out a particularly busy day for me with six rides and two winners.

In the race immediately before Dragoman's, I won on Moidore's Token for Ken Oliver and, after sharing my delight with the owner and trainer, I was a little late returning to the weighing-room and slipping into Dragoman's colours.

It was while putting them on that Gandolfo's envelope worked its way free and dropped on the floor in front of me. Not knowing where it came from, I thought at first it was another bookmaker trying to buy me off. Then I realized it was so fat there couldn't be one alive who would be that generous.

On tearing it open I couldn't believe my eyes. Talk about the Dead Sea Scrolls, I think Gandolfo helped to compile them. His letter was a masterpiece, a mind-boggler. Every tiny detail laid out and underlined, and repeated several times.

There was such a stack of information, written in wavy, spidery longhand, I found it practically impossible to read, and I had finished only four sheets of it when the bell rang for the jockeys to leave for the paddock.

Dragoman started a well-fancied 5–1 and he jumped and behaved impeccably.

Not surprisingly, with so much to digest, I had learnt little from Gandolfo's screed, so I was left to rely on my own tactics in the race, and I kicked for home three flights from the end and felt sure we were going to win.

All went perfectly for us until we cleared the last flight; we were half-way up the run in and barely a hundred yards from the post when I suddenly felt his stride shortening dramatically under me. At the same time I caught a glimpse of Pat Buckley and his 100–6 outsider Apocalypse gaining on us rapidly, and they swept past and left us trailing by half a length.

With the rest of the weekend free I took Gandolfo's letter home and spent most of Sunday trying to decode it. In fairness to Gandolfo, he knew his horse well, and nothing was excluded in his vast volume of instructions. His monumental mistake was heaping the lot together on twelve sheets of notepaper instead of making a short, simple telephone call to me on the night before the race, which is customary practice for a trainer when he knows he will not be attending a race-meeting where his horses are listed to run.

On decyphering Gandolfo's message it became clear that Dragoman needed to be held up for a late challenge, and that to take him to the front the way I did was the worst move imaginable.

By now it was too late to repair the damage, but I promptly

drew Gandolfo's attention to his costly blunder, jokingly suggesting he should sell his pen and install a telephone.

Immediately the 1967–8 season finished, Tommy Stack and I flew to Rimini and rented an apartment for £70 for thirty-one days. For me, from start to finish, it was just wine, women and song. I was even well-boozed when I collected the key and took the bags in.

Tommy and I ate out every night. The Embassy was our favourite. The admission price was slightly above average, but every customer was given a free bottle of champagne. Thankfully, Stacky was abstemious. He never touched a drop of alcohol, so I sat on the balcony night after night happily sipping my bottle away and then quickly following up with his.

It was at the Embassy that I met a gorgeous Dutch girl from Amsterdam. I had a fortnight's obsession with her. She was a tall, elegant brunette with a beautiful body. I definitely fell in love with her, and I really believed I was going to marry her. Hordes of Italians and other Europeans fancied her, too, but I was determined she would be mine.

It took me ten agonizing days to pluck up enough courage to approach her and break the ice, and I persuaded her to come back to the apartment with me. It was one hell of a night, and I remember catching Stacky peeping through the keyhole, a randy, frustrated young man.

I walked her back to her hotel at six in the morning and desperately wanted to meet her again, but she adamantly refused to see me. For the next four days I just drank and drank while thinking about her. Eventually, while well-boozed, I stormed into her room and told her I couldn't live without her. I caused a terrible rumpus and she called the manager and had me ejected.

I remember waking up next morning minus one of my best shoes. It took me two to three weeks to get her out of my system.

During my stay at the apartment, Stacky and I met up with Newmarket trainer Ben Hanbury and his wife, Moira. Ben and I often indulged in long, boozy sessions. Stacky and I used to take a taxi back from Rimini every night. I would always fall asleep and Stacky would stop the taxi about two hundred yards away from the apartment and jump out and leave me to pay the fare. Stacky hated parting with money.

On leaving Rimini, and before starting the 1968 season, I again stayed with Stacky's parents in Ireland; one night I became so dreadfully drunk I couldn't find my way home and slept in the hotel.

Next day, and with only £10 in my pocket, I went all alone to a greyhound meeting at Ballybunion, picked all seven winners and left it winning £137. With the money burning a hole in my wallet, I made straight for an hotel, ate a huge meal, drank champagne and got into a terrible state. Luckily I had telephoned Tommy earlier in the day and arranged for him to meet me, so he escorted me home.

After that holiday I returned to Jedburgh to live with the MacTaggarts and ride as first jockey to the Olivers. Mainly because of booze and big-eating I was having terrible trouble with my weight, and I frequently shot up to 12 st, stripped to my socks.

MacTaggart and his close friends, Bill and Di Bruce, were keen shots; I bought a gun and often joined them on the moors. I remember one occasion, after a heavy drinking lunch, setting off into the fields to bag a few pheasants. I didn't know at the time, but for five years Bill had been bothered by a blackcock feeding off his land, and he and his friends had been trying to shoot it. A blackcock is a rare bird in Scotland and a bit of a lone ranger.

Anyway, we had been stalking around for an hour or so when the blackcock suddenly flew up in front of my face and I raised my gun and shot it stone dead. Bill hailed me as something of a hero, and it became a standing joke in the Borders about Brogan's blackcock.

'Have you seen Brogan's blackcock?' raised plenty of laughs at parties and dinners for a very long time.

It was during the 1967–8 season that I received the first of countless offers to make sure a horse was beaten. I was engaged to ride Merry Stranger for Ken Oliver in a handicap chase at Ayr on 16 October 1967. When I arrived at the racecourse, a certain bookmaker approached me in the car-park and ruffled £700 in notes under my nose and said they were all mine if I could guarantee that Merry Stranger would not win. There were only four runners in the race, with two of them, Mirval (Ron Barry) and Saundby (Johnny Gorman), having no possible chance of winning. It was a straight contest between Merry Stranger and Cortachy Sand, ridden by Ken White.

To say 'Yes' to the bribe would have allowed the bookmaker to make a handsome profit by laying mine and backing the other. But I remembered what my father had told me in my younger days – that once a jockey falls into the clutches of a bookmaker he'll never let him go and he's finished for life. With this in mind, I turned him down and went out to do my very best.

Merry Stranger started favourite at 11–10, with Cortachy Sand at 5–4. As usual Merry Stranger settled down in front and we led comfortably to the third-last where he suddenly made a dreadful mistake and Cortachy Sand took over in the lead. We all knew Cortachy Sand was not a very genuine horse and, after being in front for a while, he threw up his head and decided not to race. He was half-way up the run in when he slowed up and I excitedly saw the faint possibility of catching him napping. I made a furious effort to close the gap and gave Merry Stranger a brutally hard race, but we were just a short head away at the post.

In another stride the race would have been mine. I was determined to win, not only because I turned down the offer, but because I was hungry and greedy for success. The bookmaker claimed I was mad and he came back on several other occasions to try to change my mind.

It was in the autumn of 1968 that I first set eyes on the beautiful Mary Christine Briggs, later to become my wife. I had walked to the last hurdle at Southwell to watch a race when I noticed her close by. I was told she was the girlfriend of fellow-jockey Johnny Haine.

After a lot of hotting and trotting I made sure I was introduced to her before I left the course. I learned that she lived with her mother at Bucklebury near Newbury and that she worked as secretary for royal trainer Ian Balding at Kingsclere.

Though I succeeded in finding her telephone number, I didn't have the courage to ring her up and, eventually, it was a sheer accident and a spell of bad weather that brought us together.

On Friday, 13 February 1969, I travelled down from Scotland with the Olivers to ride Drumikill in the Schweppes Hurdle at Newbury next day. Drumikill was nicely handicapped on 10 st 10 lb and I thought he would win if the ground were soft. The Olivers had arranged to stay with Rhona's sister Ann Mackie, whose son John later worked and rode for the Olivers. As there was no accommodation at Ann's, they arranged for me to stay nearby with Danny Mellon, then assistant trainer to Toby Balding and later employed by a multiple bookmaking organization.

Unfortunately for us all, a severe frost fell at Newbury that Friday night, and when the stewards assembled for their early-morning inspection next day they found the course to be bone hard and had no alternative but to abandon the meeting.

The Olivers fancied a break in the south so they decided not to return until Sunday afternoon. This left me a little high and dry; Danny Mellon thought I should find a girlfriend and trotted out a few names to me. The only one I recognized was Mary Briggs, so I asked him to ring her up. She lived just a mile or two up the road and she came over in the afternoon.

She had been invited to a party at trainer Paul Cole's house in Lambourn that night and I went with her and we chatted pleasantly all evening. She told me there was nothing serious in her relationship with Johnny Haine and this was just the encouragement I needed.

From then on, I virtually arranged my racing programme so that I could see her regularly, and this went on for several months.

When the summer of 1969 came round, I persuaded Mary to come with me to Elba for a riotous fortnight's holiday. It was made even more outrageous by the presence of Terry and Bridget Biddlecombe, Richard and Myrtle Tate, and Bob Davies, who wasn't married and didn't have a girlfriend.

Terry and Richard were excellent drinking companions for me, and it was on that holiday that I learned to water-ski. Bob and I had a small side-bet on which of us would learn first. Bob trounced me, and I took it badly and became very dejected. On numerous occasions, just after getting up on the skis, I would plunge forward and fall head first into the waves.

On one miserable, overcast afternoon, Richard, Terry, Bob and I left the girls playing cards in the hotel and became involved in a hectic boozy session. Then the girls went for some exercise on the verandah and while they were strolling along they saw Terry and Richard down below them having a piddle in the garden.

Bridget was furious with Terry and made him sleep in the bath all night.

The weather improved later in the day and we decided to try some more water-skiing. I was three-parts drunk, but I still wanted to ski. And, for the first time in a hundred attempts, I actually stood up and stayed up.

Towards the end of that holiday I became jealous of Terry because he kept fancying and flirting with Mary. I got so bitter one night that I stormed off, got well-boozed on vodka and slept on the beach.

I also remember love-struck Bob Davies falling for an Italian hairdresser who couldn't speak a word of English; he would sit on the beach every day, talking to her with the help of an Italian-English dictionary. Bob was absolutely hooked on her.

At this stage Mary was working as secretary to a trainer in Switzerland and after our crazy holiday she flew back to Lucerne. We wrote to each other every day and I telephoned her at least once a week. Then one night she rang me in an awfully distressed state and said she had broken her wrist in a fall from a horse. So, at the first available moment, I flew to Lucerne and brought her home. There was no obvious job for her, so I praised her secretarial talents to the Olivers and they agreed to appoint her at the beginning of season 1969–70.

She lived in with the Olivers and shortly after she arrived I paid £5,000 for a small farm, comprising two cottages and fourteen acres, in the outskirts of Jedburgh. A few outbuildings went with the place and I soon converted them into loose-boxes to store young horses for the Olivers.

So the season opened with Mary as secretary for the Olivers and me on my farm. But my drinking sessions were accelerating, and in October I became so concerned about my problem that I went to Ken Oliver and told him about it, but he simply brushed me aside and told me not to worry.

I travelled to the races a lot with the Olivers and win, lose or draw, a huge booze-up was always guaranteed on the journey home.

I was drinking heavily and tried every conceivable method to stop, but I couldn't. I was living on my own in the cottage and night after night I would lie awake, unable to sleep. I had stepped up my pace of life, and I remember fellow-jockey David Mould telling me that if I didn't slow down I'd crack up or even kill myself. But I wanted to be race-riding every day, and I wanted the championship. I would travel anywhere for a ride. Often I would drive alone from Scotland to Devon for just one mount, and sometimes clocked up a thousand miles in a day.

# 5
# The First Big Bribe

FOR A FEW YEARS AFTER MY FATHER'S DEATH I WAS CONVINCED I was fated to die the same way as he did. A sharp pain, a sudden collapse and the lights would go out. I was so obsessed with this fear that I ended up mesmerizing psychiatrists both in Ireland and England. I saw sixteen of them in all.

One of my worst moments came on 13 July 1968, while riding a mare called Bubbled Over for Deryck Bastiman at Southwell. We parted at the last hurdle in a heavy fall and I was left flat-out on the ground with severe concussion.

I couldn't cope. The injury to my head, the enormous drinking bouts and the permanent fear that I would drop dead any second drove me so mad that I went to see Dr Roger Bannister in London. I really believed I was going insane. He wired me up and gave me a long and careful brain-scan.

I thought the fall had aggravated my mental disorder, but it hadn't. Alcohol was the complete and only cause. The more I drank, the more anxiety panics I suffered. And I couldn't find a psychiatrist to understand the gravity of my illness. The fears always troubled me at night, when alone and in the dark.

I would go short of breath, gasp for air, turn white and pray to God to let me live. It was torture. It frightened me so much I went to Dublin and met the brilliant Dr Austin Darragh, father of Paul Darragh, the exciting young show-rider. I explained in detail about the panics and fears, and how I felt a pain shooting down my left arm and across my chest. He listened intently for an hour, examined me from head to toe and passed me A1. I reckon I've had more physical examinations than any other human being alive.

Everything was functioning normally, but I still couldn't accept his professional assurance and the fears continued to haunt me so badly that he arranged for me to see a top Dublin psychiatrist, Professor Ivor Brown.

Right from the start there was little doubt in Professor Brown's mind that I was suffering from delayed reaction following my father's death, and he settled me in a soft, reclining chair and put me under hypnosis. Within minutes he had cleverly taken my subconscious mind back to the moment of my father's death and reduced me to tears, something I never did when he actually passed on.

I also told him about the pains in my arm and the grim fears I had of dying from a coronary thrombosis. But Professor Brown skilfully removed these thoughts from my mind.

Since that afternoon with him I've accepted death much more readily, but even now I occasionally suffer the panics and fears and the thought that I have to die one day.

Besides suffering these fears in bed I often found them overwhelming me while driving the car along a busy road. I remember one afternoon carrying jockey Stan Murphy back from a race-meeting at Thurles and the fears got worse and worse and the sweat poured down my face, and I kept praying silently to God to ease up and give me a break.

I kept coughing nervously and taking my pulse, and I lowered all the windows. I had a terrible habit of taking my pulse. And all the time Stan Murphy kept looking at me in amazement.

On another occasion I was driving along the Navan–Dublin road after riding some exercise for Nigel Longstaff when the panics began so fiercely I had to stop the car. I was so scared I didn't know whether to run to a telephone-box or hitch a lift to a doctor. I was frantic. In the end I was so confused I dropped on my knees at the side of the road and prayed to God to let me live.

It was nearing lunch-time and I knew I was only half a mile from the Grasshopper Inn at Blanchardstown, where I often called for a meal and a drink. I had only recently been dried-out, but this was yet another of those desperate occasions when I had to consume some alcohol to stop the feeling of panic and bring me to my senses.

I eventually reached the Grasshopper and drank, and suffered the inevitable alcoholic slip.

All the time I knew the fears were real. It was not muddled imagination. I knew my pulse went fast and slow. I knew I went short of breath. But, instead of working it out in my mind that

I wasn't going to die I succumbed to it, and this made me panic even more. It ran away with me.

Fortunately they were not all gloomy days; luck and providence did occasionally shine brightly on me. 17 January 1968 was one of them. I rode a five-year-old gelding called October over two miles at Newcastle. It was owned by George Weir and trained by Ken Oliver.

George Weir was married to the daughter of Lord Kilmany, who has owned and trained horses for many years. He was very loyal to me in my ups and downs, and always tried to keep in touch with me until it became impossible.

I studied the runners meticulously the night before the race and was certain October would win. I had hacked up on him at Teesside ten days earlier and was convinced he was still improving. I put £200 on him at starting-price.

The only horse I had been unable to rate was a six-year-old gelding called Irish Rain. He was trained by Arthur Stephenson and ridden by Paddy Broderick. Like so many shrewd judges over the years, I've always shown the utmost respect for any horse saddled by Arthur. When he was running a horse for the first time, it was essential to scrutinize it with the care and patience of Sherlock Holmes.

As soon as I reached the weighing-room I asked Broderick – better known as Brod or Jape – 'How good is this thing you're riding in the last?'

'Oh, that,' he drawled. 'No chance. He's still big and backward.'

I took this with a pinch of salt, because no one ever knew what to expect from Arthur Stephenson. Then when I saw the horse in the paddock I was very impressed. He definitely looked the part. Arthur had bought him from Tom Costello in Ireland.

While milling around at the start I couldn't miss noticing how small my horse was compared with Irish Rain. He could almost fit inside him. Even Brod, big as he was, looked like a pimple on a mountain. He was a super-looking horse, and I said to Brod, 'If that's any good, you're bound to beat me.'

But Brod continued to keep his mouth sealed. I didn't pursue the interrogation any longer because I knew he wouldn't open up.

Though October was a gutsy little chestnut, he was certainly no speed merchant, so when the starter lifted the tape and sent us on our way I decided to make the maximum use of him. We led at the third and the fifth flights and, turning into the straight, approaching the second-last, were back in front again.

But October had been flat-out for too long and was beginning to show signs of tiring, so I started to niggle him. Then I looked up, and there was Brod looming alongside me, with Irish Rain just cantering. It was a Rolls-Royce against a Mini, and I decided it would be mad to hammer my horse and give him a hard race to try to beat Broderick's giant of an animal.

Broderick kept looking across at me, taking the mick, which was typical of him at the time. He had an infuriating habit of doing that. He did the same to me at Ayr one afternoon and beat me by a head.

So I turned at him and shouted, 'For God's sake kick on. Leave me alone. I don't want to give my horse a hard race.'

But he wouldn't listen, and we went to the last flight bang in line, with me on the inside and Broderick on the stands side.

October was a splendid jumper and when I asked him for an extra-special leap he really stood back and answered my call. Irish Rain did the same and landed about half a length ahead of me. But he was new to the game, and landing awkwardly he veered towards me and I crashed straight into him.

As October was so small and Irish Rain so big, he spun me round until I ended up facing the wrong way. Broderick quickly straightened Irish Rain and they cantered away and won by three lengths. I stormed into the weighing-room and told the Clerk of the Scales I wished to lodge an objection for crossing.

I was thinking a lot of my £200 bet and realized I had a great deal going for me as October was owned by the son-in-law of Lord Kilmany, one of the acting stewards. Also, coming from a non-gambling stable, October would be more kindly considered than a horse from Stephenson's yard, which was renowned for heavy punting.

Even before they received news of my objection the stewards had decided that they had seen enough and were preparing to hold an inquiry.

Broderick, of course, marched confidently into the room and put on the act that his horse had won very easily. He was correct. The better horse had won!

Racing's 'bible', *Chaseform*, said in its report of the race:

*October*   looked well, led third, led fifth, every chance and ridden two out, unable to quicken flat; finished second, three lengths; awarded race.

*Irish Rain*   good sort; looked well; led fourth, led after three out; jumped left at last; cleverly; finished first; disqualified and placed second.

When going in for the inquiry I didn't know that word was buzzing round the course that Stephenson and his associates had gone for a massive gamble on Irish Rain. It had been knocked down from 20–1 to 3–1, and returned at 5–1. To lose the race would be a financial disaster for him and his supporters.

Stephenson was always very much against complaining, and never allowed his jockeys to object. He would always leave decisions of this sort to the stewards. Only this time he could never succeed. Brod had no chance with me at the inquiry.

Throughout my life I've always had the gift of the gab, and poor Brod could hardly put three words together. It was a verbal walkover. Arthur was very bitter about the outcome and never forgave me. I cost him and his connections a veritable fortune.

One of the biggest bribes ever tried on me involved Even Keel in the National Hunt Champion Chase at Cheltenham in March 1969. A well-known bookmaker telephoned me from his home in Berkshire late on the evening before the race and offered me an astronomical £7,000 in cash to make sure Even Keel was beaten.

The horse was certain to be favourite, and the bookmaker tried every persuasive trick to get me to accept. But no money in the world could buy a Cheltenham Festival winner, and I stressed this to him, telling him in no uncertain terms what to do with his £7,000.

Even Keel was very much in the public eye as a flying-machine. He had built up a sequence of four wins earlier in the season, although in his race immediately before Cheltenham we were trotting up at Doncaster when he fell at the second-last and I remounted and finished third. It was entirely my fault and I accepted full responsibility.

His price fluctuated dramatically at Cheltenham. He opened at 6–4, drifted to 9–4, and then settled at 2–1. Although I didn't tell the bookmaker, I knew there were two very large question-marks against him. He had run badly in a previous visit to Cheltenham, and we had just learned that he was an early-season horse and tended to lose his sparkle in the spring.

Despite these doubts I still couldn't see anything in the race good enough to beat us. Unfortunately I had reckoned without the prospect of Even Keel making a string of stupid and enormous mistakes. He had a peculiar kink in him and, on a moody day, would pull himself up when you least expected him to.

*Chaseform* said of his performance: '... mistakes, lost ground five out.'

He lost this ground mainly through diabolical blunders, and any distance he might have made up completely disappeared when he became reluctant to race and dropped back to be last. It was only when we turned into the straight that he started to fly, but by then our hopes had vanished and we were trounced ten lengths by Ben Hannon on Muir, which had been my first winner as an amateur when riding for Tom Dreaper.

Not surprisingly, the bookmaker wasted no time in telephoning me that night and insisted that I had been an ass to reject his £7,000, particularly in the light of Even Keel's dismal performance.

This bookmaker was the most persistent man I ever encountered in racing. He pursued me and pestered me throughout my career to fix races for him.

Obviously the most satisfying day of my life will always remain Monday, 11 November 1968, when I rode five winners from five rides for Ken Oliver at Wolverhampton. Unknown to the press and even to those who rode against me, I was absolutely knackered. I was on my knees through lack of sleep and being boozed up to the eyeballs.

An outrageous forty-eight hours of non-stop drinking had started at Newcastle on the Saturday night after I had completed a four-timer on Ken Oliver's magnificent hurdler Billy Bow. After the races I went berserk and indulged in bottle after bottle of my favourite vodka.

I was naturally late to bed, but on Sunday morning I somehow managed to wake on time and rode out at the Olivers. Mrs Oliver, with her usual efficiency, organized the despatch of the stable's five horses to Wolverhampton. It was the first time for the Olivers to run a horse at this Midlands track, and the first time for me to ride there.

Midway through that Sunday morning, Ken Oliver went to see a friend, Geoff Elliott, about some auctioneering business and I drove him over in his Rover 3500. I owned a Mercedes 250SL at the time, and later that day we travelled down to Wolverhampton in it.

Mr Oliver told his wife he would be back by 12.30 because he had arranged to pick up Lord David Crichton-Stuart, owner of Ballycurragh Lad, and Mrs Agnes Ogilvy, who owned Shingle Bay, at the Buccleuch Arms, St Boswells, en route to the Midlands.

When we reached Mr Elliott's isolated farm the whisky and gin bottles soon came out, and being a generous host he kept topping up the glasses. Though I didn't enjoy gin, I had such a dreadful hangover and thirst from the previous night I thought a drop would do me some good.

After leaving the Elliotts we called in on another farming family, and the booze bottles came out again. After knocking back a few more glasses it was well past one when we eventually arrived home at the yard, and Mrs Oliver was furious.

It was around 2.30 when we finally arrived at St Boswells to pick up Lord David Crichton-Stuart and Mrs Ogilvy, and by now I was in a state of advanced inebriation, although I continued to drive. I didn't help my condition either by sinking two large vodkas before pulling out of the Buccleuch Arms.

Our next oasis came at the Scotch Corner Hotel, about a hundred miles from where the Olivers lived. We ate a snack and enjoyed even more drinks. Then we drove on to the Bridge Inn at Wetherby, where we sat down for a large steak and consumed several bottles of wine. I now felt very tired from all the drink and lack of sleep, and I had not given a moment's thought to my five rides next day.

Not surprisingly, I had clipped the pavement several times with my erratic driving and frightened the daylights out of everyone. So on leaving the Bridge Inn, Mrs Oliver decided to take over for safety's sake and I fell asleep in the back.

I had suggested we booked in at the Albany Hotel in Birmingham as I had stayed there many times when riding in the Midlands. As we approached Birmingham, Mrs Oliver woke me as no one knew the way to the hotel. It was now 3.30 on Monday morning. On entering the hotel I felt absolutely dehydrated from all the alcohol I had consumed, and I had to drink six lagers before I could get to sleep. I was in a desperate state.

I also left a message at reception to be called at seven o'clock. I had to visit a Turkish bath early and swallow some Lasix diuretic pills to drain the excess fluid that had accumulated inside me in the past thirty-six hours. I had to shed 10 lbs before the first race at one o'clock!

On entering the baths, I was 11 st 5 lbs stripped, and I had to burn it down to 10 st 9 lbs. I swallowed the pee-pills, read *The Sporting Life*, and sweated furiously. By midday, the 10 lbs had gone. I felt very weak and weary but still just fit enough to ride five horses over a total of eleven miles and fifty fences. Given the chance, I'd have offered £10,000 to a penny that I'd never win on them all.

Glenkiln was my first, a big, bay gelding, and having his first race over fences. We had ten to beat and we started 100–30 favourite. I put up a pound overweight to ride at 11 st 2 lbs. It could have been 14 lbs for it wouldn't have mattered. I sent him ahead at the third fence, and we trotted up by ten lengths.

Even Keel came next. We had struck up a great partnership and during his magnificent career I won on him no less than twenty times. The Olivers left him hurdling a little too long, so that it took him a spell to master the art of fencing. I schooled him twice around Ayr, and twice around Kelso, and many hours at home. He was such a big favourite of mine I didn't want him to tackle the very stiff fences until I was absolutely certain he was ready for them. He was owned by David Heilbron, a director of Long John Whisky.

At Wolverhampton he flew from the 'gate' and went like the clappers. He didn't lift a leg at a fence. He crashed through them all, and made it seem he'd never been schooled in his life.

*Chaseform* reported: 'Made all, blundered last, ran on gamely.'

We started 6–4 favourite, and stayed on by two and a half lengths to beat second favourite Sweet Score, ridden by Phil Harvey. It was obviously the outing Even Keel needed. In the next seven weeks we went on to complete a four-timer at Carlisle, Doncaster and Ayr.

A gap of two hours elapsed between my winning on Glenkiln and riding Even Keel and I stretched myself out on the weighing-room bench and felt I was about to die. I had terrible palpitations and I thought my heart was going to stop. They were all chronic withdrawal symptoms from the alcohol I had consumed. I felt so ill I sent out for a few bottles of lager which I often hid in the weighing-room. It was a habit I picked up from several other top jockeys.

Obviously drink is strictly forbidden in there, but the valets will usually nip out and come back with the bottles tucked under their aprons.

The lagers perked me up. My needle had dropped to empty and my tank needed replenishing. The perspiration streamed down my cheeks and I could practically taste the alcohol as the sweat found its way between my lips. It was not a new experience. There were many times when I turned up with a hangover and risked my life riding over fences at thirty-five miles an hour, not fully understanding what was going on.

After Even Keel came Drumikill – and my hat-trick! Peter Easterby saddled a fancied horse in the race called Nothing Higher, ridden by David Nicholson. It had won a 22-horse race at Nottingham a month earlier, and we were set to give it 15 lbs. It was a lot of weight to concede, and I knew we would be hard-pressed to win. My fears became a reality at the second-last where we started a ding-dong struggle which continued right up to the line.

Drumikill led at the second-last, but Nothing Higher was very strong and had inched in front by the time we jumped the last. At this point I galvanized every ounce of energy I had left and Drumikill responded like the good horse he was. We regained the upper hand fifty yards from the post and drew away to win by a length.

In a strange betting-market, I thought Drumikill started rather generously at 4–1. Nothing Higher was the 6–5 favourite, after being backed from 2–1. It was rumoured that Cyril Stein, chairman of Ladbrokes, had some connection with Nothing Higher, so this might explain the sudden rush of late money.

Four months later I had the thrill of riding Drumikill at the Cheltenham Festival when he left no one in doubt about his exceptional ability by running second to the great Persian War in the Champion Hurdle. We led at the second-last and, except for a bad blunder at the last, I'm certain we would have won.

My Wolverhampton four-timer came on Ballycurragh Lad, a young grey gelding who could be hopelessly unpredictable. Although the season was barely two months old he had already run three times, winning his first race at Perth, falling at Wetherby and finishing second at Carlisle.

There were just six runners at Wolverhampton, but the bookmakers were left scratching their heads about who to make favourite. In the end they settled on three – Eddie Harty's mount Black's Bridge, Roy Edwards' mount Hozelock, and mine. We all started at 5–2; I beat Roy by eight lengths, and Eddie finished last.

Four rides, four winners! I was ecstatic. I had ridden four winners in a day three times before, but never five. The excitement grew, particularly as Shingle Bay came next, and I regarded him as my nap of the day.

In his three previous outings that season he had won once and been second twice. He was wonderfully consistent, and a smooth, fluent hurdler. The bookmakers confidently made us 11–10 favourite, and I thought this reflected our excellent chances. We were never extended over the two miles, led three flights out and won, easing up, by five lengths.

A remarkable five-timer had been accomplished both for me and the Olivers. I was as pleased for them as I was for myself. It was a magnificent training achievement. How I attained it all with such a prodigious hangover and feeling so desperately ill will remain one of the great mysteries of my life.

The Olivers generally enjoyed a long and heavy drinking session after race-meetings but, ironically, this was one occasion when no time was available to dive into a celebration. They were booked on a flight to Dublin where they planned to spend a few days with trainer-cum-horse-dealer Padge Berry. They flew out in great heart because Even Keel, Ballycurragh Lad and Shingle Bay had all been bought from him.

After dropping them at the airport, I drove on to Huntingdon where I'd arranged to stay with Macer Gifford and his mother. Macer knew my form and, having heard I'd ridden five winners at one meeting, was sure I would want to go out on the town and celebrate. He never made a bigger mistake. I was shattered. It was a struggle to breathe. All I wanted was a long sleep and plenty of rest. For once, alcohol didn't interest me.

After twelve hours of deep, undisturbed sleep in Macer's spare room, I drove back to Scotland. My next mount was Brogeen Lass at Carlisle on the Thursday, so I had plenty of time to savour my success and prepare to come down to earth again. And I did – Brogeen Lass, a 100–8 outsider, finished ninth!

Throughout my career I was always acutely superstitious about sleeping with women the night before I was due to race. Sleeping with them was always very pleasant, of course, but I usually paid for it next day with a few broken bones and a spell in hospital. No matter how safe the horse was said to be, I consistently ended up with a fall.

A perfect example was my first visit to Kempton in November 1967. Tommy Stack and I drove down to London and stayed overnight in a flat with two female friends. Tommy had a Mickey Mouse ride next day on a hurdler called Lady Glenorchy. It was just an excuse to go racing – and they were tailed off when they fell. Luckily for Tommy he escaped unhurt.

Connie O'Keefe, who trains in County Cork, had booked me to ride Doneraile's Glory, one of the safest jumpers in training. He had won practically every point-to-point race in Ireland, jumped the stiff Cheltenham course three or four times, and never fallen in his life.

There were fourteen runners at Kempton and we went off at a tremendous lick . . . and I fell at the first! A terrible fall; I bruised my shoulder, got kicked in the ribs and cringed as just about every runner stepped all over me. I was carried back in the ambulance, black and blue from head to toe.

As soon as I could be eased out of my colours and into my clothes, I made a bee-line for Park Street in London for treatment from sports-injury specialists Bill Tucker and Alun Thomas.

I reached Dr Tucker before he locked up for the night and he started working on me immediately, and again on Friday. I was terribly sore, and I had to decide late on Friday whether to risk riding at Doncaster next day. I had six mounts, but I knew I couldn't physically manage them all. So I settled for two – Drumikill and Merry Stranger.

On Saturday morning, I caught the first fast train out of King's Cross and arrived at Doncaster just in time to ride Drumikill in the opener. I was in awful pain throughout the race and I had to work desperately hard to win by a neck.

Thank God, I had no problems with Merry Stranger. He jumped impeccably, led all the way and beat Alan MacTaggart's outsider Ted Broon by a length.

Naturally, I was glad to see Sunday. I stayed at home and relaxed and vowed never again to indulge in sex before racing as long as I remained a jockey. Of course, it was a ridiculous resolution because with so many temptations and plenty of willing women, it was a promise I couldn't hope to keep. Inevitably, I had more sex, more fun ... and more falls. And, quite honestly, I can't say I'm complaining.

I got close to another sex-before-racing session in a Paris hotel on the night before a big hurdle race at Auteuil. I was there to ride the Oliver star The Spaniard.

After The Spaniard had been flown out, I met Mrs Oliver and the horse's owner, Bill Rimmer, at Heathrow. Mrs Oliver was in great form and opened a bottle of champagne.

I had been wasting hard for three weeks to ride the horse at 10 st 3 lbs, but Mrs Oliver insisted a few drops would do me no harm. I had no food in my stomach but got stuck into the champagne; soon I was floating. Ken was due to fly out later, having been delayed at the Doncaster Bloodstock Sales.

By the time we boarded the aeroplane I was well and truly soaked. We sat at the back while I continued to devour the champagne. When we touched down in Paris we were really swinging.

We took a taxi to the Hotel La Silva and booked in for six days. We soon met Josh Gifford and Althea Roger-Smith, Josh being there to ride Major Rose. Althea and Josh were engaged at the time. Mrs Oliver and I, in high spirits, crept along the corridor at two in the morning, knocked on Josh's door and tried to peep through the keyhole. Josh was too smart for us. He had stuffed it up with a cigarette packet!

Bill Rimmer and I shared a room, but before we went to bed I suggested to a bird staying in the hotel that I should nip along to see her as soon as Bill was asleep. Bill was very tired and soon dropped off, and I tip-toed to her room. I stayed with her until four in the morning. We were disturbed by a clatter in the corridor and I got out by climbing down the fire escape clutching my underclothes.

Right up to the time of the race Ken Oliver badgered me to make the correct weight or he'd ask Willie Robinson to fly out to replace me. So, to be sure of keeping the ride, I slipped into a tracksuit and ran three miles round Chantilly park and came back at 9 st 13 lbs.

The race was run over three miles and a furlong, but after jumping the fifth the French horses swept past me as though The Spaniard was stuck in clay, and we finished plum last. Josh pulled up Major Rose and Jimmy Uttley came in fourth on Persian War.

As a race it was disappointing, as a holiday it was superb.

# 6
# Getting Rich Quick

I MET 'THE SWAN' IN LONDON IN 1968. HE APPROACHED ME secretively in a club called Ruby's. He was a toff and I never found out his actual name. He wanted to tap me for tips. I was riding for the Olivers in Scotland then, and he arranged to telephone me at a kiosk in Denholm at nine every morning to know what I fancied in the day's racing. If they won, there was always money in the post for me. If they lost, he never complained. Overall, he won a packet.

Our arrangement continued until I spent a weekend riding in Scotland. I was riding at Kelso on the Saturday and Ayr on the Monday. 'The Swan' flew up to both meetings. My main mount at Ayr was in a four-horse race, and he offered me £5,000 to make sure it was beaten. I refused, and told John Banks about him; he warned me to be careful.

I later saw him in London several times. He would meet me at the airport and drive me to his flat, furnish me with cigars and booze, and take me out to dinner. He knew what I liked. He knew a lot of people in racing. He knew the wealthy men in London who do business with our top flat jockeys, giving them vast sums of money for information. I could have earned a fortune if I had agreed to do the villainous things he suggested. Or if I'd been a flat jockey.

There was one very powerful man behind the scenes and a number of top flat jockeys conferred with him several times a week. I knew who he was, but I refused to jeopardize my job by becoming involved with him and his demands. I didn't want to get in the hands of those people.

The position has not changed to this day. A lot of our leading flat jockeys are still building up huge bank balances on the strength of the information they are supplying these men.

Up to fifty per cent of jockeys bet on horses every day. Some get the valets to nip out and put the cash on for them, and many have wealthy punters who provide presents in exchange for information. It goes on every day, every meeting, and almost every race.

If every jockey who bet on horses was called before the stewards of the Jockey Club the sport would grind to a halt. There wouldn't be enough riders left for racing to continue in the way we know it at present. Two fixtures a day would probably be the maximum.

There is no end to the ways in which gullible, unsuspecting punters are ripped off by the professional fixers. Favourite methods include deliberately running horses with sore shins, sore backs, sore withers, pulled muscles, over the wrong distance, on unsuitable ground conditions and when they simply aren't fit enough to do their best. Even worse, many horses are sent to a racecourse without ever being taught to jump fences. This is not only unfair on the public but is grossly dangerous to the brave, unsuspecting jockey who frequently finds himself badly hurt as a consequence. I have often ridden horses that have never seen an obstacle of any description before they reach the racecourse.

The Jockey Club should take a large share of the blame. Licences are granted far too freely to trainers and permit-holders. In the interests of safety I would urge a prompt and considerable tightening-up in this quarter.

I have frequently been asked about my views of the integrity of people in high places, particularly those employed by racing's controlling body, the Jockey Club. It must be remembered, of course, that stewards of the Jockey Club, and any other members of the Jockey Club, are all liable to the same human and material temptations as you and me.

I can recall one instance when a senior member of the Jockey Club challenged me about my misconduct and I quickly drew his attention to his own dubious activities with a woman of ill-repute in Soho.

On another occasion, a senior and well-known local steward in the north of England was caught, stripped naked, in the back of a horse-box with a stable-girl.

I don't wish to condemn or expose these men of trust and power, but it does seem strange and illogical that people who have sat and smirked when passing judgment on me over the years have been guilty of their own private moments of indulgence and never had to face a disciplinary panel in their lives.

As for betting, stewards and officials are as keen as Alec Bird. Not a day goes by without one steward or another investing a few pounds on a horse of his fancy. During my career I rode for scores of stewards and racecourse officials and am fully conversant with their interests and habits.

Again, I'm not objecting to stewards having a bit of fun, but it does seem absurd that a local steward who bets £5 on a 10–1 winner is suddenly called to an inquiry to adjudicate on an objection from the rider of another horse in the race for a possible infringement of the rules.

Before I left college I had long formed the opinion that bookmakers are born vultures forever circling around, greedily waiting to swoop on easy pickings. Like my father, I have always resented their arrogance, the casual way they strut around buying up information and transforming it into vast acres of personal wealth and power.

I have no respect for bookmakers, and whenever they offered me huge sums to stop horses I often said 'Yes', knowing full well that the horse I was riding wasn't good enough to win anyway. There were other times, too, when I agreed to a proposition, but if I found myself in a winning position I would say 'to hell with the bookmaker' and go flat out for the line.

Winning meant more to me than any money I could accumulate from bookmakers. I loved the applause, the adulation, and the prospect of winning the Championship.

I would have given my right arm to win the Championship. But every time I came within striking distance, alcoholism would get in my way.

I remember taking a bookmaker for a ride at Teesside in December 1968, and it cost him a fortune. I agreed to stop a horse, but I double-crossed him and won by six lengths.

Dennis Yeoman had booked me for a bad mare called The Treatment, and the bookmaker offered me £1,000 to make sure she was beaten. I said I would. I thought it was money for jam. She was a dreadful jumper, always wore blinkers and was a right bitch.

There were four runners: Big Noise (R. Barry), Marcello (J.

Fawcett), Air Commodore (R. Greig) and The Treatment. They bet: 13–8 Marcello, 5–2 Air Commodore, 100–30 The Treatment, 9–2 Big Noise.

I led from the start and, with Air Commodore falling at the second, I was able to coast in, unextended.

I regarded the bookmaker's £1,000 proposition as a gift. The Treatment was such a bad mare I couldn't possibly see her winning, but once the opportunity arose to score, I couldn't resist it. Needless to say, he was livid, but it didn't deter him and he kept coming back with many other tempting offers.

Throughout 1968 I struggled furiously to keep my weight under control. When I was not riding, drinking or travelling, I'd be slumped in a sauna sweating off pounds and pounds of surplus flesh or dosing myself with diuretic pee-pills and trotting to and from the loo, hosing away gallons and gallons of excess fluid.

It was a rotten, vicious circle. If I drank, I put on weight. If I put on weight I lost rides. If I lost rides I locked myself away and plunged into long, black depressions. So I drank to perk myself up. And it worked. And the whole dreadful merry-go-round started all over again.

It played hell with my nerves. The best judges applauded my skills. After all, riding racehorses was my trade, and it came naturally to me. But weight or booze, and bloody frustration, kept getting in my way.

I used to look round the weighing-room and envy the lads who could go home and enjoy a happy, normal life. Even lads who were lucky if they could put together a dozen winners in a season

Oh yes, I might have been doing well on the racecourse, but the torment I suffered privately I wouldn't wish on my worst enemy.

Many times I arrived at the course unable to ride at the weight laid down in the calendar, and I would deliberately set out to deceive and cheat the officials.

My favourite trick was to weigh-out minus the pad the trainers put under the saddle, and on one desperate occasion at Catterick I actually fooled the Clerk of the Scales by placing the number-cloth over a light piece of cardboard and sat in front of him on the scales and successfully pretended that I had the saddle on my knee.

Unfortunately, I was not so lucky at Ayr in October 1968 when I rode a young steeplechaser called Lothian Prince for Wilf Crawford. I was supposed to weigh-out with 11 st 11 lbs, but with all my drinking I found it impossible, so I decided to cheat the pad again.

I weighed out with only the 4 lb saddle and told the lad in charge of the horse to put the pad on in the usual way, keep his mouth shut and be close at hand when the race was over so that I could pass it back to him without the officials getting to know about it.

But I reckoned without the vigilance of the stipendiary steward, a real Highland hawk-eye if ever I saw one. He noticed that my horse was carrying the pad in the paddock, and he tipped off the starter who confirmed I had the pad at the gate and rode with it.

Lothian Prince finished third and after weighing-in I was summoned to the stewards' room, where they cautioned me for cheating with the pad and suspended me for the rest of the two-day meeting; it cost me three winners.

I was finding it intolerably difficult to live two days alike. Fresh problems kept springing up in the most unexpected ways.

A short time after the Ayr incident I had a good few drinks after finishing third on the 3–1 favourite Glenmavis for the Olivers at Nottingham and Mrs Oliver drove me back to Newcastle, where I had been booked in at the General Hospital for a cheek-bone operation. I waved goodbye to Mrs Oliver through a window as she drove off in my Mercedes – and five miles up the road she crashed it at a roundabout and caused extensive damage.

Nothing would go right for me. Even when lying in hospital minding my own business my car was being smashed up! It cost Ken Oliver a packet to repair it and he did his best to hush it up.

My hospital stay was brief and I was out by the end of November, just in time to ride the brilliant Billy Bow in the Ladbroke Handicap Hurdle at Newcastle.

Billy Bow was always something special to me. I adored him. It's strange, but sometime, somewhere, in every jockey's career, he falls in love with one particular horse. Perhaps it's for his courage, temperament or speed, but usually for all three. Billy Bow was blessed with the lot. A kind, honest gentleman of the racecourse.

He won that Ladbroke Hurdle at Newcastle, making it six

victories from seven races in four months. But just two strides after passing the winning post he sagged ominously under me, collapsed, and died in my arms.

I'm not normally the sobbing type, but I got down off his back and stroked his head, and the tears trickled down my face. I had lost a friend.

In honour of Billy Bow's remarkable record, the Newcastle racecourse later had the wisdom to rename the race the Billy Bow Handicap Hurdle, and it's now affectionately known as the 'Billy Bow'.

Like Billy Bow, the enormous Flyingbolt gained a special place in my heart, and I had the honour of riding him to victory on his very last appearance in public in the Gamekeepers Handicap Chase at Haydock on 3 January 1969. What a valedictory performance he put on – he carried a massive 12 st 7 lbs, gave runner-up Hal's Farewell a colossal 19 lbs, and beat him by six lengths! It seemed he knew it was his last curtain-call, and he put on a show no one would ever forget.

In my view Flyingbolt was probably the best horse I ever rode – even better that Arkle! I honestly believe he would have beaten Arkle in the 1966 Gold Cup if Tom Dreaper had allowed him to run.

Unlike most people, my memories of Christmas are generally unpleasant. I stole the £5 from my father's drawer over Christmas, and the Christmas of 1969 was even more traumatic.

The warning lights were flashing as early as 16 December. I rode 2–1 favourite Another Guy in a two-mile chase at Kelso and we were well clear at the third-last when we came down with a bang. Ironically, the winner, Tarik, was ridden by my brother Peter for his first success in England.

My fall was due entirely to alcohol. I was too weak to control the horse. Too dehydrated. I was frantically worried about my drinking problem, but I knew of no one who could help me. I was also keyed-up at the prospect of riding Flyingbolt in the King George VI Chase at Kempton on Boxing Day. To be sure I was sober I spent all Christmas Day in my sauna and didn't touch a drink.

Ken Oliver picked me up and we stayed overnight in Glasgow

to be ready to fly to Kempton next morning. I suffered a terrible night. I couldn't sleep, and the sweat poured off me. I felt a wreck. I would have loved a few drinks.

I accompanied Ken Oliver to the airport next morning without telling him a word of my condition. My ticket was checked out at the desk and we made our way to the barrier, where I couldn't keep silent a moment longer.

'Guv'nor,' I said, 'there's no way I can ride this horse today. I feel terrible. I have an awful tummy bug.'

If I had told him the truth, that alcohol was to blame, he would have brushed me aside and said as usual, 'Oh, God, that's nothing, Barry. You'll be all right.'

Of course he got into his usual flap, rushed to a telephone and rang Josh Gifford and booked him for the horse. Ken then flew on to London and I stayed in Glasgow. I watched the race on television, and saw Flyingbolt finish second to Titus Oats. Then I spent the rest of the day in bed.

Looking back on that day, if I had swallowed a few drinks at the airport I would probably have been fit to ride. But, having tried not to drink for forty-eight hours, my withdrawal symptoms were chronic.

Yet no matter how sad I felt about missing the ride on Flyingbolt, I certainly didn't want to miss the mount on Drumikill in the Irish Sweeps Hurdle at Fairyhouse next day. So when Ken Oliver flew back to Glasgow from Kempton I assured him I was over my illness, and we flew from Glasgow to Dublin together. I walked the track and got myself ready to ride Drumikill.

Unknown to Ken I still felt tired and dehydrated; Drumikill ran badly and Ken Oliver criticized me for not riding him well. It wasn't a very smart piece of observation; for six weeks I'd been riding well below my best because of the alcohol.

After the Sweeps Hurdle I went back to my mother's house, where she was putting on a twenty-first birthday party for my sister Ann. There must have been a hundred people there, including Ken Oliver, Padge Berry, and the Dreapers, so I had to behave myself, although I was still able to keep myself topped up by nipping into the kitchen for some wine.

As the night wore on and the visitors started drifting away, I went to the kitchen for longer spells and knocked back several drinks.

When I returned to the drawing-room, Ken Oliver was there, and he fell against the mantelpiece and split his head open. It was so bad we had to call a doctor, at two in the morning. The wound needed six stitches, but Ken was so full of drink I doubt whether he felt the blow. However, it caused a nasty gash and the scar is still there today.

When the doctor left I went straight to the fridge and grabbed a bottle of champagne and drank the lot. My mother found me an hour later, blindly unconscious from alcohol, stretched out in front of the Aga, sleeping with the dogs.

Having now seen me at my worst, my mother was desperately worried about my drinking and next day drove me to Dr Byrne's house in Drogheda. He spoke to me about my drinking and concluded I was nothing more than physically and mentally rundown. At the back of my mind I knew there was a lot more to it than that.

Within forty-eight hours I was admitted to Our Lady of Lourdes Hospital in Drogheda, where I was tested for ulcers and all sorts of other illnesses. After three weeks there I felt a great deal better and Dr Byrne suggested I should meet Dr Wilson, a psychiatrist at the Ardee Mental Hospital in County Louth.

Dr Wilson was the first person to tell me I was an alcoholic. I was stunned. I had feared it for a very long time, but I never wanted to believe it.

In the ensuing six years, constant hospitalization, loss of jobs, going skint, a broken marriage, and practically ending up in the gutter, left me in no doubt that Dr Wilson's diagnosis was bang on target. I was a chronic alcoholic.

During my stay at Our Lady of Lourdes, Ken Oliver and my mother covered up every day for me, and the press were fed a string of stories that I was suffering from ulcers.

One distinguished national newspaperman was so imaginative he even wrote that I had developed the ulcers the previous year, and that they had flared up at a Christmas party. He also wrote that I was on a diet of milk puddings, and it was these that had sent my weight soaring. I received sackfuls of mail recommending cures and treatment, and some 'fellow-sufferers' even offered to post me medicines and herbal concoctions. Of course I've never suffered from ulcers, but the fairy-story has stuck and to this day I still receive countless inquiries about them.

On leaving Our Lady of Lourdes, I went home to my mother, and the Olivers wrote to say my job was safe. But in my absence the stable's second jockey, Peter Ennis, had started winning on Even Keel and Drumikill and all the other good horses in the yard, and I knew I faced a stiff battle to re-establish myself.

I arrived back in England on 1 February 1970, and rode out for the Olivers right away. As early as the second day back, they called me indoors. Ken did most of the talking. Suddenly he had decided that I was a better hurdles jockey than a steeplechase rider, and that Peter Ennis would have the chasers and I would have the hurdlers.

He was entitled to his opinion, but it seemed rather a strange decision considering I had ridden so many winners over fences for him. What gratitude, I thought. However, I saw the Olivers had plenty of chasers but very few hurdlers, and I could have told them to 'stick your job up your jersey' as many jockeys in my position would have done.

But I knew Peter Ennis's limitations. I knew it was only a matter of time before I got back as number one again. Peter was a friendly sort, and he once lent me £1,000, which I paid him back. He was always very cool, and very lucky. Peter came from Garristown, the place that spawned Tommy Carberry, and he served his time with my father and later worked for Charlie Weld, father of Dermot. He followed me over to the Olivers, but has now retired from the saddle and has a flourishing business breaking horses in Middleham.

With Ennis in the driving-seat, I grafted hard and lived like a monk with little food and no drink, and my weight plummeted dramatically to a mere 10 st 7 lbs.

Slowly, the top trainers came back for me. I rode my first winner, Tudor Times, for Fred Rimell at Nottingham on 14 March. The previous day I rode Red Rum in a handicap hurdle at Teesside and we finished fifth. I considered him an average horse, and certainly not brilliant.

Winners were now steadily trickling in, and it was getting through to the Olivers that this guy must be good.

My first winner for them after my illness came on Dunmore East in a two-mile hurdle race at Carlisle on 28 March. Mentally and physically I was in excellent shape. I was completely off the drink.

But I still needed the big breakthrough to convince people that I was back at my best. Astonishingly, it came at the tremendous Aintree Grand National meeting when the whole world is riveted to every tiny piece of action.

Again I was grateful to a so-called small trainer for providing the leg-up. Peter Ransom, who trained at Leominster, booked me for Tenterclef in the Mildmay Chase, and we went to the front three fences from home and pulled clear to win by fifteen lengths. As a result of that win, David Coleman interviewed me on BBC television and questioned me about my remarkable loss of weight and general state of fitness. In turn, I gave all the credit to Dr Austin Darragh in Dublin and this prompted a lot of other heavy jockeys to ring him up and join his medical register.

Even the fastidious Ken Oliver was now satisfied I had something to offer over fences and asked me if I'd like the pick of his four probables for the Scottish Grand National. An amazing climb-down when you remember he dropped me from his chasers and I hadn't ridden one fencer for him since being in hospital.

Anyway, there was only one horse I wanted to ride – The Spaniard. I was frank with Ken Oliver and told him I couldn't get down to 9 st 13 lbs, but I would make 10 st. He said, 'Fair enough. He's yours.'

Then three days before the race, I had a terrible scare when I fell from Dunmore East at Newcastle and was rushed to hospital with a suspected broken right arm.

Thank God, the X-rays showed I was only badly bruised, so I rushed down to London for ultra-sonic treatment and prayed I'd be fit to ride The Spaniard on 18 April – my twenty-third birthday! I put up 4 lbs overweight to ride the horse at 10 st 3 lbs, and we dominated the race over every yard of the four miles, cantering home by eight lengths to provide a fairy-tale ending. I also bet £150 each way on the horse, so I collected about £1,600 as a pleasant bonus.

It was my first ride over fences for the Olivers for more than five months. It was a great personal achievement and I was absolutely delighted. I was winning the fight back. It injected enormous confidence into my system and I started to believe in myself again. I didn't give drink a thought.

But my abstinence couldn't last forever. Inevitably, I was soon back on the bottle again, drinking like a maniac.

Nothing silences a weighing-room more effectively than the death of a fellow-jockey, particularly when the fatality happens on the racecourse. Thankfully, it occurs very rarely, but I have the sad memory of being at Chepstow on 9 May 1970, when poor Freddie Dixon was killed in a fall from Pernie, trained by his guv'nor Roy Whiston.

His death probably hit me more than any other jockey's because I actually changed alongside him, cracked a joke with him, and we discussed each other's chances. I even walked to the paddock with him.

Freddie and I were tremendous friends and I greatly admired the way he grafted year after year for his winners, which usually amounted to twenty-five or so a season.

I rode Gravel Lodge for Earl Jones in the race and missed seeing Freddie's fall as I was leading at the time. I fell at the second-last, but bounced up without a bruise. That's the luck of the game.

Freddie had taken a fall from Chantaway in the first race and later complained to me of feeling a bit heady. But Freddie wasn't the type to miss a ride, and wouldn't think of consulting a doctor.

His terrible death knocked us cold and taught us never to take our job for granted. The risks are enormous and frequently underestimated.

# 7
# Hitting the Bottle

THROUGHOUT MY CAREER, BOOKMAKERS DIDN'T GIVE ME A moment's respite. They pestered me to stop this horse and that horse, and hounded me like bees round a honey-pot.

In October 1969 I had just strolled into Ayr racecourse when a bookmaker offered me £2,500 to stop Winterguide from winning a three-horse race. I said I would.

My only rivals were Tipperwood (I. Watkinson) and Matts Moon (R. Greig). The betting went: 4–5 Tipperwood, evens Winterguide, 100–7 Matts Moon.

It was, I thought, a two-horse race. I agreed to accept the bribe because I knew Winterguide was a stupid, ignorant horse and unlikely to stay on his feet for two and a half miles.

I did my absolute best but, true to form, Winterguide came crashing down at the second-last, leaving Tipperwood to canter home by a distance. I remounted to finish second, and later on met the bookmaker in the car-park and cheerfully collected the £2,500 in notes.

Yet a further £2,500 came into my hands at Perth when I rode the temperamental Ballyroan in a four-horse race. Again the bookmaker propositioned me, and again I said, 'Yes.'

My three opponents were Persian Fancy (T. Stack), Tipstaff (S. Hayhurst) and Air Commodore (R. Greig). Bookmakers listed Persian Fancy 5–4 favourite, with Ballyroan the 7–4 second best. When saying 'Yes' to the bookmaker I knew full well that Ballyroan tended to be a problem at the start. Tommy Stack usually rode Ballyroan, but this time he wanted to be on Persian Fancy. Tommy was no fool.

As expected, Ballyroan was left stranded at the gate, and although I eventually drove him hard into the race we could never make up the leeway and Persian Fancy cantered in by fifteen lengths. Pocketing the £2,500 was absolute child's play.

Though I was riding every day and consistently landing winners, my drinking habits were once again driving me insane, and in the summer of 1970 I flew out to Greece for a holiday with Mary Briggs and hit the bottle in a way I'd never hit it before. In a fortnight of outrageous drinking I went through £750 and ended up penniless.

It was one of those weird arrangements where the honeymoon came first and the wedding later. I had signed to ride for Colin Davies and Ken Oliver, so there would be no time for a break during August when Mary and I had planned to be married.

Before leaving for Athens I drew £300 in traveller's cheques, which I passed to Mary, and squeezed £700 in notes in my pockets to be sure I'd have enough money for drink.

On our first day in Athens I did a reasonable job of staying sober and I tried hard to stay that way. But it couldn't last. Soon I began deliberately losing Mary in the crowd so that I could nip into the nearest restaurant for a few large vodkas to keep myself topped up. We trudged tediously to all the famous historical places, but I saw little, and appreciated nothing. I was drifting around in a permanent alcoholic haze. On the third day we hired a boat and steamed off to a nearby island called Idhra and booked in at the Idhra Beach Hotel. By now, I was drinking non-stop, taking just a brief break to answer the call of nature, and a second or two to light my Havana.

I remember on our first night we went down to the restaurant and I bought two bottles of wine; a young honeymoon couple called Halfhead from Yorkshire came across and joined us. Mary was an excellent host.

As usual I started bringing in the wine and soon got them on the tonic, and we all ended up in a jolly, happy mood. Feeling quite merry, we left the table and made our way through the trees to the beautiful, floodlit swimming-pool.

While I stared into the pool, I developed a touch of the giggles. I was very inebriated and crept up behind Mrs Halfhead and pushed her in. I don't know why I did it – it was just the insanity of the drink. Then her husband jumped in because the frantic, astounded girl couldn't swim. Water splashed everywhere and I just stood at the edge and looked in at them.

Although I could swim, I wasn't going to get wet. That's how wretchedly selfish I was. It was terribly embarrassing for Mary. The couple scrambled out, soaked to the skin, and excused themselves. They had known me a few hours and I had pushed the young wife into the pool. Her dress was ruined.

Mary was furious and insisted I apologized next day. I found this a huge problem, but I did as she asked, simply to keep the peace. Needless to say, Mr and Mrs Halfhead didn't join us the following night.

Mary liked to go to bed early, so I would sit at her side, well-intoxicated and smoking a cigar, and she'd usually be asleep by half-past nine. As soon as her eyes were shut I'd rush off to the bar, grab a bottle of Remy Martin and some ginger ale, and sit alone and drink steadily into the early hours of the morning. I followed the same routine night after night, and it cost me a bomb. I was the bar's best customer. Then on the seventh night I almost keeled over with shock. I strolled up to the bar and found the doors were locked; it was the staff's night off.

So here was an alcoholic desperate for a drink. I was parched. I paced up and down like a panther. I went to reception and practically begged for a bottle of brandy. But everyone ignored me. I was brushed aside. Then I remembered a little bar down on the beach. This was also closed, but it had a flimsy plastic shutter that was simple to prise open. I did a swift, neat job, climbed over the bar and, by using my lighter in the dark, picked two brandy bottles off the shelf.

I suppose I was, strictly speaking, stealing the brandy, but that's how uncontrollably desperate an acoholic can become. I intended to pay for it the next morning, and I did. And I paid for the damage to the shutter as well.

With the brandy safely in my hands, I settled on the beach under a warm, star-filled sky and got stuck into the drink. All I can remember is waking up at six in the morning, flat-out on the sands, and with only a quarter of one brandy bottle left at my side. I promptly finished it off, stumbled back to my room, put on a clean shirt, shaved and was ready for action again.

This routine continued night after night, day after day, and Mary became quite accustomed to it. She was also beginning to worry about me. After all, we were to be married in two months' time.

After ten days I had drunk my way through all my spare money and had to coax Mary to cash some of our traveller's cheques in order to buy more booze. She argued violently with me, but I was so desperate she finally gave in.

One scorching afternoon we took a boat trip to a nearby island. Mary had met some friends who wanted to visit a monastery high in the mountains. It was so isolated the only way to reach it was on a donkey. From the moment Mary mentioned it, I knew I was snookered. How could I get up there and back without a drink? The thought was horrifying. So while the others hired the donkeys, I sneaked off to a bar and knocked back four double vodkas.

Donkeys had to be used because deadly snakes lurked on the hillside and it was too dangerous to walk. It took us two hours to reach the top. I was so dry I'd have paid £200 for some brandy, but there was nothing. Just sheep and goats, and miles and miles of silent desolation. The heat was intense and the sweat ran down my cheeks to my chin. My withdrawal symptoms were chronic.

In desperation I thought of the monastery. Surely they'd have a stock of wine for mass? So I got 'lost' – I slipped into the monastery and rummaged through cupboards and lockers ...

Then I heard a soft shuffling noise behind me, and turned to look into the ebony eyes of a bearded priest in long black robes. I knew he didn't speak English, so I tried frantically to explain that I needed a drink. I raised my hands to my lips and poked out my dry tongue. I was praying he would get the message before Mary and her friends came along to collect me. The priest then went away and I thought my prayers were being answered. But in a short time he came rushing back with the two worst things for any alcoholic – a jug of water and a slab of Turkish Delight!

I hoped he would go away so that I could hunt around and find the wine I knew had to be there. Eventually he did leave and, although I searched with the skill of Maigret and the speed of light, I still failed to find the bottles. Mary and her friends remained outside, taking photographs and nattering about historical values and all that junk. I couldn't stand all that nonsense. But I had to stand it because I was stuck up there with them!

For a moment I thought I'd skip off down the mountain on my own, and I was just about to leave when I remembered the snakes and realized that if I were bitten by one of them it would be the end of me.

As the seconds ticked by I became more and more agitated. I told Mary I had to return to the bottom because the heat was killing me. I made all sorts of absurd excuses. So we scrambled back on our donkeys and made our way down the mountainside. It was the longest ride of my life. The moment we hacked into the village I leapt off the donkey and vanished. I was supposed to be crippled with stomach pains and diarrhoea. I darted into a bar, and I was shaking and shivering. People already sitting around thought I was mad and I probably was.

Anyway, I didn't bother to measure the drink. I just told the waiter to pour the vodka straight from the bottle into a half-pint glass. He filled it to the top and left a bottle of bitter-lemon at my elbow. I sat there for half an hour and I drank and drank and finished off the whole bottle. It put me right; I stopped shaking. I rejoined Mary and we headed back to the hotel.

Twenty-four hours later, I was up to my antics again. Mary and I went on a midnight cruise around the islands and someone on the boat made a pass at her. In my alcoholic madness I burst into a jealous rage and threatened to jump off the boat and into the sea. I climbed down to the rudders and crowds of people pressed against the safety-rail and stared over the edge at this inebriated fool stepping closer and closer to suicide.

Screams of panic pierced the night and the boat was brought to a standstill.

I had a huge audience, and Mary was escorted through the crowd to the rail. She pleaded with me to stop my nonsense and climb up to her. It was mortifying for Mary, and it contributed to the ruin of a holiday-honeymoon that had been a massive booze-up from beginning to end.

We arrived back in London at midday on Sunday and I had no money left to buy 'duty free'. I had drunk every penny. And I still wasn't satisfied. I knew British pubs opened at midday and tried every stroke to stop the car and plead with hotel managers to let me have some vodka on tick.

My luck was out, and we continued on our way to Mary's mother's home near Newbury. She knew I had a drink problem and wouldn't risk me with a wine-gum. I had stayed there a few months earlier and had crept downstairs in the middle of the night and devoured a whole bottle of gin. Mary's mother noticed it was missing and quizzed me about it. I denied being involved and protested at her cheek in considering me a thief.

When I reached Mary's mother's home, I couldn't sit still. I couldn't speak clearly, and I kept trembling and wincing. I said I was unwell after the holiday. That I had a touch of sunstroke. And I made excuses to go for a walk.

I covered miles and miles in every direction, but there wasn't a pub in sight. So I returned to the house, and made some excuse to take the car for a drive.

Eventually I found my oasis. I sank six large vodkas, bought a large bottle of brandy and hid it in my pocket. This was typical of an alcoholic. Cunning and devious. Scheming for the future.

I bought the brandy because I could drink it neat, which I couldn't do with vodka. I put the brandy inside my clothes in a suitcase under the bed so that I could take a swig whenever I felt like it. It kept me going until we left on Monday morning.

After coming back from Greece, I took a call from Colin Davies asking me to school some horses at his stable in Chepstow. I was trying desperately hard to stay off the drink, but it was impossible. I just had to consume a certain amount of alcohol every day. It was like five-star petrol. Without it, I'd grind to a halt

At the end of July 1970 I again called on Dr Ford Simpson in Hawick as a matter of urgency about my drinking, but all he gave me were anti-booze tablets. Thank God I had the good sense not to take any. If I had, and drank, I'd have been dead.

I was booked by Colin Davies to ride Farmer Giles at Market Rasen the following day, the first meeting of the season. I had schooled him over fences several times, and he was a brilliant jumper. I was sure he'd win, but I worried like hell about the race. I failed to sleep on the Friday night and had terrible diarrhoea. I was a mental wreck.

On Saturday morning, just as Colin Davies was preparing to leave for the races, I rang him up and told him I was in agony with my stomach and that I couldn't take the ride.

He put Graham Thorner up in my place and they cantered in by eight lengths. When I heard the result I was depressed even more. Mary knew how I felt and took the keys from the car, but that couldn't stop me. Nothing could stop me. I walked three miles into Jedburgh and stayed there all day and all night, just drinking myself stupid.

I don't remember much of what happened, but I do recall waking up behind the Royal Hotel in a bramble bush with a whisky bottle in my hand. It was three o'clock in the morning and I staggered to a telephone-box and rang Mary. She was fast asleep, but she came out, drove me home and poured the whisky down the sink.

Alcoholism had overpowered and wrecked me. I couldn't fight it any longer. So early next day I took an Aer-Lingus flight from Glasgow to Dublin and began my first horrific drying-out session at St John O'God's Hospital.

I was met at the airport by Jack W., a good friend and a member of Alcoholics Anonymous. Four years earlier he had cleverly detected I was developing a drinking problem, although I had then been on the bottle only four months. I had never forgotten the autumn of 1966 when Jack had told a friend I was drinking too heavily and needed close watching.

I entered St John O'God's on 2 August, was dried out until 6 August, and then amazingly got married four days later at the Church of St Francis of Assisi in Ascot.

The service, followed by a reception at the Berysted Hotel in Sunningdale, was nerve-racking. I was dead scared to take a drink; I still had the shakes.

Then, if this were not enough, my mother had spent three hours on the telephone the night before trying her hardest to get me to call the wedding off. To this day my mother doesn't accept that I have a drink problem. She believes my trouble is nothing more than immaturity, a personality flaw that prevents me from facing up to reality. She's wrong. I have a disease called alcoholism, and I wouldn't wish it on anyone.

I ask for help every morning, and I give thanks every night. I'm not fanatically religious, but I certainly believe there is a good Lord up there somewhere keeping a close eye on what we do.

As the wedding drew closer, I knew my mother was right about calling it off, but I couldn't make the decision because I was afraid of letting so many people down at the last minute. Of course these were ridiculous grounds for entering into a marriage, and, with hindsight, I'm the first person to agree that I was a fool to to go ahead.

It wasn't that I didn't love Mary. It was just that I was unstable and had not come to terms with my drinking problems. I should have cancelled the wedding, but I didn't have the guts.

Tommy Stack was my best man and we had 150 guests, including jockey friends Jimmy Uttley, Bob Davies, Stan Mellor, David Mould, Macer and Josh Gifford, Terry Biddlecombe and my brother Peter. Trainers Ken Oliver, Colin Davies and Earl Jones were also there.

Several photographs were taken of me holding a glass of champagne to my lips, but I didn't touch a drop of alcohol all day. On the surface it seemed such a happy gathering. Behind my mask the tension and torment were tearing me apart.

The honeymoon night was even more disastrous. We stayed in an hotel in Castle Combe and we sat on the bed and talked and cried. Secretly, we both knew our mistake. We both knew we had just gone through the most important moment in our lives, made solemn pledges, committed ourselves to each other, yet all the time we weren't really equipped or ready for such a big step.

We left the hotel after two days, and I started riding work for Colin Davies. A short time later I was reunited with Farmer Giles in a Novices Chase at Market Rasen and we won by twenty lengths. Obviously it was a great fillip.

While at St John O'God's, I was introduced to the tranquillizer Valium 5, a small, yellow tablet on which I eventually became hooked. When I wasn't drinking I was on tranquillizers. I was swallowing pills like Smarties.

I took Valium at the first sign of approaching anxiety, and when not swallowing a pill I would rush to the nearest pub and sink two large brandies, which would eliminate the fears right away. Yet, once I realized I was a progressive alcoholic, I no longer wanted to drink to remove the panics. Valium was the only alternative, although it was painfully slow and took time to work through the system. Booze, on the other hand, stopped the fears instantly.

I believe too many doctors are too liberal in the way they

prescribe Valium and other tranquillizers. People become too dependent on them. There is an obvious need for tighter control.

On top of all my drinking and pill-swallowing I was still gambling heavily, and in September 1970 I turned a modest mid-week meeting at Teesside into a rattling good benefit day. A bookmaker offered me £2,000 to stop King Dolphin in the seller, and in another race I bet £5,000 on Arctic Explorer to beat my mount Dixies Double.

King Dolphin had only three opponents: Touch Line (C. Boothman), Golden Fancy (P. James) and Chroniquer (D. Atkins).

Basically, it was a two-horse race between King Dolphin and Touch Line. I said 'Yes' to the bookmaker because I thought Touch Line would win on merit, and that King Dolphin wouldn't require any stopping from me.

To the bookmaker's despair, I was wrong. He splashed £20,000 on Touch Line and King Dolphin won! He was naturally furious, but eventually cooled down and forgave me, and came trotting back with further tempting offers.

Then I moved on to Arctic Explorer. This was a snip! The Olivers trained both Arctic Explorer and Dixies Double and they decided Peter Ennis should ride Arctic Explorer and I should ride Dixies Double. As Dixies Double had won two races over fences in recent weeks, he was weighted to give 10 lbs to Arctic Explorer. However, having ridden both of them, I knew better than anyone that Arctic Explorer was far superior. He also loved the fast ground that prevailed on the day.

Because I, as stable jockey, was engaged for Dixies Double, the betting public naturally thought I was riding the better horse and made me the 2–1 favourite. To my delight, and despite my £5,000, Arctic Explorer was allowed to start at 9–4. As expected, he led every inch of the way, and left me and Dixies Double painfully prostrate at the second-last. It was a crashing fall and I was lucky to escape without breaking my back, but thoughts of collecting the handsome £12,500 profit certainly helped to ease the pain and speed my recovery!

Obviously a good race for any bent bookmaker is the one that has only two runners. If he can buy up the jockey of one, he can earn himself a mint by betting on the other.

Such a bookmaker once approached me before a two-horse race

at Nottingham and offered me £2,000 to make sure my horse Royal Slave was beaten by Pollock Fair, ridden by the luckless Jimmy Harris, who sometime later broke his back in a shocking fall and now trains bravely and successfully from a wheelchair at Melton Mowbray. I promised the bookmaker I'd fall in with his plan, but knew in my heart I'd win if I could.

Pollock Fair started 4–5 favourite, with Royal Slave at 11–10. I decided to sit in behind Pollock Fair. He led me to the seventh and then suddenly tried to run out, crashed into the wing and fell.

Again the bookmaker went berserk, but behind my apologies I was able to smile. I had covered myself with a single bet on Royal Slave, and also included it as the third leg of a lovely £100 treble!

To emphasize my mania for riding winners, I must recall an incident a fortnight later, when I received an SOS from Colin Davies after breakfast to travel six hundred miles from Jedburgh to Chepstow to ride Colditz Story in the last race because his stable jockey Bob Davies had pulled out with injury.

Without stopping to consider the distance, I threw myself into my BMW, filled it up with petrol and rushed to Wales and beat John Williams and Cheroot by a neck. I had no time for a chat; I was like a clockwork toy and kept charging on.

After changing out of my colours, I went straight to my car and drove back to Jedburgh without a stop – a round trip of 1,200 miles for one ride, and very little profit. That's how greedy and insane I'd become for a winner.

# 8
# The Wrath of Walwyn

OVER THE YEARS I HAVE MET OR RIDDEN FOR EVERY CONCEIVable type of trainer. The best by a furlong was the immaculate Fulke Walwyn.

He was a pleasure to work for. Dedicated, efficient, and a tremendous judge of a horse. He was always understanding with my drink problem, and I maintained the highest admiration for him.

My first ride for the guv'nor was on a spare called Almirene. It was a five-year-old gelding owned by John Banks. We finished eighth of twenty-four, but two weeks later I rode him again at Worcester and we won by fifteen lengths.

Between these two rides I received a telephone call from Mr Walwyn's secretary, Liz, to ask me if I would like to ride The Dikler in the Tony Teacher Handicap Chase at Cheltenham.

'Good God!' I said. 'I can't believe it.'

I knew The Dikler was a difficult horse, but I looked on it as another challenge in my life. I spoke to Mr Walwyn and he wanted me to travel down from Jedburgh to Lambourn to sit on the horse before I rode him in public. I was pulling out of the garage before Mr Walwyn had time to put down the receiver.

I schooled The Dikler over three fences on the Lambourn gallops early next morning, and we were just turning for home when a thick blanket of fog swept across the Downs and blotted out the whole landscape.

The Dikler was feeling full of himself, and he suddenly took off and pulled so bloody hard I couldn't hold him. He tore into the fog and frightened the life out of me. I was lost and we were going hell-for-leather. I had visions of finishing up in Wantage or wrapped round a telegraph-pole.

Thank God my fears weren't realized. The Dikler, the crafty blighter, knew his way back, and he eventually pulled himself up at the foot of the hill and quietly made his way home.

In the race immediately before The Dikler's at Cheltenham I was booked by John Edwards to ride a little mare called Bay Tudor. Mr Walwyn was very worried about this ride and kept asking me whether Bay Tudor could jump. He practically pleaded with me not to take the mount.

In the end I reluctantly asked John to release me. I hated turning down rides, no matter how dangerous they were supposed to be. But John stood firm, and I went back to Mr Walwyn and assured him Bay Tudor was a safe jumper, and that there was nothing to be worried about.

Within twenty-four hours my confidence was justified. We led from the seventh and won by six lengths at 14–1. The victory couldn't have come at a better time. It put me at my psychological best for The Dikler.

Because of his top weight of 12 st and the boggy ground, Mr Walwyn advised me to hold the horse up and get him settled, to make sure he didn't run away with me. I followed these instructions to the letter.

The Dikler jumped superbly, and coming down the hill we cleared the third-last with only Ashgate and Jimmy Bourke ahead of us. Slowly, I moved The Dikler closer and joined Jimmy at the fence. The Dikler was cruising, and loving every second. I had no alternative but to give him his head and let him go to the front.

In making the move I realized I could be making a lot of trouble for myself. The Dikler had a monstrous habit of running down his fences, and without a horse ahead of us to lead him he would be more inclined to get up to his antics again.

He had tried his tricks with Willie Robinson and Stan Mellor long before I teamed up with him. I watched him at Newbury on a bad day running down every fence on the far side, and always jumping from left to right.

So, turning into the straight at Cheltenham, and with the race at our mercy, I decided that if he tried to run down the last fence I would fight him in a way he had never been fought before.

I locked both hands tightly on one rein and refused to budge. We approached the fence in full stride, flat-out, and with fear a forgotten word.

He felt strong and aggressive, and his balance and rhythm were perfect. Then, with the throttle wide open, and just five yards from the fence, he suddenly slammed on the brakes, cocked his head and used every ounce of his gigantic frame to duck and dive to the right.

'Okay, you bastard!' I screamed, and I gripped him hard, kicked him in the belly, and drove him violently at the fence. My muscles were jammed rigid with determination. This was one test of strength he was not going to win.

In the few seconds it takes to cover five or six strides, he capitulated like a sensible schoolboy, obeyed my command, jumped the fence dead straight and trotted to the line a convincing fifteen-length winner from Eddie Harty and Jimmy Scot. One partnership had been established. Brogan was boss.

I rode The Dikler in the Gold Cup that season and we finished third behind L'Escargot. The ground was bottomless, and he hated it. He was never able to produce his best.

As time went on, I began having other rides for Mr Walwyn. One terribly difficult horse was Charlie Potheen. We first teamed up in the Bibury Chase at Cheltenham. He started even-money favourite and we had to concede 12 lbs to the useful Balinese, trained by Bob Turnell and ridden by Jeff King.

Charlie Potheen was a dead ignorant, powerful front-runner, a brute. He would charge like a bull at everything. And he tended to hang badly.

Going to the last open ditch at Cheltenham, Jeff was sitting ominously on my tail and Charlie Potheen approached the fence like a Centurion tank. He burst right through it and landed vertically on the other side. Luckily, I rolled clear and miraculously avoided being trapped under his massive frame. I thought this accident would teach him a lesson, and seeing that we were both all right I jumped on his back again and we finished third.

Mr Walwyn wasn't at the meeting, but when he heard I had remounted he broke into a rage. Because the horse wasn't hurt I thought it only right and prudent to finish third and earn the owner Mrs Joy Heath a little prize-money. Mr Walwyn didn't support this theory, so whenever I fell on a Walwyn horse in future I took great care never to remount, even if it meant turning down good money.

I later rode Charlie Potheen in the Totalizator Champion Chase and we finished a respectable third after the bridle had slipped through his mouth. So I suggested to Mr Walwyn the horse should be fitted with a cheek bridle in future to help me restrain him. I had used it with enormous success on Even Keel, another terrible tearaway.

Our next adventure came at Newbury in the Kencot Handicap Chase. The Queen Mother's Inch Arran was one of several front-runners in the race, so I thought I might get my chap settled for a change. But by the time we reached the stands he was scorching in front and pulling my arms out. All along the far side he dropped his jaw and hung violently to the left, and I screamed in his ear and cursed hell out of him.

He was still hanging badly as we turned into the straight, and as we jumped the fourth-last, I kicked him in the belly to keep his mind on the job. His response was electrifying. He flew thirty lengths clear and I knew for sure he was an exceptional horse.

We jumped the final fence twenty lengths in front, but he hung so badly we careered off the track. I had to summon up every ounce of strength to drag him back onto the course, managing to get him going again just in time to beat Garrynagree three lengths.

In the meantime my association with The Dikler continued to prosper. I taught him to settle to Mr Walwyn's satisfaction, and in the middle of March we went in search of steeplechasing's principal prize – the 1972 Gold Cup at Cheltenham.

Crisp headed the Gold Cup market at 11–4, and in a star-studded line-up Leap Frog and L'Escargot, the two Irish giants, were the other major contenders.

Despite this illustrious opposition, The Dikler matched them for speed, skill and overall class. We jumped the last three fences in front, and I was confident we were poised to pull it off. Then, just thirty yards from the line, my compatriot Frank Berry stormed up the far side with Glencaraig Lady, and Nigel Wakley came with a rush up the stands side with Royal Toss. I was the cold meat in the sandwich.

Glencaraig Lady was shortly declared the winner, with Royal Toss second and The Dikler third. Distances were given as three-quarters of a length and a head. But before the huge Irish contingent could reach the bar to celebrate, the racecourse announcer advised punters that all betting tickets should be retained as two objections had been lodged.

Speculation in the weighing-room was firm that Frank would lose the race. Once I heard that Nigel had objected to him, I decided to object to Nigel. Not because he had hampered me, but because I thought Frank had won fairly and squarely; by lodging an objection myself, I might help him keep the race. Happily, my tactics worked.

'Placings remain unaltered,' blared the loudspeaker, and the Irish backers went berserk and fled in droves to the bars and devoured gallons and gallons of Guinness.

When the Gold Cup came around the following year I was sadly off the scene, being dried out for the sixth time at the St John O'God's Hospital in Dublin; the nearest I got to the action was watching the race on television.

Ron Barry stood in for me on The Dikler and they pipped Pendil by a short head in the most thrilling finish ever known in the history of this famous race.

It was from the same hospital bed that I watched Terry Biddlecombe deputize for me on Charlie Potheen to win the John Smith's Great Yorkshire Chase. Richard Pitman won the Hennessy on the same horse, and Ron Barry completed my misery by capturing the Whitbread on him.

My craving for drink had cost me four important victories. I had done all the hard graft in educating this massive animal, and then three other riders had stepped in and reaped the benefit. I was terribly dejected, although each time I wired my congratulations to the owner, trainer and jockey.

Coming up to Christmas 1970, I was desperately short of cash, and I faced a stack of bills after a disastrous spell with my gambling. Then, on 17 December, I went to Carlisle to ride four horses, and came up with a brainwave that made Drumikill the biggest certainty in the history of the sport.

He was set to carry 11 st 5 lbs in the Corby Handicap Chase, with his biggest danger, Rossglass Lad, on 11 st 3 lbs. Rossglass Lad had won two of his previous three races, and his regular partner Stan Hayhurst was again in the saddle.

The Carlisle weighing-room is significantly different from any other in the country. It has a long, dark, narrow corridor that leads from the main room to the doorway, and I exploited it in a manner it had never been exploited before.

On my way out to saddle the horse I nipped smartly into the toilet half-way down the corridor, but instead of zipping open my pants I grabbed 10 lbs of weight from the lead-cloth, pushed it in a plastic bag, and went out and hid it under a sack which I had left conveniently behind the weighing-room door. With 10 lbs off his back, Drumikill was an absolute certainty. Barring a fall, he couldn't be beaten. And I put £10,000 on him!

Up to the sixth fence I was happy to let him amble along. I knew that once I unleashed him he'd never be caught. His light weight was ridiculous. I was toying with the opposition. Eventually my patience ran out and I kicked for home. He flew, and although he blundered slightly at the last through travelling so fast, he raced away to win by an easy ten lengths from Michael Dickinson and Charming Fellow, with Rossglass Lad in third.

Drumikill was returned 5–4 favourite, and I picked up a handsome Christmas profit of £12,500. It was a great stroke, and I have never revealed it to anyone until this day. Trainers galore have boasted of saddling handicap certainties all over the world, but I doubt if any of them ever compared with my Drumikill coup at Carlisle.

With victory safely in the bag, I returned to the weighing-room; on entering the corridor I pretended to stumble and dropped all my tack over the floor near the door. The girths, stirrups, breastplate and saddle were spread all over the place.

As I fumbled to get them together, I made sure of slipping my hand under the sack behind the door, grabbed the lead from the plastic bag and made my way to the scales. Once there, I looked the clerk straight in the eye and weighed-in without the slightest suspicion.

Two hours later I completed a marvellous day with a win on October after Fooseboot was disqualified for bumping on the run in.

Tony Gillam owned, trained and rode Foosaboot, and I was reluctant to lodge an objection because I had sold the horse to him and wished him luck with it. The stewards came to my rescue by announcing an inquiry before they received my objection, and this took a lot of strain off me. On seeing the camera-patrol film we were all satisfied Foosaboot had given me a resounding thump and deprived me of certain victory.

By coincidence, two of my many successes on the gutsy little October came in the stewards' room after trouble from other horses on the run in.

I greeted 1971 in hilarious fashion. I spent New Year's night in London with the Olivers, and we joined the many thousands singing and dancing in Trafalgar Square, and I pushed Ken in the fountain.

He was drenched to the skin. He was as wet outside as I was inside. I had been twenty-four hours on the drink, mainly nipping to and from my car where I had bottles of vodka topped up with lime-juice hidden in the boot.

We were in London for the Express Chase at Sandown on New Year's Day and, although I felt like death going out for the race, I led all the way on Even Keel and beat our solitary rival Gay Trip by an easy length and a half.

My drinking bouts were accelerating again, so with several fixtures cancelled through frost, I seized the chance to re-enter St John O'God's for a few days to be dried out.

In flew to Dublin on 5 January, and returned on 8 January . . . and the very next day rode two winners at Market Rasen. I don't know how I achieved it, and I don't want any medals. But I was amazed at my resilience. My constitution was absolutely indestructible. I just kept bouncing back.

The Olivers had no idea where I had been. I told them I was going for a spell of hunting. Then, after two days at St John O'God's, I telephoned Ken and said I'd suffered a fall but hoped to be fit to ride for him at the weekend. Thank God, I was.

By keeping silent about my stay at St John O'God's, the public and the press were not aware that I was pickled in drink again. I was using my wits, a facet of a jockey's make-up that must never be under-estimated. There is no worthwhile jockey in racing history who has reached the top on talent alone. Brains are an essential asset, and I remember pulling off a priceless con-trick on a jockey at Wolverhampton one day, when Earl Jones saddled both Hard Nut and Gravel Lodge.

Barry Brogan, young – and innocent. When he first landed in England aged nineteen he was keen to learn about life. (*Bespix*)

Barry's mother, Betty Brogan, was determined, alert and industrious. She and Barry fell out over a fiver when he was still a schoolboy. (*Peter Sweetman*)

Celebrating an early success with Rhona Oliver, wife of trainer Ken Oliver, who was Barry's first regular employer in England.

Even Keel raring to go at Cheltenham. Barry was offered £7,000 to stop him in the Two-Mile Champion Chase. (*Racing Information Bureau*)

A favourite grey, Ballycurragh Lad, who helped Barry clinch an unforgettable five-timer at Wolverhampton in November 1968. (*K. Bright*)

The incomparable Billy Bow, who died in Barry's arms just after winning the Ladbroke Hurdle at Newcastle in 1968. There is now a race named after him. (*J. E. Hedley*)

Better than Arkle – that was Flyingbolt. Barry rode him to his last success at Haydock in 1969. (*Central Press*)

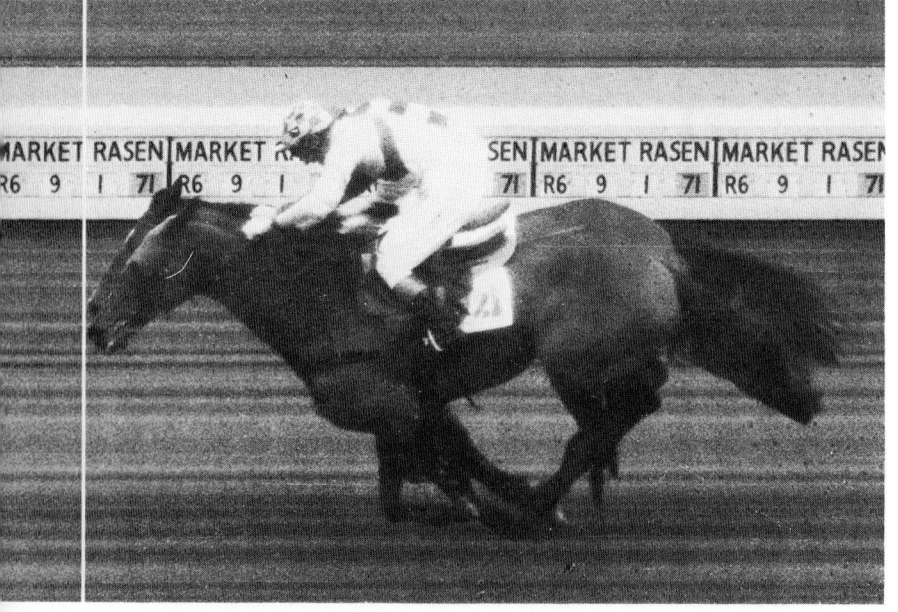

Barry on Arctic Explorer (no. 21) in a dead heat with Roy Edwards on Dungarvan Jewel at Market Rasen in January 1971. (*Copyright Racecourse Technical Services Limited*)

On the way down ... Menehall, in the lead, about to drop Barry at the last at Windsor in 1973. (*Sport and General Press Agency*)

Barry and Mary Briggs after the wedding; four days earlier Barry was being dried out in Dublin. From left to right: Tommy Stack, Jimmy Uttley, Stan Mellor, David Mould, Macer and Josh Gifford, and Barry's brother Peter.

Leaving the Jockey Club headquarters with his licence tucked into his hat after an awkward interrogation into his betting habits. (*Press Association*)

The Dikler lurches and Barry is too weak from boozing to keep him straight with Spanish Steps breathing down his neck. An enquiry was inevitable. (*London Photo Agency*)

Barry touches down on Moidore's Token, (no. 13), ahead of David Mould on Different Class in the 1978 Grand National. Barry beat him by a neck for second place, Red Alligator winning by twenty lengths. (*Sport and General Press Agency*)

Sitting tight on Flashy Boy, hell-bent on winning the Black and White Chase at Ascot in November 1975. (*Sport and General Press Agency*)

A moment to savour: the Queen Mother congratulates Barry on his win on Flashy Boy. (*Wallis Photographs, Doncaster*)

I rode Hard Nut, and a young claimer, Bill Hannon, rode the other. Both horses were natural front-runners, but I knew Gravel Lodge was a lot faster than mine, so I had to come up with some Machiavellian move to adjust the balance.

Turning into the straight, with only four fences left, Gravel Lodge was almost fifty yards in front of me. I had to act quickly. After jumping the third-last I put my plan into action. I shouted to Bill to take his time, and that if he continued at that speed Gravel Lodge would tire rapidly and end up on the floor. I prayed he'd listen to me.

Secretly, I knew that if Bill eased up early enough and I could get Hard Nut ahead of him, Gravel Lodge would give up and never fight back.

Bill was young and naive; swallowing the bait, he took a pull. I swept past him at the second-last and drew clear to beat him by three lengths.

Back in the weighing-room he knew he'd been conned, but was too embarrassed to talk about it. I left him suffering in silence.

Besides being the lucky owner of Persian War and other good horses like Clever Scot and Bowie's Brig, little Henry Alper was a cantankerous, self-opinionated gnome of a man.

I crossed him badly in the Champion Hurdle at Cheltenham when he booked me to ride Bowie's Brig, pacemaker for Persian War. Bula started favourite at 15–8, with Persian War third best at 9–2 and Bowie's Brig out with the washing at 50–1.

Unlike Alper, I refused to accept that Bowie's Brig was an also-ran, so I ignored his instructions to ride the horse as a moderate pacemaker and set out to shock the racing world and win the race for myself.

When it came to racing, Mr Alper wasn't considered a knowledgeable observer or good reader of a race, and his views were rarely taken as a serious appraisal.

Bowie's Brig had tremendous ability and was far too good to be wasted on setting the pace. He was a genuine contender.

I set him off in front, and we led them all a merry dance until reaching the second-last at the bottom of the hill where Bula, Persian War and Major Rose struggled to pass us. Bula possessed devasting speed and he flew up the hill to beat Persian War by four lengths, with the so-called no-hoper Bowie's Brig a mere six and a half lengths off the winner in fourth place. Some performance for a pacemaker!

I felt my confidence in the horse was more than justified, and that I had acted correctly in trying to steal the race. This opinion was not entirely shared by the irate Mr Alper, who reckoned I had ruined the chances of Persian War by not obeying his instructions and setting the 'appropriate' pace.

If God gave me nothing else, he instilled in me the gift of speech, and Ron Atkins, in particular, still has nightmares about the race I stole from him in the stewards' room at Cheltenham. Ron rode Lord Henry for Ifor Lewis, and I rode Dulwich for Colin Davies.

There were eight runners, and Dulwich started 2–1 favourite. The drama didn't really unfold until I started making progress coming down the hill towards the sixth flight. By now I had Dulwich in top gear and, going to the last hurdle, I could see Lord Henry on the far side, with me on the stands side, and poor Stan Mellor and Double First blatantly squeezed between us. The run to the line was a frantic free-for-all, and Lord Henry and Dulwich definitely bumped before Ron passed the post the clear and worthy winner.

I didn't back Dulwich that day, but I was ravenous for winners, so when I heard that the stewards were holding an inquiry I sharpened my tongue for the best piece of post-race oratory ever produced.

Talk? I bamboozled them!

The stewards stared at me, mesmerized. They accepted my explanation that Ron bore in on me, and they disqualified Lord Henry and gave me the race. Ron Atkins couldn't believe it, and Stan Mellor confessed he had never heard anyone talk so convincingly in the stewards' room.

# 9
# Betting to Lose

I SPENT THE NIGHT AFTER THAT RACE AT TERRY BIDDLECOMBE'S house in Tirley, and on the Friday we drove to my farm at Jedburgh to prepare for Saturday's big meeting at Ayr.

Terry was riding Gay Trip for Fred Rimell in the Scottish Grand National, and I was riding San-Feliu for Neville Crump.

Because San-Feliu was set a particularly light weight of 10 st 2 lbs, I had to stay off the drink, a necessity, alas, that didn't apply to Terry.

As usual, Terry was quickly on the prowl for birds, and shortly before midnight I rang Bob and Maureen Bruce, who owned a farm near Jedburgh, and they arranged for a girl called Tonia to drive down to stay with us.

For once, I kept completely out of the front line, but Terry and Tonia had a great time, and before he left for the races they had drunk a dozen bottles of champagne between them.

When riding in the Midlands or the West Country, I often stayed with Terry and his ex-wife Bridget. One memorable day was 29 March 1971. I drove down from Scotland and stayed overnight with them before travelling on to Taunton where I had two rides on a ten-race programme. John Edwards had booked me for Bay Tudor, and Colin Davies for Fake.

Terry was also riding at the meeting, and we indulged in an unprecedented booze-up on the way to the races. We warmed up as early as eight in the morning when we walked into a Gloucester sauna with a bottle of champagne and a bottle of Guinness.

As my first mount didn't come along until the seventh race, I felt free for a good drink on the way down. Terry drove, and we enjoyed a great pub-crawl.

Terry had a favourite pub on the route, about three miles from the course, and he went in and sank his customary couple of brandies and a Babycham.

We drank far too heavily, and Terry got into a giddy mood. We stopped at six pubs altogether, and I kept running out with large brandies for him and the same stuff for myself.

By the time we reached the racecourse, I was well and truly shattered. As my first mount was still some three hours away, I told Terry I was going to sleep on the back seat and try to sober up. I asked him to come back and shake me about forty-five minutes before I was due to ride Bay Tudor.

Terry had a ride in the first race on the joint favourite Many Ways for his guv'nor Fred Rimell. It finished sixth, beaten by more than thirty lengths. But no one could blame our pub-crawl because Terry had an amazing capacity for drink. He knocked it back like Lucozade.

When Terry returned to the car my head was numb, but I felt reasonably sober and ready for action on Bay Tudor, which the bookies were making 15–2 second favourite.

Terry had told a few jockeys in the weighing-room about our pub-crawl, and some of them couldn't resist taking the mick, Jimmy Uttley in particular. Ironic really, because he was an indefatigable drinker. We figured in many late-night sessions together.

While cantering Bay Tudor to the start, I felt terribly dizzy. The withdrawal symptoms were chronic. A few lagers at the starting-gate would have solved all my problems. Bay Tudor wasn't at her best. She blundered badly at the second fence and never fully recovered; I had no option but to pull her up after the ninth.

I was still staggering about a bit, but thirty minutes later I was back on track with 20–1 Fake, and we finished a respectable fifth, beaten by less than three lengths.

Terry remained perfectly sober. He was able to ride perfectly. All the time I have known him Terry has drunk some form of alcohol every day, but it never seemed to affect him in the way it affected me.

Unfortunately my drinking was getting worse by the day, although I still remained in front in the championship. My hopes were high and I was flat-out to clinch it. But then disaster struck me in a novices chase at Perth where I had the ride on Hardemon.

Even before the start of the two-day meeting Ken Oliver had complained that he was not satisfied with the way I was riding. I knew the drink was to blame, but his comments niggled me, so I went out determined to give Hardemon the ride of my life. I came crashing down at the fifth-last.

Though I felt sore and groggy, I still rode Arctic Explorer and Polar Prince the following day, but I couldn't do them justice. They both started favourite, and both were beaten. I knew my shoulder needed early treatment, and I hurried to London to have it X-rayed. The fracture was confirmed, and I was advised to have a complete rest.

Mary suggested we should fly to Malta for a few days. Her motives were good, but the result was disastrous. Having no riding commitments, I was free to drink, and it escalated out of all proportion. After seven days I returned to England deep in the horrors from alcohol. I was terribly depressed.

I was still top jockey, and I carried on without luck at Wetherby on the Wednesday, Carlisle on the Thursday, and then decided I had no alternative but to forfeit the Championship in order to come to terms with my drinking problem.

With me out of the way, Graham Thorner quickly seized the advantage. In the final weeks of the season he drew clear to clinch the title, with Terry Biddlecombe finishing second and me close-up in third. Graham ended with seventy-four winners and I was right on his tail with sixty-seven.

My whole ambition while riding had been to win the Championship. With it virtually in my grasp I had allowed it to slip through my fingers because of my addiction to alcohol. I was heartbroken.

It was on that last visit to Carlisle, in May 1971, that I backed myself to win a large sum of money because I knew I was certain to lose a two-horse race! I was booked to ride Bobby Corbett for Ken Oliver and our only rival was Kilmogany Five, trained by John Dixon and ridden by Maurice Barnes.

Bobby Corbett had run at Ayr three weeks earlier with Peter Ennis in the saddle and was outclassed and finished sixth. But inferior ability was not the only reason for his defeat; he had navicular, a crippling, progressive disease of the foot.

I knew Bobby Corbett well. I had won on him at Sedgefield in March. The day before we raced at Carlisle, I worked him at the Olivers and was disappointed with him. He didn't move well and was clearly feeling the pain. The navicular was getting to him. On returning to the yard I suggested to the Olivers that they should withdraw him from the Carlisle race for two very good reasons: he was sure to be odds-on favourite, which would be unfair to the betting public, and it was cruel to run a horse when he was in so much pain and not able to do his best.

But Mrs Oliver was adamant the horse would run, and that was that. The Olivers wouldn't listen to me.

I also pointed out that the advanced 'going' for Carlisle was firm, and that this would definitely aggravate his condition, and jar him up, yet they still wouldn't be swayed.

After lunch, I rang *The Sporting Life* for the final list of declared runners and discovered it was just a two-horse affair between Bobby Corbett and Kilmogany Five. I rang my betting partner in Newcastle right away. Whatever money I bet, he bet the same. He was magic at finding bookmakers who would accept large bets and keep their mouths shut. Rarely, if ever, did our money reach the racecourse to ruin the starting-price.

I explained the navicular position to my partner and assured him there was no way in which Bobby Corbett could win. We agreed Kilmogany Five was a financial dream and we each splashed £10,000 on him. My partner assured me he would organize the bet in such a way that not a penny would return to the track.

Oh, yes, he was a genius at placing cash. The secret is to open a large number of credit accounts with bookmakers right across the country. The backer can then invest his money in comparatively small amounts; instead of placing £10,000 with one bookmaker he splits it up between ten or more. It's also imperative to put the money on just five to ten minutes before the race. Never give the bookmaker time to 'blow' the cash to the course. And the smaller the stake, the less likely he is to smell a coup. Spread it around, that was our motto.

Kilmogany Five excelled on firm ground, jumped like a cat and, with Maurice's 3 lb claim, was receiving a colossal 19 lbs from Bobby Corbett. In normal circumstances I suppose a fit Bobby Corbett could have given him the 19 lbs without much trouble, but this was a sick horse and I couldn't see him finishing the race, let alone winning it.

Bobby Corbett's first 'show' was 4–6. Then he drifted to evens and finally ended up at 4–5. Kilmogany Five was far more generous. He opened at 5–4 and wound up at evens. There was nothing in the betting to indicate a coup. My partner excelled himself. He had superb contacts.

I went out on Bobby Corbett to do my best. Not once did it cross my mind to stop him. Even cantering to the start he stretched out 'feelingly' and was clearly finding the ground too firm.

Maurice had Kilmogany Five in front from the start. As he was such a good jumper they were sensible tactics. I managed to stay in touch for the first mile and a half, but Bobby Corbett wasn't jumping well. He was afraid to take off and land on his sore feet.

Three times in the race he slithered on his knees and on his belly, and I was lucky to stay aboard. If I had any thoughts of rolling off and making the bet a certainty I had plenty of opportunities out in the country.

But rolling off and jumping off was something I never did throughout my career. It was enough to smash yourself up accidentally without deliberately looking for a fall.

At the fence after the water Bobby Corbett made an appalling mistake and Kilmogany Five quickly drew ten lengths clear. We had no chance of getting back on terms. I suppose I could have pulled him up, but I decided to struggle on. Then, at the fourth-last, he made another dreadful mistake, and Kilmogany Five widened the gap and eventually passed the post some fifteen lengths ahead of us.

Three of Ken Oliver's lads were standing near the fourth-last and they saw the horse's terrible mistake and how badly he was 'feeling' the ground.

*Chaseform* said of the race: 'Kilmogany Five: looked well, made all, went clear from 10th. Bobby Corbett: looked well, mistakes, no chance from 10th.'

When I returned to the enclosure to dismount, Mr Oliver was waiting for me. He was flushed with rage and accused me of stopping the horse. Several angry words were exchanged and he remained adamant that I had deliberately prevented the horse from winning.

I was very upset, but determined not to let him go round the north saying that I had ridden a horse for him and stopped it – although to this day he never actually knew that I backed the winner.

I didn't stop Bobby Corbett. The horse was so crippled he stopped himself. I knew this would happen twenty-four hours before the race. That's why I exploited the situation.

As soon as Ken Oliver accused me of stopping the horse I reported him to the stewards of the meeting. They included John Marshall, in the chair, Alan MacTaggart, whom I lived with for two years, and Claude Berry, who also lived in the Borders and was a very good friend of mine and the Olivers. I had to report the incident in order to keep matters right and to protect my good name.

The stewards promptly sent for Mr Oliver, and when he entered the room he immediately backed down a little and looked rather sheepish. In front of the stewards I told him, 'You accused me, in the presence of Mrs Oliver and your stable-lad Arthur, of stopping the horse, and now I should like you to repeat those accusations for the stewards to hear.'

It was obviously embarrassing for a trainer to be reported in this way by his jockey, and to be told he should not have run the horse, but he left me no alternative after slandering me in public.

Bobby Corbett was owned by Simon Fraser, a London stockbroker, who was unable to travel up to see his horse run. Mr Fraser always enjoyed a bet, but he didn't have a penny on his horse that day; he usually listened to my advice.

When Mr Oliver was officially confronted, he tried to sidestep the fact that the horse had navicular. Unfortunately for him, the stewards had already formed their own opinion after seeing the horse cantering to the start. They were unanimous that it went down very 'feelingly' and was not striding out well. After hearing evidence from Mr Oliver and me, the stewards asked us to leave the room while they considered what action to take. Reading between the lines, I was already sure there was very little the local stewards could do about it.

I reckon that up to forty per cent of horses racing today have some known physical defect. Mr Oliver might have known the horse had navicular, but believed it could still go out and win what was, after all, only a two horse-race. On many occasions I've ridden horses with serious physical problems but, because I wasn't so close to the stable, I knew nothing about them.

When we were called back, Mr Marshall admitted he had never witnessed a complaint like this before, and said it was such a serious matter it would have to be passed on to the stewards of the Jockey Club. It was an embarrassing situation for Marshall, MacTaggart and Berry because they all knew Mr Oliver and myself personally, and we were all close friends.

But the stewards had a job to do, and I had my reputation to protect. I regarded this as a definite case of defamation and couldn't allow it to pass without protest. So they asked us to leave the room again so that we could consider the consequences before I finally decided on whether I wanted the matter to be reported to Portman Square for a top-level investigation.

When I got outside, every tiny detail flashed through my mind. I knew that if the case went to the Jockey Club I had enough grounds to win it because all Ken Oliver's lads knew the horse had navicular, the vet knew it, and so did Mrs Oliver. There was no denying the fact. Later, after Bobby Corbett was sold at the Ascot Sales, his new trainer, Mrs Nina Whitfield, also had problems with the horse's navicular.

Once outside the stewards' room I told Ken Oliver I would not press charges provided he apologized to me. I knew full well he had little option because he was entirely in the wrong. I also knew he would not forget the incident and that it would create a hostile atmosphere between us for as long as we remained together.

We returned to the stewards' room and I said, reluctantly, that I would drop the charges. The stewards sighed, and thought it might be a good idea if we shook hands in front of them and left the room without any ill-feeling between us.

That was impossible. Ill-feeling was inevitable because Mr Oliver was not the type of man to be spoken to in that manner without reacting bitterly. He was the leading trainer in Scotland and a nationally-known auctioneer. For instance, I lost a ride to Swanny Haldane at Newcastle two days later on the Saturday, and to

Tommy Stack at Hexham on the Monday. Swanny was unseated at the first, and Tommy fell at the fifth. Need I say more?

The Olivers made all sorts of excuses about the owners wanting a change of jockey, but it was only what I expected from them.

On 25 May, I had no alternative but to re-enter St John O'God's and was dried out in the infirmary before spending four weeks in the Richard Pampouri Unit, a group-therapy section set aside for the rehabilitation of alcoholics. I stayed in hospital four weeks and then went straight back to England to school horses for Walter Wharton and Alan Jarvis. I also bought a lot of nice horses at this time, including Mulligan, Blue Snake, Amigris and Grangewood Girl, and they all won many good races.

Wharton asked me to take two horses to Ireland for the big Galway meeting, and I won on Sea-Robber. Unfortunately his other runner, Future Fame, broke down while cantering at the fourth-last and we were robbed of victory.

Sea-Robber was a certainty. I put £500 on him at 6–4 to replenish the tank before returning to England.

The English season opened two days later and I began in great form with a treble at Market Rasen on Mulligan, Dundoyne and Royal Recorder.

It was a sizzling start to my first season as a freelance and gave me the perfect encouragement. I eventually drove a hundred thousand miles between August and May in a frantic bid to capture the 1971 Championship. I ended up with seventy winners in England, a further five in Ireland, and twelve in Scandanavia. In all, I accepted 561 rides in the British Isles alone. To boost my score, I often rode at two meetings a day. I'd hire a plane or a helicopter and rush from one end of the country to the other.

On Bank Holiday Monday I rode Sea-Robber in the 3 pm race at Huntingdon and tried to reach Warwick for the 4.15. It was impossible. I was in such a dash that I left the Huntingdon weighing-room without knowing whether I'd won or lost. I had finished virtually in line with Stan Mellor and Country Retreat and when I took off in the helicopter the judge was still studying the photograph.

I arrived at Warwick one minute too late to ride Mulligan.

Graham Thorner deputized for me, the horse started at a ludicrous 4–11 and then was beaten by a length and a half by The Roamer.

Meanwhile, I checked on the result of the Huntingdon race and found I had won it by a short head. At least my expenses were paid!

My first really substantial bet of that season was reserved for Sedgefield on 5 October, when I invested a fat £20,000 on Vimy Rock to win the Woodhouse Novices Chase over two miles.

Gordon Holmes rode Vimy Rock, I rode Jane's Heir, my brother Peter was aboard Carntyne, and Tommy Stack was on Whitsun Joe. Vimy Rock was the heavily-backed 1–2 favourite, with Jane's Heir easy at 2–1.

Gordon Holmes was beyond reproach as a jockey, and his name had long been struck out by those who recruited riders to stop horses.

Apart from Vimy Rock, the other runners were nothing more than selling-platers, so I was simply using my brains to boost my bank balance. Vimy Rock was in a different class.

I looked on it as a gilt-edged chance to pocket £10,000 in four minutes – 4 mins 22.2 secs to be precise.

I had Jane's Heir in front from the seventh to the run-in, with Vimy Rock in hot pursuit. For a moment I thought I had miscalculated. It was Vimy Rock's first run over fences and he jumped much slower than I had expected. My £20,000 seemed doomed.

But Gordon Holmes is a great battler, and once Vimy Rock had touched down over the last he roused the horse to such effect that they pulled away to beat me two lengths. Again my judgment had been vindicated and my bank manager was delighted.

I was bubbling with confidence, and two days later was booked to ride Crackaseal for Alan Jarvis in a hurdle race at Ludlow. There were seven runners, but I reckoned on three with a chance.

One of them, Prims Boy, was a bit of a rogue, so I discounted him, and then learned that a connection of the remaining danger had accepted £400 to make sure his horse didn't win. This left the way open for Crackaseal, and I made him a good thing. So I waded in with £10,000 and stunned the bookmakers; his price dropped from 5–2 to even-money favourite.

For once, Jeremy Glover was superb on the hooded Prims Boy, third favourite at 3–1, and they led from the sixth flight and beat me by three lengths. I was flabbergasted. I'd lost the lot!

Still, it took more than one defeat to break my spirit, and I set out on a recovery mission at Uttoxeter two days later.

Five runners lined up in the Weaver Novices Hurdle and I made my mount Whistling Sea a snip. His chances improved even more when I heard that a connection of another horse had accepted £1,000 to play a spectator's role.

Whistling Sea started 6–4 second favourite; I put £5,000 on him and won by three lengths, doing handsprings.

With my pockets bulging, I moved on to Sedgefield and stuck £10,000 at starting-price on Nice Shoe, ridden by Peter Morris. Again there were just four runners, and I partnered Baytown Willow, the second favourite, for Peter Milner.

Once more my judgment was infallible. Nice Shoe beat me by two lengths, starting at 8–11, although I'd have been a great deal closer if not hampered by another horse at the last.

An hour later, I copped again. Alan Jarvis ran Nell's Son in a hurdle race, and I rode Strident for the late Noel Robinson. I had seen Nell's Son work, and knew he was a bit special. I put £5,000 on him at starting-price, and he plunged from 20–1 to 9–1.

Red Weaver rode him and, despite swerving badly on the run-in, they trotted up by two and a half lengths. I finished fifth, just over seven lengths away. Someone had a tickle on mine, too, shortening him from 10–1 to 5–1.

Still not content with my day's work, I followed up half an hour later with another £10,000 to win on Red Ruler, an absolute lay-down in a three-horse race. Again, word had reached me that a connection of one runner – not the jockey – had received £500 to stay out of the firing-line.

Red Ruler was ridden by Brian Fletcher, and they sauntered up by thirty lengths at 5–4 after Tommy Stack and Corseal had fallen at the third-last.

In just ninety minutes that day I pocketed £67,000 – and, remember, jockeys aren't allowed to bet!

Section 62 (ii) of the Rules of Racing states categorically:

During the terms of his licence, a jockey or an apprentice jockey may not

(a) Be the owner or part-owner of any horse being entered or run under these rules or the rules of any recognized Turf Authority with the exception of horses taking part in hunter steeplechases only.

(b) Bet on horse-racing; this rule applies to a bet wherever placed and to a horse-race wherever run.

(c) Receive presents in connection with a race wherever run from persons other than the owner of the horse he rides in the race.

Any rider who may be proved to the satisfaction of the Jockey Club stewards to have contravened any of the above conditions appropriate to his licence or permit will have his licence or permit withdrawn.

Without doubt, the biggest and most absurd offer I ever received from a bent bookmaker was before a race at Doncaster. He tempted me with £20,000 in cash to fall off Dad's Lad in a two-horse affair. The horse had won for Graham Thorner at Hereford the previous week, and my only rival was Fairy Music, a useless twelve-year-old ridden by an amateur called Bill Bennion.

On the morning of the race, *The Sporting Life* forecast the price of Dad's Lad at 1–8, with Fairy Music at 10–1. Then came the bookmaker's call, and his preposterous proposition. To make matters even sillier, the race was being televised, so even if I had wished to go along with his potty idea the whole country would have enjoyed a close-up of Brogan the fall guy.

Dad's Lad was a superb jumper and we led all the way and won by thirty lengths – and no betting was returned.

At that time I was building up for a gigantic gamble on Traite de Paix in a hurdle race at Warwick. He was a French-bred three-year-old colt trained by Alan Jarvis. The public knew nothing about him, and this was his first appearance in England.

In the week leading up to the race he worked brilliantly at home, and I knew he was far superior to anything he would meet. Jarvis booked me to ride him, and I put £15,000 down at starting-price.

In ten minutes to the 'off', his price dived from 6–1 to 5–4 favourite, and the result was never in doubt. We skated up by six lengths.

But even this £15,000 was chicken-feed compared with the huge bet I placed on Nether Edge to win at Uttoxeter.

Ron Barry rode Nether Edge, I rode Lighter for Reg Hollinshead, and Jimmy Uttley partnered the only other runner, Pattered. Knowing that Lighter was badly off form, I put £25,000 to win on Nether Edge ... and he miraculously got home by a neck from Pattered, with Lighter a further ten lengths back. Nether Edge was returned desperately short at 4–9, but I was still delighted with my £10,000 profit.

I returned to Uttoxeter for further good business a week later, when Nether Edge, Pattered, Inishmaan and Unit Trust all lined up in the Burton Hurdle.

Though Nether Edge had beaten Pattered a week earlier, I now had good reason to switch my allegiance to Pattered. So I staked £10,000 on him at starting price, and I was right yet again.

Pattered and Uttley won by five lengths, and the horse was returned at 11–8 from 7–4. Yet another £13,000 was thrust into the Brogan kitty.

Meanwhile, squeezed between all my gambling and rushing across the country, came a win that pleased me immensely. I raced away with the King George VI Chase at Kempton on Boxing Day with my immaculate friend The Dikler.

It was a truly memorable occasion. We trounced such outstanding horses as Spanish Steps and Titus Oats, and those Gold Cup heroes L'Escargot and Glencaraig Lady. This victory established The Dikler as the great horse he really was.

My next bit of business came at Catterick where I confidently placed £10,000 on Jim Leigh's chaser Eagle's Nest to win a four-horse race in which I rode second favourite Mulligan for Alan Jarvis.

Unknown to the public, the track suited Eagle's Nest, but didn't suit Mulligan. And the other runners – Hibiscus and Zabarat – couldn't have won with a hundred yards start.

David Moorhead rode Eagle's Nest and they led at the eighth, and slammed me fifteen lengths. Hibiscus trailed in third, a further ten lengths away.

It was money for old rope. I simply used my wits to take advantage of a golden opportunity. There was nothing illegal about it – except, of course, that I wasn't allowed to bet!

A similar gilt-edged opportunity soon came my way at Market Rasen, and yet again it underlined how easily British racing can be fixed. I was assured that a trappy two-horse race was crooked, and that the odds-on favourite Permit would definitely not win. A £1,000 'arrangement' had been made for Permit to finish second, and I knew the information was accurate.

Jimmy Bourke rode Permit, and Brian Fletcher rode Castle Walk. But let me stress a million times over that neither Bourke nor Fletcher could be bought, and that the fix didn't concern either of these bold, brave riders for whom I had the highest admiration.

Brian, in fact, underlined his skill as a horseman by collecting three Aintree Grand Nationals. The first on Red Alligator, and then two in a row on the bionic Red Rum. Besides being a marvellous jockey, Brian used to amuse me with his tight handling of money. He and Graham Thorner were probably the meanest jockeys I ever met. They wouldn't buy you an ice-cream. In fairness to them both, all the money they earned they locked away. They were frugal and sensible. In recent years they have used all their cash to buy large plots of land and property and one day I hope to emulate them.

# 10
# Northern Jockeys in a Fix

IT WAS DURING 1970 THAT A SHREWD GROUP OF NORTHERN-based jump jockeys put their heads together and hatched an infallible scheme to fix races and build up gigantic bank accounts.

I rode against them every day and knew every trick and every stroke they were playing. They would place huge bets on horses, knowing they could never lose.

The gang had two 'Generals', both senior and trusted jockeys. And to be certain nothing went wrong with their coups, they provided irresistible 'fees' to a small ring of other riders to co-operate whenever required. Gangleaders usually staked up to £20,000 at a time on a fixed result. They set themselves up for life.

Fixed races were generally confined to four or five runners. To exceed this number would have meant buying off more jockeys, risking security and causing a drop in profit.

Immediately I knew a fixed race was coming up I would ring my betting partner and he would invest a substantial amount of money for us without giving a hint of the villainy involved.

Again, I simply took advantage of privileged information. I never actually organized the rip-off myself. Owners, trainers and punters had no idea of what was happening. Even some jockeys were kept in the dark.

Fixed races were always very carefully selected, mainly in the Midlands and the North. Wetherby, Uttoxeter, Ludlow and Wolverhampton were popular racecourses for jobs.

The two 'fixers' were backed by a team of eight to ten jockeys, men at the peak of their profession and respected everywhere for their integrity. The whole huge operation was so skilfully handled that details of the gang and their enormous and regular killings have still not leaked out – and never will. Too many people in high places will see to that.

Jockeys who co-operated were usually paid £300 'assistance' money. They simply made certain they finished anywhere but first.

And knowing the result well in advance, they would put the whole lot on the 'winner' and laugh all the way to the bank.

Certain northern jump jockeys were driving rather flashy and expensive cars at the time, and this was the only clue to the perpetrators. As I hope I've made clear, I promised to co-operate only when I knew the horse I was riding had no chance of winning. I considered it a few hundred pounds for doing nothing, and my betting partner and I soon multiplied it.

Some jockeys, inevitably, made a fortune. The main 'fixers' could paper their homes in fivers. They were printing money. It was a faultless scheme. When a horse was supposed to win, it did. Every time!

At the end of the 1973 season, Peter Smith, then secretary of the Jockeys' Association, whom I respected immensely for all the hard work he put in for riders, came along and marked my card. He warned me to watch my betting. I was rather naive, and I remember thinking, 'How the hell can anyone know?'

Then a couple of jockeys mentioned it to me, and I suddenly had trouble getting my licence. I didn't take much notice at first, and thought the Jockey Club weren't satisfied with my physical fitness.

I was freelancing at the time and based at Bedworth in the Midlands. I was riding mainly for Alan Jarvis and sharing a house with fellow-jockey Steve Taylor, who later quit after a terrible injury.

A month before the 1973 season was due to open I flew to Ireland and asked Dr Austin Darragh for a full physical examination and a thorough check on my weight. He passed me A1. Shortly afterwards I returned to Bedworth and ten days before the season's first race meeting took the medical cerificate to the Jockey Club in London and handed it personally to Harry Marshall, the licensing officer.

With this done, I thought it a formality for him to issue my licence so that I could get the worry off my mind and prepare for the start of the season. But, to my shock and disgust, he refused to give it to me, and made a lot of silly excuses. He said the stewards would have to examine the certificate before I would be allowed to ride. By now I could detect something strange going on and I began to lose sleep over it. After hearing nothing for three days, I rang

Harry Marshall and asked him if my licence was now on its way. He said I would receive it within the next three days, and that he would post it to me personally.

Time had dragged on, and it was now only four days before the start of the season. While waiting, I offered to drive Alan Jarvis to Redcar races on the Wednesday and, on returning to Bedworth, I found a letter had arrived from the Jockey Club saying the stewards would like to see me the following Monday regarding my application for a licence.

I was worried stiff, and I went to Jarvis and told him about it. I had to mention it to Jarvis because he had booked me for four rides at Market Rasen on the Saturday, and there now seemed no way in which I could get my licence in time.

So at first light on Friday, an angry Jarvis and I drove to Portman Square to confront Harry Marshall about my licence and ask him point-blank why they were continuing to keep me waiting. When we arrived, Harry Marshall told us all the licensing stewards were at Goodwood and that there was nothing he could do for me.

Jarvis became even more annoyed and kicked up a rumpus. He told Harry Marshall that one of the four horses he intended running next day was a temperamental grey called Amigris, and that if I couldn't ride him he would take him out in protest. I also kicked up a row, but Marshall wouldn't flinch, and I had to walk away without my licence.

While Jarvis and I were in London, a Sunday newspaper reporter telephoned the Jarvis stable and spoke to Alan's wife, Anne. Without thinking too seriously about what was happening, she told him we had gone to London, and said it was a disgrace that I had not received my licence to ride next day.

And it was only when I read his story on the Sunday that I realized what was happening. Under a huge headline, 'Brogan Ban Sensation', the paper reported:

> Top jockey Barry Brogan has been sensationally banned from riding in the new National Hunt season ... Brogan, who has been given no reason, has been ordered to see the Jockey Club's chief inspector of security tomorrow. The move is an unprecedented step by the Turf authorities.

I was stunned. Reporters rang me from everywhere, but I refused to be drawn. I told them bluntly: 'I have no comment. There is nothing to say.'

Basically, I had not been refused a licence as stated in the newspaper. The letter from Harry Marshall simply said that the licensing stewards and the Jockey Club's chief investigator, Bob Anderson, wanted to see me. There was no mention of being banned. Yet it was still a huge mystery, and I was a bundle of nerves.

I thought deeply about it, and suddenly a picture began to emerge. I could see what was happening. So I decided on some positive action. I took the telephone and rang some jockeys who I thought were using me as a scapegoat because they knew I liked a bet.

I was furious. I told them that it was scandalous that I wasn't being allowed to ride and that I would keep my mouth shut no longer. I was ready to blow the gaff on the lot of them and cause the biggest sensation in British racing history. I left them in no doubt that if the stewards sent me down next day the rest would go with me. I would name the whole damn lot.

One particular jockey was very friendly with a lot of stewards at the Jockey Club and I made him well aware of the consequences if his name were linked with the series of race-fixing. He got the message all right! Without wasting a second he rang one of our leading National Hunt stewards, and a member of the licensing commitee at the time, and explained his embarrassment and the risk to everyone concerned if I decided to expose the conspiracy and name the participants. Besides being on friendly terms with our stewards, the panicking jockey was riding for them every day of the week.

On that Sunday night, I stayed at an hotel in Stow-in-the-Wold, and around ten o'clock the jockey rang me and said I was guaranteed to receive my licence when I turned up next morning. Besides being an expert at fixing races, he was evidently pretty adept at fixing licences, too. He had obtained his guarantee from the Jockey Club steward. I now knew that picking it up was a mere formality.

The daily newspapers were now plastered with big headlines like,

'Brogan, the George Best of Racing' and 'Brogan Says He's Never Pulled a Horse'.

As usual, the inquiry ran late, and after parking my car I walked to Portman Square and rushed straight into a mass of reporters and photographers. My solicitor, James Johnson, was with me.

Bob Anderson, the Jockey Club's chief investigator, met me in a private room and quizzed me about my betting partner. Then he asked me if I gambled, and I said 'No', which of course was a lie. I wasn't with Mr Anderson more than ten minutes, but I was made to wait an hour before I was called in to face two of the licensing stewards, 'Sonny' Richmond-Watson and Major Michael Wyatt. They apologized profusely for all the inconvenience I had suffered and for all the bad publicity I had received while waiting for my licence.

They obviously realized that if I wanted to be vindictive I could have taken legal advice with a view to suing them for loss of earnings. The stewards hadn't exactly refused my licence, but they had made it extremely awkward for me, and done nothing to enhance my reputation.

I now knew for sure that Bob Anderson was trying to flush me out about what I knew of the jockey fixers. There were all sorts of rumours going around and Anderson's snooping put the wind up them.

Before I left the room the stewards asked me if I would be making a statement to the Press. My solicitor said 'Yes' and the Jockey Club's senior Press Officer, Tony Fairbairn, carefully prepared a statement which I eventually read and approved. It said:

> At a meeting of the licensing stewards this afternoon, Barry Brogan was granted his jockey's licence for the 1973–4 jumping season. The delay in granting the licence arose partly due to the late completion by Barry Brogan of the formalities connected with his application, and partly by reason of an outstanding appointment with Mr Bob Anderson, chief investigations officer of the Jockey Club.

After my solicitor had read this statement to the press, I waited nearly three hours before poking my head round the door, hoping every reporter and photographer had left.

But once I walked out of Portman Square, four or five photographers converged on me and pleaded with me to turn round and give a V-sign to the Jockey Club. I refused and strolled on, happily puffing a huge Havana to the place where I had parked my Ford Granada. To my horror I found the police had towed it away to their pound at Hyde Park, and it cost me £6.50 to get it back!

Throughout the five months preceding my fight for the licence, all sorts of rumours were rampant about race-fixing, and official inquiries often came too close for comfort.

Chief Superintendent John Collinson, head of Co. Durham CID, was specially appointed to head top-level investigations together with Harold Prescott, the Director-General of Racecourse Security Services, and a former Assistant Chief Constable in charge of crime with Lancashire CID.

In one interview Collinson confirmed to a pressman: 'Racing personnel are involved. That is all I am willing to say.' In fact, that is all anyone would allow him to say! If precise details were revealed the whole racing world would have been rocked with an unprecedented scandal and the entire integrity of British racing would have disintegrated overnight.

Because of the VIPs involved, frustrated and angry police officers found their hands tied. They were forbidden from making logical progress and the vast probe gradually died a natural death.

Perhaps the nearest anyone ever came to revealing the exact identity of the 'Generals' was on 21 March 1973 when a report in the *Sun* began: 'An artful Irish gambling syndicate is believed to be behind "bent" horse-racing in Britain. The teams have an uncanny knack of backing certainties.'

I have little doubt that the first tiny crack in the lucrative system occurred in October 1972, after a few privileged newcomers, including a top Irish trainer and a leading Irish bloodstock agent, were given some information.

I met them on the evening of 10 October at a party at the home of a wealthy racehorse owner in the stockbroker belt near Wentworth in Surrey. Inevitably, the conversation soon got round to the best methods of stacking up some easy money. I took them into my confidence and told them they could make a start by betting on Golden Blue, ridden by Ron Barry, to win the first race at Wetherby the next day. Golden Blue's trainer, Donald 'Ginger' McCain of Red Rum fame, was naturally confident in the horse's ability but of course knew absolutely nothing of what was being arranged behind the scenes.

They questioned me about the strength of my mount Ross-Babur and Pat Buckley's mount Archook, but I told them not to doubt my word, and to bet Golden Blue with every penny they could lay their hands on.

And they did! The Irish trainer put down £20,000, and the bloodstock agent wasn't far behind him. The catastrophic influence on the market can be judged by Ross-Babur drifting from 7-4 to 11-4, and Golden Blue shortening from 5-2 to 4-5. Archook was also clearly unfancied, and took a long walk from 3-1 to 5-1.

The racecard listed five runners, with Kevin McCauley's mount Scotch Briar (10-1 from 12-1) and John Doyle's mount, So Long Sam (33-1) making up the quintet.

From the public's point of view there were five possible winners. In reality, there was only one. Golden Blue could not be beaten!

With such a vast amount of money staked on Golden Blue, and the blatant drifting of my horse and Buckley's, suspicion was inevitable. All five riders being Irish didn't help matters either.

The form-book's official account of the race read:

Ilkley Selling Hurdle £204 (£54, £24) 2m

Golden Blue (fav) 7-11-10 R. Barry (always close up, led three hurdles out, driven out) – 1.

Ross-Babur (H) 8-11-5 B. Brogan (led to 3 out, every chance last, ran on towards finish)...1½L – 2.

Archook 7-11-5 P. Buckley (lost touch fifth, stayed on from 2 out)... 4L – 3.

Scotch Briar 7-11-5 K. McCauley (headway fifth, ridden 3 out, never reached leaders)... 3L – 4.

So Long Sam 8-10-12 J. Doyle (behind from fifth, finished lame)... 15L – 5.

Ron Barry went on to complete a treble that day, including a twelve-length victory on the magnificent Red Rum.

But all the gossip centred on Golden Blue.

I took great care not to be drawn into any public wrangle with disgruntled punters and brushed them aside and ignored their taunts of 'Stitch-up! Fix!'

Golden Blue was a good thing. If every backer had used his head and followed the market they would have cleaned up in the same way as my two Irish friends.

The trainer I'd tipped off was so thrilled he gave me £1,500 and raced off to Heathrow to catch the first flight back to Dublin. He was dead scared of being caught up in a scandal.

Unfortunately, as weeks went by, this fear didn't stop him making a few indiscreet remarks about the race. The Jockey Club then unleashed their bloodhounds, and the more they sniffed, the more the riders got the jitters and dropped out.

The great gold-mine was in jeopardy, and the 'Generals' realized it. One man's slack tongue had threatened to expose everyone involved. Reluctantly, they decided it would be too risky to continue much longer.

# 11
# Dr Hines and a Bitter Pill

AFTER ALL THIS ADVERSE PUBLICITY I FOUND IT EXTREMELY difficult to make a living, and in December 1973 I had no alternative but to relinquish my licence and return to Ireland to work as a stable lad.

I was in touch with the famous Mr B.J. Curley at the time. He was from Irvinestown in Northern Ireland and the biggest professional gambler in the United Kingdom, the most successful I have ever known and even more professional than Alec Bird.

I had first met Barney Curley in Mungret College when I was a schoolboy and he was studying for the priesthood. He was a scholastic; scholastics were confined to one side of the College while the lay-boys, of which I was one, were restricted to the other.

After a while, Curley found a way to introduce himself to me, although scholastics and lay-boys were not supposed to mix. At first sight he seemed a nice fellow, and gave no indication of his motive for coming to see me.

While I was at College my father wrote to me every Sunday and always told me how the horses were working at home. He knew I was mad keen to have every detail.

At the time Curley found me my father was training a grey called Paddy Field, which he rated very highly. He had been a difficult horse to educate, but I had worked on him a lot and eventually taught him to settle. Paddy Field was entered to run in a 'bumper' at Navan in November 1961, and the famous J.R. 'Bunny' Cox was booked to ride him. The horse had never run in its life and my father and his owner, Bill Pilkington, thought he was certain to be a 20–1 chance. Yet, to my father's amazement, when he walked to the paddock, he noticed the bookmakers were quoting the horse 2–1 favourite. He was dumbfounded.

Unfortunately, Paddy disappointed that day, and he finished in the pack. Some big investor had obviously burnt his fingers.

Then, several months later, and with the race long forgotten about, my father called me into his office and asked me whether I knew a fellow called Curley.

I said I did and he asked me whether I ever mentioned Paddy Field to him. I thought hard and remembered telling Curley, in all innocence, that Paddy Field was expected to win at Navan.

My father was very shrewd. The stupid short price about Paddy Field had puzzled him for weeks. He couldn't rest until he had found out the truth, and he told me Curley had backed the horse at all rates from 12–1 down to 2–1.

And he was a scholastic at Mungret College!

My father was furious with me and stressed that every bit of business in the yard was strictly confidential at all times. It was my first slip and, to be fair, I had no idea Curley was such a ferocious gambler.

Curley eventually left Mungret College and the priesthood, and I never saw him again until I returned to Ireland after relinquishing my English licence in 1973.

For several months I virtually vanished off the face of the earth, and when I eventually surfaced in the Easter of 1974 I was granted a licence to ride in Ireland.

It was at this time that a flurry of writs started pouring in concerning all the debts I had accumulated in England through gambling, and being unable to cope because of drink. In all, they exceeded £50,000. I owed a racehorse owner £10,000, a bank £8,000, a bookmaker £2,500, and a garage £2,500. The list was endless. On top of this, my Ford Granada 3,000 XL was on hire-purchase and I hadn't paid a penny on it for fourteen months, so a man from the HP company called one morning and took it back.

A short while later I became involved with Colette Brosnan, then secretary to bloodstock agent Jack Doyle, a brilliant judge of a horse. Colette and I flew over to England and we stayed at the Washington Hotel in London. We went out and enjoyed ourselves and I was taken over by alcohol again.

I managed to sober myself up in the morning and went to the Ascot Sales to meet a leading Irish National Hunt trainer. I wanted him to buy a horse called Lord Nut. I had bought the horse some years earlier at Goffs Ballsbridge sales when he was an unbroken three-year-old. I paid a record £9,000 for him, and I bought him specifically for Henry Zeisel, of Rheingold fame. But Zeisel dropped out at the last minute and left it on my hands. Fortunately I found a new owner eventually, and the horse went on to win two races before returning to the Sales.

When the horse entered the ring, the trainer said: 'Bid for it, Barry.'

So I did, and it was knocked down to me for £5,200. But I had no money to pay for it. I couldn't even pay the hotel bill!

The auctioneer, John Botterill, asked me who the horse was for, and I told him the truth. But the trainer never paid, and Botterill sent me a writ. I approached the trainer, but the matter was never resolved.

My life was unmanageable at this time. I didn't know where I'd be from one week to the next. In England or Ireland. I was being dried out so often it was impossible to have a regular job. So I disappeared again. No one could find me for up to three months.

When I did emerge, I rang Brian Lusk, a well-known trainer, and arranged to meet him at the Royal Dublin Hotel in O'Connell Street. I was absolutely frank with him about my problems. We chatted for hours and he offered me a job as a stable-lad. I agreed to start at the bottom again, mucking out and doing all the grimy, menial tasks.

Brian was about to leave for Cheltenham with Skymas, and he suggested I took my bags to Naas racecourse next day and travel with his assistant, George McGrugan. I was to start work on the Sunday.

I met McGrugan as planned, but his sheepish look told me something was wrong. He said Lusk wanted me to telephone him urgently as some trouble had cropped up.

I was speechless. But I rang Lusk the moment he returned from Cheltenham and he told me CID officers were in the area looking for me, and that he didn't want me anywhere near him.

I knew this was untrue because my debts were a civil matter. I also knew Lusk was a straight man and I was determined to find out the truth. I soon did. Someone had put the boot in.

Knowing Lusk was a softie, this man had told him the CID were on my trail and had thoroughly alarmed him. I was at rockbottom, and the job with Lusk might have provided the vital uplift I so badly needed. I never forgave this man because what he did put me under great pressure and strain. I had no job and I was very dejected.

So yet again I went back to Liam Brennan, a trainer of immense skill and patience, and he saw my plight and gave me another chance. He said stable jockey Ben Hannon would have the main rides and I could have the spares.

One of Liam's owners happened to be Barney Curley, the man whose whole life has revolved around horses, dogs, cards and every other means of gambling. He's a millionaire, a 'stroke' player, and he's brilliant. He's known as the 'Silent Man' of racing, and likes to be called Kojak because of his bald head, dangling cigarette and his pale, cream raincoat. He had a string of good horses in training with Liam.

Though he never understood my drink problem, he picked my brains a lot. It was my idea that he should send horses over to England to run in the names of small-time trainers in non-gambling stables, and to have large bets on them at starting-price; it was a brilliant ruse and earned him a fortune. I have always expressed a high opinion of his gambling skills but, as a person, I have a lot of resentment against him because he caused me many major problems.

In the summer of 1973 I went to Ireland on holiday and I rode out with Liam to get fit for the coming English season. At the time, Liam had a yearling in the yard called Dr Hines. It had just arrived from Las Vegas. Curley had been to America and met a man called Hines, from whom he had bought the horse.

Little did I realize that some time later I would be riding the horse in a massive starting-price gamble at Bangor-on-Dee.

Dr Hines ran without distinction as a two-year-old on the flat, and again as a three-year-old, both on the flat and over hurdles.

The plot developed the moment I suggested to Curley that he should begin to consider sending a few horses to England to pull off some attractive starting-price jobs. Nothing trivial, but coups that could make him a fortune in a very short time. The horses would be specially selected and, as a vital part of the plan, they would be put with trainers who rarely had winners and whose horses normally started at very long odds.

To do the job properly it would be essential to choose non-gambling stables to ensure the odds weren't affected in any way. So I introduced Curley to Ray Peacock, a modest, friendly, hard-working man who was training about twenty horses at Tarporley in Cheshire. Ray came to Ireland, visited the yard and went through the procedure of buying Dr Hines.

After a few months had passed Curley came to me and said he wanted to do me a favour. I resented this hollow gesture because I had done him countless favours over the years. He had picked my brains time and time again. And as he got richer, I got poorer.

The favour was to offer me the ride on Dr Hines at Southwell on 10 March 1975. It was the Monday before the big Cheltenham Festival meeting, but the course became waterlogged after torrential rain and the fixture was abandoned.

In the meantime I had collected a few mounts at the Festival, so I stayed over until Thursday evening, then travelled back on the B & I Munster ferry from Liverpool to Dublin.

Jessica Willis, daughter of Waring Willis for whom I rode many horses, was with me, and I was supposed to be seeing her home safely. So I boarded the boat, sank a few drinks, and then a cashier upset me over a few pence in change. I immediately became stroppy and all hell was let loose. Alcohol had taken over again and I provoked the staff, resulting in the captain having to come and speak to me.

In my alcoholic haze I finally pulled myself together, apologized, and went up to the bar and bought everyone drinks. When I got up next morning I couldn't remember how I went to bed. I was still in my clothes and suffering a terrible hangover. I eventually spent three or four days drying out at home.

Dr Hines was next entered for Bangor-on-Dee twelve days later. There was considerable talk in Ireland at the time that I would not be allowed to ride the horse because of the troubles surrounding my licence in England in 1973. These doubts were comprehensively removed when John Edwards invited me over to ride High Ken in the Greenall Whitley Chase at Haydock. In my enthusiasm I arrived a day early, and rode three for John at Ludlow on the Friday. They were my first mounts in England since I relinquished my licence in

December 1973, but the best I could manage was third on Crack O'Doon.

Next day I went on to Haydock where High Ken led them all a merry dance until he hit the eleventh fence, where he lost his impetus. Ron Barry drove The Benign Bishop past us to win, all-out, by a length.

That ride on High Ken gave me tremendous publicity. I began to ride a lot in England again, and commuted regularly from Ireland, mainly to ride for Ray Peacock and John Edwards.

On the Saturday I rode High Ken, the wily Curley was organizing his first big starting-price job in England. He ran Fair Rambler in a long-distance conditions race at Hereford and with some superb tactical manipulation managed to extend the horse's price from 5–2 to 7–2. God knows how much Curley won. Fair Rambler skated up by eight lengths from Master Blarney.

With Fair Rambler's earnings safely in the kitty, plans switched to Dr Hines. Curley called at my flat in Dublin and said the horse would run at Bangor on Saturday, 22 March, and he wanted me to ride it. I accepted the booking because I was also engaged to ride there for John Edwards, Ray Peacock and Owen O'Neill.

I rode in a flat race at Leopardstown on the Wednesday, and met Liam Brennan outside the weighing-room after racing to discuss final plans for Dr Hines before I set off to catch the overnight boat to Liverpool. As usual with Liam, I took care not to ask whether the horse was fancied. The reply would have been the usual rude glare and absolute silence. Liam was renowned for his tight lips and secrecy. I was going over for a specific job, and the horse was obviously there to do its best.

By coincidence, John Edwards had booked me a week earlier for Topping in the same race as Dr Hines; I had to ring him at the last moment and say I was no longer available. John was naturally a bit puzzled because Topping was in good form and certain to be a fancied runner, while Dr Hines hadn't produced a flicker of ability in his five runs that season. Obviously I didn't dare divulge my reason for wanting to swap.

We bamboozled the public even more by deliberately delaying the announcement of my switch until barely an hour before the race. My name was cunningly left alongside Topping in every morning newspaper, and no jockey was shown for Dr Hines – yet another example of the thorough and detailed preparation for a well-organized coup.

A few minutes before the race I met Ray Peacock in the paddock and he looked tense and pale.

'We can win,' he said. 'Do your best.'

In the racecard, Dr Hines was down as owned by Mrs Mary Kelly, but I can assure you it was Curley who paid the bills.

I asked Ray for instructions because I knew Liam had passed them to Curley. But Ray had heard nothing. Apparently all Curley had said was, 'Tell Barry to ride Bangor as he knows it.'

Bangor is a tight, sharp track, and although I had seen Dr Hines at work I had never actually sat on him in a race. I had watched him school and was very impressed with the way he jumped.

There were eighteen runners, with Tom Corrie's hooded Doodle Bug the favourite at 2–1. Topping started at 3–1.

When the tapes flew up I decided to settle Dr Hines in the pack. He pulled hard early on, but I didn't allow him to go to the front until we were striding out down the far side. Then I confidently set sail for home.

Because Bangor is so sharp, a horse has to be close up all the way round to stand any chance of winning, so we jumped the fourth-last in front. We were cantering. I had a double-handful. We then pinged the second-last, still ambling along, but I suddenly heard a rush of someone coming quickly behind me.

I worked furiously with hands and heels and we flew the last, landing about a length and a half ahead of whoever was pursuing us. I wasn't worried in the slightest. I was certain it was simply a case of asking Dr Hines to accelerate and he would stroll in. But he stuck his head in the air, found no speed and I was quickly passed and beaten by Doodle Bug and my rejected Topping.

Immediately we passed the post I felt awful. I knew I'd have won if I had delayed my challenge a moment longer.

Dr Hines finished third, beaten by a total of four lengths, and was returned by the bookmakers at 16–1.

I was furious with Curley for not relaying the instructions from Liam.

Shortly after the race, Curley came charging towards me and

started abusing me for making too much use of the horse, leaving him in front too long. This was both unfair and untrue.

So I bawled back at him: 'I've ridden scores of winners around here, so don't tell me how to do my job. If you'd played your part and passed on Liam's instructions I'd have trotted up.'

As far as I know, Curley backed the horse each-way all over England and Ireland, and stood to collect £300,000 if the horse had won.

Exactly a week later, Dr Hines was entered to run in a very bad novices hurdle at Southwell and, on his Bangor performance, he was entitled to be well-fancied by the public. But, on this occasion, form was to prove no guide to his chances. The horse would not be doing his best. Those who backed him would lose their money before he left the paddock.

As expected, practically every punter on the course went for him, and he ended up 6–4 favourite. Only this time Curley didn't have a penny on him.

During the week between riding Dr Hines at Bangor and then at Southwell, I went to Roscommon races and hauled professional gambler Billy Maher out of trouble when he was losing £10,000. I tipped him 7–2 chance Scarva, and he went home winning £5,000 Before leaving the course. Maher slipped me a cheque. I stopped off at the Forge Inn at Naas and cashed it for £20. Then I started drinking, and didn't stop until I blacked out. At three in the morning the barman flung me into the street – right opposite the police station.

I was seething, so I picked up a gas cylinder from the pavement and hurled it through the pub window. Glass splashed everywhere, and pandemonium broke out. The police were so close they couldn't miss the din. In a flash two burly officers came out and threw me in a filthy cell. Excreta and urine covered the walls and coated the floor. It was revolting. I asked for a hanger to put up my clothes, but the police wouldn't give me one. Then a young constable started taunting me.

Next morning, Liam came down and bailed me out for £50. I had been charged with being drunk and disorderly, but I quickly countered it with an official complaint against the constable.

I was bailed to appear at Naas court, but I was advised to hand over £50, which would be passed to the 'right' person and the whole matter would be hushed up. So I did. And I never heard another word about the case.

On leaving Naas police station, I went to Nenagin where I was rescued by Paddy G., a member of Alcoholics Anonymous. Paddy understood my problem and immediately began drying me out on tablets in his tiny back room.

It was now Thursday, and I was penniless. There were just forty-eight hours left before I was due to ride Dr Hines at Southwell. Luckily Billy Maher popped up again and lent me £100. I drove to Dublin and boarded an aeroplane to London, where I was met by two great Irish friends. In thirty minutes the booze was flowing faster than the Thames. I drank so much they had to drag me up next morning and lead me, like a blind man, to the Turkish baths in Jermyn Street. My head was like a lump of lead, and I struggled to sober up.

I faced a fairly low weight of 10 st 8 lbs on Light Master for Ray Peacock, and felt like death. I gulped a handful of pee-pills, and sagged with dehydration. A careless undertaker would have boxed me up and wheeled me away.

Later on I rang the racecourse and told Ray I had been trapped in traffic and that I would not be there to ride Light Master in the 4 pm, although I would definitely arrive in time for Dr Hines in the last.

When I went out to ride Dr Hines, poor Ray was petrified, literally trembling. There were just nine runners, and I had been given explicit instructions not to finish in the first three. Dr Hines usually wore a tongue-strap because he gurgled, and the contraption always improved his performance. This time it was decided to leave it off. The heavy ground didn't suit him either.

I obeyed my instructions to the letter. I left no room for complaint. I finished stone last!

As I passed the post – some fifty lengths behind the winner, Night Talk – the angry crowd gave me a terrible reception and shouted at me, 'Go back to Ireland!' and 'Take the brake off, Brogan!'

When I dismounted, Ray was too scared to come forward in case the stewards asked us to explain the horse's absymal running.

Fortunately they saw nothing wrong with it, and I was able to return to Ireland without a question being raised.

Dr Hines then left Ray Peacock and went back to Liam Brennan, and on 25 August he was lined up for a massive bet in the Directors Maiden Hurdle at Downpatrick.

Curley also ran Cannon Gun. As part of the plan, stable jockey Ben Hannon was put up on this horse, and an unknown youngster, Steve McNally, was engaged for Dr Hines.

With Hannon aboard Cannon Gun, it inevitably ended up 4–5 favourite, but finished fourth.

I was in England at the time and not aware of the plot. A week later I learned that Curley had bet on Dr Hines at the starting-price well away from the track. The horse was returned at 16–1, but Curley was out of luck – by a centimetre! There was no photo-finish equipment at Downpatrick and the harassed judge had given the race to second favourite Caroline's Dream, by a short head.

Many knowledgeable people close to the line were certain Dr Hines had won, and that Curley had been deprived of yet another gigantic pay-out.

With Dr Hines now exposed as a job horse, the whole world would be watching for him, so Curley sent him to Sedgefield to run in a seller worth just £272 to the winner.

Though I had ridden him at Bangor, and obeyed instructions to stop him at Southwell, I suddenly found myself jocked off, and replaced by my best friend Tommy Stack.

Dr Hines was now very much dropped in class, and he trotted up by four lengths at 8–11. Ironically, I finished third on Sharmaggie for Dennis Yeoman.

Before leaving Ireland I was assured by Liam that if Dr Hines won Curley wanted the horse off his hands, so I put George Berry in to bid at the auction because I knew the horse could go on and win more races. George liked to buy selling-platers. He secured Dr Hines for 2,100 guineas, and the horse went into training with Owen O'Neill at Cheltenham.

Whenever he warmed up for a killing, Curley was always incredibly patient. He was methodical, meticulous and arrogant. Nothing flustered him.

For sheer unadulterated coolness, Curley really excelled himself with a young horse called Yellow Sam.

He selected a bad handicap hurdle over two miles at Bellewstown. He deliberately chose a race for amateur riders, and made sure he picked the best man in Michael Furlong, now a competent professional and first jockey to Padge Berry. Yellow Sam had tons of talent, but it was imperative that he ran on good or firm ground to produce his best.

Before Michael rode him at Bellewstown I worked him at home, and he moved exceptionally well. But even then it didn't dawn on me that he was being wound up for the wages on a 'gaff' track just four miles from my mother's home at Rathfeigh. It stretches high across the top of a bleak hill, and is a favourite resting-place for campers and gypsies.

I arrived late at the meeting, and missed the first two races. I asked the gateman what had won, and he replied, 'One of Brennan's took the second. At a big price, too!'

It was Yellow Sam – and at 20–1!

One of the first people I met was Liam, and I said, 'Well done!'

'Oh, don't talk to me,' he replied. 'I'm sick. Michael came through on him, and we didn't expect him to win. Barney is furious.'

After racing, I called in to see my mother, and a lot of other racing people came along. My mother was always glad to see visitors and she organized a small party with drinks and a buffet. Jim Dreaper, Liam Brennan and Curley were there, but not a word was uttered about Yellow Sam. Curley even borrowed £5 off my mother to buy petrol for his BMW to drive back to his place, St Boswell's Stud near Ashford in Co. Wicklow.

By now, Yellow Sam's surprise win had slipped completely from my mind. I rode out next morning at Liam's, and again nothing was mentioned about the horse.

I then left Liam's for an evening meeting at Gowran Park, and on reaching the racecourse bought the evening newspaper. I practically collapsed with shock. Splashed across the back page in the largest headlines possible was 'Biggest SP Job Ever Landed in Ireland – Yellow Sam at 20–1'! Curley and Liam had excelled themselves as masters of the art of secrecy. Not once did they offer the tiniest clue that a penny had been won.

Even now, they hadn't let the secret slip. It was the bookmakers who were screaming. They had been caught with their trousers down, and I didn't feel a bit sorry for them. I was delighted for Liam and Curley.

The bookmakers, all black ties and sobbing, held an emergency meeting to decide whether to pay out on the result. The arrogance of the men.

Eventually they had to pay up and cancel their holidays. Curley had slayed them. It was reported that he collected in the region of a colossal £350,000, the biggest coup Ireland has known.

Curley landed several other successes, including one with Tommy Joe at Bangor-on-Dee. Ben Hannon had the mount, and the horse started at 5–2, winning by six lengths. Tommy Joe later joined the powerful Tony Dickinson stable in Yorkshire and won a string of high-class contests, confirming the talent Curley knew he possessed. Another horse that swelled Curley's handsome bank account was the magnificent I'm A Driver. Curley collected at 6–1 with him at Punchestown when he was in training with Liam. The horse was then sold, and again went to Tony Dickinson's yard from where he won several big races.

Curley later sold his stud farm and bought a huge estate at Mullingar. His schemes flourish and he continues to own a large team of excellent horses. He is the most professional gambler I have ever known, and I respect and applaud his skills. However, I have no time for him as a person, and I don't mind admitting it.

But Curley wasn't the only punter to gamble on high stakes. In one six-month spell in 1972 I turned over £250,000, and most of those bets involved horses I was either riding or riding against.

One such race was at Ayr one October. There were five runners, but I made it a match between my mount Arctic Explorer and Tommy Stack's ride Celtic Gold. I put £3,000 on Tommy to beat me!

Just a week earlier I had finished last of seven on Arctic Explorer at Wetherby. We could never rely on him. At his best he was a brilliant jumper. At his worst he was moody, lethargic and wouldn't do a tap.

Vimy Rock (Colin Tinkler), Hobart (David Munro) and Mischievous Monk (Stan Hayhurst) made up the quintet. I had ridden

Mischievous Monk before, so I knew his limitations and didn't give him a thought.

Arctic Explorer carried 11 st 5 lbs, and Celtic Gold was 16 lbs worse off at 12 st 7 lbs.

We had an enormous weight advantage, but in my wildest dreams I couldn't see Arctic Explorer getting the better of Celtic Gold on his dismal performance at Wetherby. So I arranged for £3,000 to be put on Celtic Gold in my name at starting-price.

I was confident. And I remember telling Stacky at the start, 'For God's sake don't hang about. Keep flat to the boards.'

Stacky knew I liked a bet, and that I didn't dabble in pennies.

Arctic Explorer loved to bowl along in front, and we jumped the first fence several lengths clear of the others. But as we set off for the second I heard a clatter behind me. Looking over my shoulder I glimpsed jockeys and horses sprawled all over the place. Tinkler, Munro and Hayhurst were all on the floor. To my relief, Tommy Stack, Celtic Gold and my £3,000 were still standing....

I continued to make the running at a steady pace, and after jumping the fourth-last I was still sauntering and wondering when Tommy was going to launch his attack.

Turning for home, I got the answer. Tommy drew alongside me, and going to the third-last both horses were stride for stride. Celtic Gold was travelling very smoothly and I waited for him to pull away and win at a canter.

But steeplechasing can be ridiculously unpredictable. Celtic Gold pitched badly on landing, lost a lot of ground, failed to recover and by the second-last Arctic Explorer had taken command; he was cruising on the bridle. My £3,000 was disappearing with every stride – I was beating myself!

Finally I reached the line with three lengths to spare from Celtic Gold. No other horse finished, and I was never headed. It was one of the easiest victories of my career.

I later completed a double on Glenzier Lad for Jack Berry, and I was chuffed to bits that losing £3,000 hadn't distressed me to the point of breaking my morale. Riding winners still meant more to me than anything else. It appealed to my ego, and I loved the applause.

# 12
# Marriage is a Disaster

HOW MY LIVER HAS WITHSTOOD THE MASSIVE ALCOHOLIC TIDAL waves is a mystery all of its own. Come to that, so is the fact that I have no lasting injury from my falls.

Being a steeplechase jockey, serious accidents were inevitable and frequent, and considered an integral part of the job. In twelve years I broke both jaw-bones, both cheek-bones, my nose, a foot, both thumbs, a wrist, collar-bone, shoulder, and every rib down my left side, plus accumulating the usual quota of concussions which lasted between thirty minutes and five hours.

Yet, despite all these bangs and fractures, I can still walk without a limp. I can still run a hundred yards in thirteen seconds. And I can still wake each morning without an excruciating pain pounding in my head to remind me of a frightening fall.

There are few steeplechase jockeys still riding or retired who can talk of luck to compare with that. To bristle with such good health must make me the luckiest jockey alive. So lucky not to end up with a broken back like Paddy Farrell, Tim Brookshaw and Jimmy Harris. Or knocked dizzy like Paddy Broderick, Noel Flanagan and Kevin McCauley. Or forced to take my life like Johnny Lehane, Cathal Finnegan, Johnny Rafferty and Nicky Brennan.

Amazingly my only scar is a fading pencil-line above my left eye, the legacy of a kick at Catterick in 1967. It was my first serious injury, and one which made me wonder whether I was tough enough to stay in the game.

I smashed my nose at the same time, and I looked a mess. But within forty-eight hours of being patched up at Edinburgh General Hospital, I had ridden two winners at Newcastle, and all thoughts of an early retirement were firmly out of my mind.

Strangely, my worst riding accident came on the Olivers' schooling-ground in January 1972 while preparing Fugal Deal for his first race over fences.

A slow learner, he crashed into the open ditch, catapulted me from the saddle and, in a thundering fall, I broke my cheek-bone and upper jaw-bone, and thought I had broken my neck. I was rushed to hospital convinced I was bound for the scrapheap. Thankfully, a quick X-ray and a kind doctor assured me my neck was perfectly sound and that I had nothing to worry about.

Determined to make a swift recovery, I flew from Newcastle to London for treatment from Bill Tucker and Alun Thomas. They checked me over, made a few notes and then rerouted me to King's College Hospital, where I stayed two days. Doctors there fitted a brace round my teeth and put me on a diet of Heinz baby-food for two months. I felt a fool, but it kept my weight down and for that I was grateful.

Despite these problems I refused to sit on the sidelines and was back in the saddle in less than ten days. Irish trainers were still eager to lure me back across the sea to ride for them, and in March I agreed to nip over to Naas to partner Dim Wit and Brendon's Road for Paddy Mullins, and they both won. I enjoyed popping over, if only to show the lads I had not lost my touch. But the Irish jockeys resented my visits. They gave me dirty looks and made it clear they didn't want me making a habit of nicking their cream.

After winning on Dim Wit, I praised it highly as a good horse, and it was soon made favourite for the Aintree Grand National. Almost immediately owner Jeremiah John O'Neill was offered an astronomical sum for him, but he turned it down. Frankly, Dim Wit had no chance of winning at Aintree, although he did go on to land the Irish Grand National at Fairyhouse, so O'Neill lost a marvellous chance of making a good profit on him.

Over the years, many jockeys enjoyed making jokes about my inclination for alcohol and my apparent ability to drink myself into the record books. So it came as a welcome change when I wrote myself into racing history while totally stone-cold sober.

I rode Almond Lodge in a handicap chase at Perth, and my brother Peter rode the favourite, Avondhu – and we passed the post together! As far as I know its the only time two brothers have figured in a dead heat on a steeplechase course.

I was completely off the drink at this stage, and I remember one traumatic night while staying with Terry Biddlecombe and Bridget before going on to race at Worcester next day.

As usual, Terry and Bridget went to bed early and left me in the lounge where I watched television until the last notes of the National Anthem faded away. When I eventually got to bed, I couldn't sleep. The terrible anxiety came over me again and I used to think I was dying.

So I went downstairs, and I prayed and prayed to God to let me live. I knew that alcohol wouldn't solve my problem, but only ease it for a while, so I tried desperately hard not to take a drink.

But the panic became so bad I couldn't stop myself from going into the kitchen and pouring a large brandy into a glass. I carried it back into the sitting-room and placed it on the mantelpiece.

I had no Valium with me, so I had to suffer mentally for an hour and a half. I kept looking at the brandy and fought with myself to stay away from it. I refused to give in. My worries were made worse because I knew I had a few fancied mounts at Worcester next day and thought I'd be too weak to do them justice.

The anxiety gradually passed away. I went back to the kitchen, put my head under the tap and drank pints and pints of water until I felt well enough to go back to bed again.

I was so pleased with my victory over the worst temptation man can face, that I poured the brandy down the sink, put my head on the pillow and slept like a baby.

Being able to stay off the drink at this time enabled me to be a serious candidate for the best riding job in the country. Ask any young steeplechase jockey which trainer he'd most like to work for and the answer will be Fulke Walwyn every time.

It was close to the end of the 1971–2 season that I had the honour of being chosen for the most enviable job of working with the Queen Mother's brilliant and highly respected trainer. I was living nearby, at Scott's Farm in Malmesbury, and I grabbed the opportunity with great excitement and optimism.

I was honest with the guv'nor from the start. As I walked into Saxon House, I told him straightaway that I was an alcoholic. I also told him I had been off the booze a year, and I truly believed I had the disease under control. Sadly, it soon became clear that I hadn't.

A lot of people have found Mr Walwyn abrupt, but it can take a long time to understand him. Like all of us, he can become irritable at times, particularly if he feels a jockey has ridden a bad race. He is the absolute professional, a perfectionist. He has also been accused of being a snob, but I can assure you he has time and patience for everyone. Over the years he's suffered badly from a nagging stomach complaint, and it's a trouble that tends to make him edgy at times.

I certainly hope I shall be able to repair the damage I did in my time with him, and that he will continue to understand my problems.

There were many occasions when I had substantial bets of up to £10,000 on horses I rode for him, and I got my fair share of rollickings if he thought I had not followed instructions.

He wasn't the world's best loser and was inclined to get ratty and pull a jockey to pieces if he thought it was deserved. Little did he realize with me that I frequently felt sicker than he did when a horse from the stable was beaten.

All he suffered was loss of pride. Defeat for me often meant thousands and thousands of pounds in disastrous bets.

He was extremely thorough with his instructions on how a horse should be ridden. And his wife, Cath, was always very charming, and a tremendous worker. Apart from her duties in the yard and in the house, she worked tirelessly in support of the Catholic church in Lambourn.

Right from my early days as a professional, I was eager to spend a working holiday somewhere in Scandinavia. Several English jockeys kept whetting my appetite with stories of big prize-money, generous owners and beautiful girls. They would whizz over at weekends, ride a winner or two, pull a bird, and return on a late flight to their wives or girlfriends on Sunday evening.

These were the type of civilized ingredients that appealed to my sense of fun and ambition, and in April 1972 the mercurial Jack Doyle made it all possible for me. Jack has an abundance of distinguished contacts all over the world, and he arranged for me to ride on contract for Karlmonger Khalstaad in Norway.

Before I left for Norway, Mary and I finally accepted that our marriage was on the rocks. Wisely, I think, we decided that divorce was the only sensible way out for both of us. A few months earlier we had settled on a trial separation, and I had gone about with Diane

Thomson Jones, the attactive daughter of Harry Thomson Jones, the Newmarket trainer. It was at this point that I received a letter from my solicitor stating that Mary was entitled to a third of my income and half of what I owned. I was staggered, but rather than hang our dirty linen out in court and provide more fodder for the press, Mary settled for a substantial lump sum and divorce proceedings were started immediately.

Frankly, our marriage was doomed from the start. We were hopelessly incompatible, and in our two years as man and wife I profoundly regret to say our relationship was never consummated. After months of tedious haggling with solicitors the divorce finally became absolute in November 1974. Mary later remarried and is now living happily near Witney in Oxfordshire.

While talking of domestic life, I must recall that one jump jockey, Ernie Fenwick, took no risks when he got married. He holds an insurance policy against it breaking up. As far as I know, he and his wife are still living happily together and the policy has never been touched.

I finally departed for Oslo from the Duke of Beaufort's private landing-strip at Badminton after riding at Stratford on the last day of the English jumping season. On arrival I moved into digs near the racecourse and arranged for my BMW to be shipped over from Newcastle. It was the most expensive car I ever owned, and I stupidly wrapped it round a lamp-post after a drinking spree back in England six months later.

I remained in Norway throughout June and July and miraculously didn't suffer one alcoholic slip, possibly because my spare time was taken up by the gorgeous Trine Melling, a delightful and curvy Norwegian ski champion.

Norwegian racing is confined to Mondays and Thursdays, and staged on a track very similar to Fontwell's figure-of-eight. Having ridden round Fontwell more times than I can remember, I quickly adapted to the place, and ended up second in the Championship.

One hilarious incident while living over there involved British jockeys Frankie Durr, now training successfully at Newmarket, and the aggressive Jock Wilson.

After a heavy night on the town, Frankie and Jock were both steamed up in the back of my car as we travelled home to our apartments. In front with me, and minding his own business, was little Dave Thomas, a committed teetotaller, and another Norwegian-based British jockey.

Dave's strongest drink was a glass of lime-juice, and Frankie and Jock started taking the mick out of him. After a few miles, Dave could take no more and asked me to stop the car and let him get out and walk home.

But as soon as he slammed the door, Frankie followed him, stumbling and staggering across the road. Frankie was terribly inebriated. He pursued Dave to the village green, caught up with him, tapped him on the shoulder and landed a tremendous right swing on his chin.

Dave sank to the ground and Frankie left him there, flattened. Then Frankie swaggered back to the car, returned to his seat and calmly told me, 'Drive on, chauffeur!' And he blew approvingly on his knuckles.

At the end of July I was preparing to return to England to take up my duties as first jockey to Fulke Walwyn when Graham Thorner and David Nicholson flew over to ride at Malmo in the King's Cup, Sweden's most notable steeplechase. They were wasting their time. The race was strictly a clash between Rodan and Overdose, both trained by the efficient, versatile Terj Dahl. Rodan was definitely the best horse I teamed up with in Norway, and in one unstoppable sequence I won five races on him.

The King's Cup was the equine heavyweight contest the whole fanatical Scandinavian racing public had been longing for. I rode Rodan, and Dahl rode Overdose. As a jumper, Overdose was certainly superior to Rodan, but I knew that if it became a question of speed, my trusted Polish-bred partner would lick them all.

The race attracted tremendous publicity and the huge crowd was not to be disappointed. Overdose and Rodan approached the last fence side by side, landing absolutely level, and full of running. I knew Rodan had the speed to outstrip him, so I opened the throttle and we accelerated so sharply we won by three lengths.

The ovation was tumultuous. Someone even placed a huge garland of fresh flowers around Rodan's neck. King Gustav watched the race, and Rodan and I were paraded in front of him. It was a for the fuse-box when we heard a frightening bang at the top of the stairs. Then came a lot of banging and shouting, and I was certain the house was being raided. I became very panicky.

The noise grew worse by the second and I visualized half a dozen thugs in nylon masks making their way downstairs to grab us. I could never hope to cope with their fists or guns, so Trish and I dashed across the room, opened a window and leaped into the drive. Gasping, and still holding hands, we raced down the lane and out on to the main road.

When we reached the first house, I was panting and breathless from shock. I banged on the door and, to my surprise, trainer Anthony Johnson and his wife opened up. I was standing in the doorway in the dark, a towel around my waist, freezing from the cold and frightened to death.

I told them a gang were trying to break into Ian's house and Anthony went straight to the telephone and rang the police. Then he and a burly friend picked up a rifle and ran down the road.

About half an hour went by before Anthony and his friend came back. We were really worried about their safety. When they left us they were all keyed up and ready for action. When they returned they were smiling and cracking a joke. Trish and I looked at them, puzzled.

Anthony explained that two car-loads of police had surrounded the house, and that the officer in charge wanted me to visit the station to make a statement. When I walked back to Ian's house I couldn't understand why the police were talking to Barry Hills and Steve Stanhope, son of Lord Harrington, an amateur rider and assistant to Fred Winter at the time.

It turned out that Barry and Steve had been on a drinking spree and, on seeing my car outside, they decided to 'frighten hell out of Brogan'. Which they did all right!

The pencil-slim Stanhope had somehow squeezed through a tiny window at the top of the house and, once inside, opened a door for Barry to go in. Then they banged and bawled, and scared the living daylights out of Trish and me. But the prank backfired on them. When they saw the car-loads of police and the growling dogs they ended up more frightened than we were. And, my God, that's saying something!

deeply emotional moment and I felt honoured and proud of my achievements.

Later that evening, I joined the country's distinguished guests at the Swedish Derby Ball and a great night was enjoyed by all.

A great Norwegian honour came my way when I was invited to stand as a stipendiary steward at a flat meeting in Oslo, and for a short time I tested my skill as a tipster on a morning newspaper.

The cost of living in Norway was astronomical. I couldn't manage on less than £150 a week which, in those days, was a substantial sum of money.

Mary had promised that while I was in Norway she would sell Scott's Farm for me and find somewhere for me to live on my return. She did well. She sold my property to actress Diane Cilento, the former wife of Sean Connery, for £36,000 – exactly twice what I paid for it six months earlier. It comprised ten boxes, eight acres and an elegant house in a picturesque spot just a mile and a half from Badminton.

In the meantime, Mary had arranged for me to live in a rented house in Lambourn and this became yet another new base in my constant nomadic wanderings.

At Lambourn, where I lived at Kapal Cottage, I frequently used the sauna at the home of Ian Williams. I was such a regular visitor that Ian eventually gave me a key to let myself in.

I went there for a sweat every Sunday afternoon, and on one ludicrous occasion I found Trish, a girlfriend of John Patterson, curled up in a chair watching television. John lived with me at the cottage, and worked as an assistant trainer to Tim Forster at Wantage.

While I stripped and settled in the sauna, Trish continued to watch television at the other end of the house. Everything was silent and normal. I remember it was late November, and it was dark long before half-past four.

Suddenly, after sweating heavily for an hour or so, all the lights in the house went out, and I thought a fuse had blown. So I leapt from the sauna, wrapped a towel around my waist and rushed to the television-room.

The house was in pitch darkness and Trish was trembling with fear. I didn't feel too brave myself, and I was still fumbling around

# 13
# Cold Turkey

AT THE END OF THE OCTOBER FOLLOWING MY NORWAY TRIP I went to Mr Walwyn and told him I was knackered. I should have taken a rest, but I didn't want to miss a ride.

I remember going off to a Windsor race-meeting with an awful cold. Before I left, Mrs Walwyn handed me a bottle of a strong cough medicine which, unknown to me, contained a fair measure of alcohol. When I returned from the races I took a few spoonfuls before going to bed to soothe my throat. But I became hooked on it, and before the night was out I had drunk the lot and felt very high.

During this time I was off the drink. My only bad habit was swallowing three or four Valium tablets a day. But two days after taking the cough mixture I began slipping back on the drink again.

I tried to conceal it from everyone, but after five days I was suffering so badly I had no alternative but to break the news to Mr Walwyn. To my great surprise, I found him marvellously understanding.

So after eighteen months of not touching a drink, and now holding the job I'd always wanted, number one to Mr Walwyn, I found I was absolutely worn out. I began to crack up, and the inevitable happened.

One night at the end of November I was so depressed I indulged in yet another heavy drinking session, although next day I was booked for two important mounts at Towcester. As a result I finished second on Bright Spartan and then fell from Beau By and shattered my lower left jaw.

After racing, Peter O'Sullevan kindly drove me to London to meet Alun Thomas who arranged for an operation at King's College Hospital. I was told not to drink alcohol for up to twenty-four hours before the operation, but I ignored his advice and finished off a bottle of vodka just four hours before the surgeon got to work.

Five days after the operation I paid my fourth visit to St John

O'God's to be dried out, and I remained there until 4 December. I then flew straight back to London and rode at Warwick just twelve hours later, landing Cooper's Green a six-length winner in the day's first race. Again I told no one where I had been.

I was thrilled with the win and hoped I had killed booze for good. But barely three weeks had passed when I was back on the drink again and I returned to St John O'God's for the fifth time on 23 January 1973. I was discharged as good as new a week later.

Again I wasted no time in returning to the action and on the very next day I won the last race at Windsor on Fulke Walwyn's hurdler Sea Tale, and added The Dikler at Wincanton next day.

I still felt terribly run down, and I knew I should have stayed at St John O'God's and gone through the Richard Pampouri Unit, but I was desperate to be at my peak to ride The Dikler in the Gold Cup the following month.

I was still betting heavily, and on 5 February I went to Plumpton and put £2,000 on my mount Red Chief, trained by Fulke Walwyn, but I was beaten by a length by Beaming Lee.

Undaunted, I raced out to a phone box on the course and confidently placed £3,000 on another of Fulke Walwyn's runners, Great Opportunity, which I was riding in the last. I had a special affinity for Great Opportunity. I had bought him from Padge Berry for Mick Holly, a new owner and a good friend of mine. Great Opportunity had won for Mick at the first time of asking at Nottingham a week earlier. I thought the horse was a certainty at Plumpton, although I realized the soft ground was very much against him. He was backed down to 4–5 favourite.

With great assurance I sent him to the front at the sixth, and I was mentally totting up my money. We continued to lead to the second-last. But he was tiring badly and he fell, exhausted. Again I had miscalculated, and I went home losing a colossal £5,000 at the meeting.

Still unbothered, I travelled up to Leicester next day and put £2,000 on my mount Night and Day, again trained by Fulke Walwyn. I was convinced he was a good thing. But I was losing a lot of money, and I was chasing it.

In a late rush, his price was cut from 5–4 to even-money favourite.

Jeff King's mount Marsac was also the subject of some furious betting and dropped from 12–1 to 9–1.

I kept Night and Day close to the leaders, and drove him to the front at the sixth. Jeff was sitting handily all the time and he came to challenge me at the second last. From then on it was a ding-dong battle to the line, until he pulled away to win by a length. Another £2,000 had gone down the drain.

Ironically, Night and Day went on to win two races that season, but I missed them both as I was back in hospital being dried out.

My ridiculous losing spell continued at Newbury four days later. I splashed £5,000 on Sea Prince, owned by the late Sir Charles Clore and trained by Fulke Walwyn. My cash had an obvious affect on the betting market and Sea Prince was knocked back from 5–2 to 13–8 favourite.

I gave him every chance, and we led from the third flight to the sixth. We were cantering by the second-last. I was sure we'd win. But when I asked him to quicken, he had nothing to offer, and we rapidly dropped out of contention, finishing fifth behind the winner, Pythium.

When we came in, Fulke Walwyn gave me a roasting. Hitting back, I told him the horse couldn't stay two miles. He didn't have the stamina, judgment that in time proved correct. In fact Mr Walwyn later saddled him to win a flat race at Epsom – over a mile and a quarter!

So, in all, I lost £12,000 in that disastrous week.

Incredibly, I never once, in all my career, failed to find a way of placing a bet, no matter where I was riding – Cheltenham, Ascot, Aintree – or how many engagements I had on the day. Martin Blackshaw called me 'The Pimpernel'. He used to stand on the dressing-room table and chant, 'They seek him here, they seek him there, they seek that effing Brogan everywhere.'

Between races I would vanish without trace. Gone, like a puff of smoke. I would slip into a long overcoat to hide my colours, don my brown titfer and dart through the crowd in search of a coin-box to telephone my next bet.

Obviously there were times when all the kiosks were occupied or out of order, and I would plead with the Clerk of the Course to borrow his telephone 'to make an urgent call to a trainer about a riding arrangement'.

Many times I have sat in the Clerk's chair and telephoned a bet involving a horse in the very next race, and he's stood just ten yards away and not had the slightest idea of what I was doing. I used to finish up with a load of old nonsense like 'Thank you, sir. See you in the morning, sir. Goodbye, sir.'

The Clerks fell for it every time. Of course, it was a preposterous risk to take, but it underlines how desperate I was to place a bet, irrespective of the consequences. I was sick and immature, and badly needing medical help.

It was not surprising that two weeks after that disastrous week, I suffered yet another alcoholic slip. I went on a ferocious booze-up at the Pheasant pub, a popular meeting place for the racing people on the road into Lambourn. I sat there imbibing with local trainers Hugh Williams and Ben Leigh.

After several hours of non-stop drinking, I soaked myself in vodka and brandy, and plunged into a deep blackout. I lost control of my senses, stormed outside and threw a brick through the window of a nearby house.

It was one of scores of blackouts I suffered over the years. My mind would go totally blank and I'd be unable to recall a single moment of where I'd been or what I'd said or done.

During one blinding blackout at Jedburgh, I destroyed twenty yards of stone wall on a bend with my Fiat 124 at three in the morning. The police swooped and I later lost my licence for a year for being drunk in charge.

The horrible mess on the car left me in no doubt that I'd been in a smash, but that was all. I couldn't remember a solitary second of the incident! I had drunk two forty-ounce bottles of brandy in ninety minutes, and I regained my senses while slumped confused in Jedburgh Police Station.

A blackout is a total loss of memory caused entirely by alcohol. During a blackout it's possible for an alcoholic to wipe out his whole family and not remember a thing about it. The ultimate and irretrievable end for a chronic sufferer is life as a 'cabbage' in a mental home. Thank God, despite my excesses my brain has remained miraculously undamaged.

As for that outrageous night at Lambourn, I couldn't recall smashing the window, and I couldn't remember going to bed. All I could remember was paying £50 next day to replace the pane.

Mr Walwyn buzzed me at eight o'clock the following morning, and I didn't stir. Eventually the telephone did wake me, but I didn't answer it. I was afraid to!

It wasn't long before Mr and Mrs Walwyn arrived to see me. They had heard of my escapade the night before, which wasn't a great surprise because in Lambourn everyone makes a point of knowing everyone else's business. We settled down to have a serious chat.

This was my third slip in four months, and Mr Walwyn was naturally deeply worried about me and my job. He had responsibilities to his owners, and he suggested that I should go away for a long, quiet holiday.

Being a weak person, I nodded in agreement, and I went off to Barbados, although in my heart I knew it was the wrong decision. Another spell in St John O'God's being dried out was what I really needed.

Mr Walwyn rang Mary and asked her to join me on the flight. She was secretary to David Tatlow at the time, and I used to meet her in Stow-in-the-Wold where I starred in endless late-night drinking sessions.

I thought it might be the ideal opportunity to patch things up with her and establish a reconciliation. I thought a Barbados holiday in the sun would be the perfect panacea.

It was only later that I realized, once and for all, that Mary and I could never be reconciled. We were poles apart. And this was just one of many terrible mental pressures that tormented me day after day, and I found them impossible to manage.

Mr Walwyn was exceedingly generous and paid both my fare and Mary's. Surprisingly, I did not drink much on the plane. I remember pleading with myself not to drink, but for an alcoholic that's like trying to stop a flood with a fork.

Immediately we touched down, I told Mary, 'You know my form, I'm drinking again. Don't let me upset your holiday. You meet your friends and leave me alone.'

We booked into an hotel called the Tamarind Cove. I was

desperate for a drink, but all the bars were closed, so I paced the streets looking for alcohol. The first few days were horrific. I discovered a new drink called Barbados rum. I loved it and was the best customer at the bar. I didn't want to speak to people, and I didn't want Mary to see me in such a revolting state of mind. I was at my worst.

Then I spotted a notice on the hotel wall giving details of an Alcoholics Anonymous meeting. I approached the manager for dates and times and he turned out to be a non-drinking alcoholic. It was simple for him to see that I was so sick from drink I needed immediate hospital attention. He dropped everything and rang another member of Alcoholics Anonymous who immediately drove out to speak to me.

He had been off the drink for fifteen years and been dried out the cold turkey way, an excruciating method where an alcoholic dries himself out without the help of tablets or tranquilizers. It is difficult and dangerous, and alcoholics have died from it.

I certainly admired the courage of this man, as I did of other alcoholics who had been dried out the cold turkey way and never returned to the wretched bottle again.

The manager booked me into hospital in Barbados. He sent me off in a taxi and paid my fare. When I arrived I was shown to my own private room and was allowed to keep my clothes.

In a short time a pretty nurse came to see me, turned me over and rammed a long, sharp needle into my backside. Then she left me there, lying on the bed almost crying like a baby for the usual drying-out tablets.

The tablets are called Hemineverin, which most alcoholics refer to as duck-eggs. They are large and yellow, and leave a terrible taste in the mouth.

Hour after hour I waited for them, but there was no sign of the nurse, and no sign of the tablets. I rang the bell so often I lost count. In time, the nurse condescended to answer and came to my bedside.

'For God's sake, where are the tablets?' I snapped at her. I was frantic, but it made no difference.

'You must wait for the doctor to see you,' she whispered.

But he never came, and I remained in that sweat-sodden bed for ten terrible hours. And, believe me, ten hours without a drink or sedation for an alcoholic is a living hell. Only an alcoholic knows the pain and frenzy that can rip you apart with hot and cold sweats, and the increasing panic.

Finally I could stick it no longer and stumbled out of bed, shuffled downstairs to the reception desk and demanded to see the doctor.

He was at home, but the nurse kindly relented and allowed me to ring him. He was a tough, short-tempered so-and-so, and he practically broke my heart when he said the hospital never prescribed tablets of any sort. Every patient was expected to dry out the cold turkey way, with just one Parentrovite injection to help speed the recovery.

I couldn't accept this primitive method of arresting my problem, so I went back to the ward, dressed myself, and returned to the reception clerk and signed myself out. I paid for my stay and booked a taxi. I pleaded with the driver to drop me at the nearest bar, and to wait there until I came out. It didn't matter how much it cost.

I clutched the glass like a drowning man. I knocked back three lagers almost without taking a breath. I just kept pouring and pouring it down.

'Oh God, this is what I needed,' I muttered. Although in reality, of course, it was the last thing I wanted.

Drink was driving me insane.

The manager soon saw me back at the hotel, and he invited me to dinner in his room. My stomach was so upset I couldn't eat. Food wouldn't stay down. I kept regurgitating and running to the loo. All I needed was another drink ... another drink ... another drink. And through it all I struggled desperately to retain as much self-respect as I could.

Later on, I made a string of excuses to slip away and be on my own with a few drinks. I crept into the bar and restarted on Barbados rum. I was desperately sick. My mind was cracking up and I realized I had to do something – urgently! I remember Mary and her friends came back and I was ashamed and embarrassed because I was so drunk that I couldn't stand up or open my mouth properly to speak to them.

I returned to my room and tossed and turned on the bed and tried to put away a couple of brandies. But I was so physically sick, nothing would stay down. So I rang Dr McCarthy in Dublin and explained my plight. He told me to board the first plane out of Barbados and he would reserve a bed at St John O'God's for me.

On reaching the airport, accompanied by Mary, I almost collapsed with shock when I noticed Mr and Mrs Nesbitt-Waddington, who lived near my mother, making their way to the same barrier. They were influential people in Irish racing and stewards of the Turf Club. I panicked. I thought, if they see me in this abysmal state, I'll nip in the loo and cut my throat.

Miraculously, and with the cunning of a fox, I succeeded in avoiding them all the way back to London. I even managed a few drinks on the plane to keep myself sedated.

We arrived at Heathrow in the early hours and it crossed my mind to have one last fling in the metropolis. Then I accepted that I had no friends in London who understood my condition, so I flew on to Dublin, but again I dillied and dallied. Procrastination was always a permanent and emphatic feature of my drinking problem.

I finally decided on one more day of freedom and booked into the Wicklow Hotel, trying to drink socially. I didn't want to be seen because I'd be quizzed why I was living in Dublin when I was supposed to be first jockey to Fulke Walwyn in England. So I found a quiet corner and hid myself away.

My tolerance was low at this stage, and I was unable to drink a great deal. My binges were becoming more frequent, but lasting only a short while. When I had drunk enough I would go upstairs and lie on the bed where I had several bottles of brandy at hand. I fell asleep and woke up in the night, shaking and shivering, with hot and cold sweats. I felt a wreck and almost suicidal. I tried to eat, but my stomach was so rotten it rejected everything. In desperation, I staggered downstairs to the night-porter and bought a few lagers and prayed they'd stay in my stomach. But they wouldn't.

I was frantic. I left the hotel at four in the morning and walked the streets, wandering like a tramp. Knowing the pubs weren't open I slipped a quart bottle of brandy in my pocket in case I got panicky. I had double cover. I had drink in my pocket and I knew I could drink twenty-four hours back at the hotel. So I stumbled into the next day, still procrastinating, still fighting off my pledge to enter St John O'God's, still marinating my liver.

I was at rockbottom. I didn't even have the right clothes for hospital. I had no pyjamas, dressing-gown or a pair of slippers. In a fit of recklessness I walked into Austin Reed's in Grafton Street and bought £70 of stuff to enter St John O'God's.

I shall never forget struggling from the Wicklow Hotel to Austin Reed's. Every time I lifted my foot it seemed I had a concrete block around my ankles. It was agony. I wanted to enter hospital and I didn't want to enter hospital. It was an awful dilemma.

I hadn't telephoned Fulke Walwyn because a million other thoughts were rattling through my head. I wasn't short of cash, because I remember going into a betting office – my mind absolutely vacant – and putting £200 on a horse. I didn't care whether it won or lost.

I went back later and found it had won at 5–2. So I put £400 on a horse in a race at Kelso and that won, too, at 6–4.

In fact I won so much that the bookmakers, Kilmartins, couldn't pay me out, and I was directed to their head office in Mid Abbey Street where they handed me my winnings.

I thought how exciting it would be if I could go out on the town and enjoy myself with it. But time was running out. Mentally and physically I was grinding to a halt.

On returning to the hotel I tried to sink a few brandies at the bar. One or two stayed down, and eventually I tried more and went up to my room. I was in a pitiful spin. All my outlets were closed. I had no friends, and didn't know where to turn.

Practically in tears, I picked up the telephone and told St John O'God's that I was on my way. I tried to sound sober, but even then I had not definitely made up my mind to go in. I was still trying to fight it.

I remember trying to go to bed early that night, but I couldn't sleep. I sat in a chair by the window and gazed out on the street, watching people chatting and smiling and making their way home from pubs and cinemas, and I envied them. I sat and sipped brandy. I mixed water with it, and I drank water on its own.

Eventually I dozed off, only to be awakened in the dark deep of night by a searing pain cutting across my chest. I knew I couldn't procrastinate any longer.

I packed my few measly belongings in a tatty blue bag, paid my bill, called a taxi and told the driver to head for St John O'Gods where they were waiting for me.

I still had a quart bottle of brandy in my pocket and, as we drove through the gates of St John O'God's, I drank the lot and slung the bottle out of the window.

After being checked in I was examined by a doctor and my clothes and cash were taken from me. It was strange, but every time I went into St John O'God's, I usually had quite a lot of money on me.

# 14
# Crash Landing

THE NEXT FEW DAYS WERE HELL. I WENT THROUGH THE painful process of being dried out and brought back to my senses. One chap in the ward died, and I was convinced I'd be the next. This worried me terribly.

By this time I had asked a nurse to ring Mr Walwyn and tell him where I was and explain what was happening to me. From then on Mr Walwyn rang the hospital every day to check on my progress. After six days of being dried out I was transferred to the Richard Pampouri Unit.

This was my third visit to St John O'God's in six months, and my sixth visit in all, and I now had a vital decision to make. Would I be fit enough by the middle of March to ride The Dikler in the 1973 Gold Cup?

Mr Walwyn made no attempt to influence me. The decision was mine, and mine alone. It was a great temptation to accept, but I knew, deep down inside, that it would be the wrong thing to do.

I telephoned Mr Walwyn and told him I would prefer to stay in hospital for a further month to try to get on some proper programme to come off the drink, and stay off it.

As time went on, Mr Walwyn engaged Ron Barry for The Dikler, but he stuck by me one hundred per cent. Reporters kept pestering him about my whereabouts, but he and my mother and the hospital staff were marvellously kind and discreet. They refused to embarrass me by telling the world where I was and what I was going through.

So on Gold Cup day I suffered the indignity of sitting up in bed, a broken alcoholic, watching Ron Barry winning the race in my place, and gaining all the glory which should have been mine for all the time and patience I had put in to teach the horse to settle and conserve his strength.

I was furious with myself. I found it impossible to accept that I had plunged into such a rotten mess, and I wondered how I would ever scramble out of the pit, and where I would end.

St John O'God's have a precise, specialized programme for treating alcoholics. As soon as a patient goes in, his blood pressure is checked and rechecked every hour. And he's put on the Heminevrin tablets. Patients are drugged and sedated by these pills and they have to drink gallons and gallons of water to help the recovery. I usually took five days to dry out and to feel on top of the world again.

The drying-out area is known as the 'infirmary', where one is forced to mix with other alcoholics and mental patients. There are no escape routes. Every door is locked, and the whole place is heavily barred. It's terrifying. Often patients would die in the night and I used to hide under the clothes as nurses wheeled the bodies out.

After dozing off one night I was stirred by a big fellow from Limerick sitting up in the bed alongside me. He was staring at the ceiling and mumbling to himself. Puzzled by it all, I asked him to share his secret with me, and he casually said he was watching colour televison. He really believed it. This was typical of an alcoholic in the early stages of being dried out. It was happening all the time.

I also remember a strapping chap from the West of Ireland who kept jumping in and out of bed, going to and from the door pretending to open it. Then he'd lash out with his boot and pretend to close it again. He went through this performance several times, so I asked him to explain. It turned out he had been a Black and White whisky drinker all his life and was now seeing a black-and-white cat entering the room, and he kept putting it out and kicking the door closed.

To anyone sane and in full control of his faculties it probably sounds funny. But when you're actually in that frame of mind, drugged and incarcerated, it's all deadly serious and no one risks a joke.

On another occasion, a very bad alcoholic rushed up the corridor and thrust his hand into a huge goldfish bowl and ate the lot. Then he burst into the television-room, grabbed the budgie, and ate his legs in front of everyone.

With so many alcoholics around, it was commonplace to see strapping young men suffering terrible bouts of the 'shakes'. They came from all walks of life: teachers, engineers, doctors, sportsmen, farmers, writers and company directors. They would say they had ulcers and stomach trouble, not wanting to admit their real reason for being there.

Shaving was a major hazard. Their hands shook so violently they nicked their necks, and when they stemmed the blood with tiny pieces of newspaper I could practically read the day's full racing results.

Mealtimes, of course, were always a pantomime. The tea arrived in a large, enamel pot and we would all wait expectantly to see who was about to pour it out. In most cases the unlucky chap would be shaking so badly he would spray it everywhere, missing the cups and flooding the table. He felt even worse about it, because a hundred eyes or more would be staring up at him. 'Whose turn to shake the tea out today?' became a standing joke at the place.

I found the infirmary sheer hell. I would lie awake at night, drenched in sweat. I often changed my pyjamas three or four times before morning. They wouldn't just be damp. They would be absolutely saturated with perspiration from all the alcohol blown out of my system. Flushed out of my kidneys.

After five days of drying out, a social worker and a psychiatrist would come to the ward and interview every patient. The social worker took a profound interest in every patient and tried to persuade us to stay on for twenty-five days in the unit to complete the course of treatment.

The unit itself was run by a woman, Mrs Terry Kennedy. She had great drive and dedication and equalled any of the vast number of psychiatrists I bamboozled along the way.

St John O'God's must rank with the best hospitals in the world for people with a drink problem. My only complaint was the bill.

After my last visit it came to £600, and I didn't have a penny to meet it. Thankfully, John Oaksey – on behalf of the Injured Jockeys' Fund – kindly came to my rescue, and settled it for me.

I left St John O'God's with the best intentions in the world to live a normal, rational life. I vowed never to go back on the drink again.

On returning to England I had one chance left; I went to Lambourn and rode out for Mr Walwyn, assuring him I felt grand and was fit enough to resume full work.

But what I felt and what I said sadly didn't comply with what I did. My life was still terribly unmanageable, and I couldn't accept the value and importance of attending Alcoholics Anonymous meetings. Inevitably I returned to my bad habits. I began to hare round like someone demented. I didn't want to miss a ride, I certainly didn't want to miss a winner. I was soon back on the drink again, and missing just about everything.

While still retained by Fulke Walwyn I used to nip over to Sweden or Norway to ride on Sundays and return in time to ride in England on the Mondays.

One weekend I flew out with Eric Eldin, then a flat jockey, and met a girl there called Eva. She and I became good friends and she used to pick me up on subsequent weekends from Stockholm Airport. We would drive into town and take a suite at the best hotel.

After racing ended on Sunday I usually had a few hours to kill with Eva before I flew back on the 9 pm flight to England. I became very fond of Eva and on one particular weekend I decided to miss the aeroplane and stay the night with her, taking the first flight out on the Monday morning.

I knew it had to be an early flight because I was booked to ride Kernel Marty for Mr Walwyn in a winners' novices chase at Wye. I had previously completed a three-timer on Kernel Marty at Worcester, Cheltenham and Fontwell, and he was still coming to his best; winning at Wye was a certainty.

I enjoyed a few drinks that Sunday night, but I didn't allow myself to get too bad. I wanted to be fresh for a bit of fun with Eva. About ten o'clock, I telephoned Mr Walwyn from the hotel and told him the aeroplane had been delayed, and that I couldn't fly out until Monday morning.

When morning came round, my luck took a dive. A thick, grey mist blotted out Stockholm. Consequently my flight was late taking off, and I arrived in London close on lunch-time, with all hopes of seeing Wye swiftly fading.

Though my car was parked at the airport I didn't know my way to Wye so, at great expense, I hired a taxi and promised the driver a big tip if he got me to the racecourse in time. I didn't ring Mr

Walwyn to say I was in a flap, because I knew I'd work him up into a worse one.

The taxi-driver did his best to emulate James Hunt, but time was stacked against him. The race was due off at 3.30, but at two o'clock we were so far from the track that I stopped the taxi. I got out and telephoned the racecourse and told Mr Walwyn's travelling head-lad, Tommy Tirely, that I wouldn't be there in time. He would have to find another jockey, and chose Johnny Haine.

I then kept the taxi waiting half an hour while I rang a friend in Jedburgh and asked him to listen to the race for me in a betting-office.

Kernel Marty won by eight lengths, and it made me feel worse. He was a snip.

My next problem was explaining to Mr Walwyn why I hadn't ridden the horse.

Whenever his horses run at meetings he can't attend, Mr Walwyn invariably rings a bookmaker at Lambourn and listens to the commentary on the telephone.

I rang him from a kiosk, and when he knew it was me he called out, 'Well done, Barry! Well done!'

I felt ashamed.

'Sorry, guv'nor,' I replied. 'I didn't ride him. The plane was late...'

The old man seemed unconcerned. He was delighted with his winner. I was disgusted at missing it.

Have horse, will travel... was a motto I pursued throughout my career. There were no bounds to the distances I'd travel in a day for a ride. Often I'd squeeze in two meetings, and they'd frequently be five hundred miles apart, right across the country. I employed my own personal pilot, Peter Ransom. He flew me all over England and Ireland, and occasionally over to Norway and Sweden. Peter was based at Newcastle, and he never let me down. Even on the tightest schedule he'd find a following wind and get me to the course in time.

18 May 1972 was one of those hectic days. Peter arranged with Kit Patterson, the genial Clerk of the Course at Perth, to land his aeroplane on the hurdles track straight after the last race at 5.15 to pick me up and fly me to Wolverhampton to ride in the 7.45.

I rode Ken Oliver's smart hurdler Acquisition in the 5.15, and we trotted up from Headship by two lengths, which put me in a marvellous frame of mind.

On reaching the winner's enclosure I caught sight of Peter circling high above and preparing to land. Without speaking to the Olivers I sprinted into the weighing-room, changed faster than Danny La Rue and raced out just in time to see Peter and his Piper Apache bumping to a halt a few yards past the winning-post. We took off promptly, at 5.25.

I was all keyed up to ride Cobbler's March. I had ridden him at Worcester a month earlier and felt he was coming to his peak.

The flight went smoothly and right on schedule until we crossed over Birmingham, when we suddenly plunged into a pea-soup fog and Peter got lost. He had permission to land at Pendeford Airport, but he couldn't find it!

With time running out, we flew on to Wolverhampton racecourse. We reached there about 7.10 and circled above just as the runners for the 7.15 race were on their way around. The horses were less than two hundred feet below us. With a decent rope-ladder I could have gone down and joined Tommy Stack on Maid of Lorien and both of us could have been on a winner!

Once the runners had passed the post, I knew I had to act swiftly. I was in the very next race, and I was still high in the air. Dramatic and immediate action was needed.

There was no hope of finding Pendeford, and we both knew that if a pilot wanted to land on a racecourse he had to apply for permission.

In fact, Wolverhampton had no landing-strip. But I got to work on Peter and convinced him there was just enough room to land on one of the many soccer pitches in the centre of the course.

I had paid him £150 for the round trip, and I didn't want to forfeit my money and miss the mount. I told Peter it was an emergency, and that the soccer pitch was absolutely safe. No one was around.

'Don't worry,' I assured him. 'I'll sort it out with the stewards.'

Peter swooped in beautifully, like a bird, and landed near the last fence. I leapt out and ran like hell to the weighing room.

Luckily for me, the trainer had seen the plane overhead, guessed it was me trying to land and didn't engage another jockey.

In the meantime, Peter flew back to Pendeford, and I arranged for a taxi to take me there after racing before flying back to Newcastle.

Still gasping, I hurried out to ride Cobbler's March, and Earl told me he thought the horse could win. This was good news. For when Earl fancies a horse it usually goes in. I don't know how he does it, but he can certainly set them alight.

Cobbler's March was a powerful front-runner and pulled painfully hard.

We cleared the first three fences with a long, extending lead. He was really flying. By the time we reached the stands I had succeeded in settling him at a sensible pace and could see our chances improving with every stride.

'If I can win this,' I thought, 'to hell with landing on the course!'

Then Bill Shoemark wrecked it all. He brought the favourite, Relic's Son, alongside me, and on seeing another horse, Cobbler's March pricked his ears, pulled fiercely, and took off at a frantic pace. Disaster was inevitable.

As we approached the open ditch he didn't even bother to lift his legs. He crashed right through it, sent me flying and I landed with a thud under the rails.

I skinned my nose, and felt shaken up. What a way to spend an evening, I groaned. Then the ambulance came along and took me off to the weighing-room. I felt rotten. But there was no time to recover before the stewards sent for me.

Bobby McAlpine was one. And he and the others ticked me off for literally 'dropping in' on the meeting.

The stewards' secretary, Lorraine-Smith, was still shaking his head in disbelief, and he told me, 'I've never seen anything like it. A bit of James Bond.'

Sadly for me, the stewards didn't see the funny side and they cautioned me for landing on the course without permission.

And there was worse to come....

On leaving the weighing-room I found an officious-looking policeman standing in the doorway waiting for me. Oh God, I thought, what have I done now?

It transpired that traffic control at Birmingham Airport were bemused and angry and wanted to interview Peter. The policeman drove me to Pendeford – kindly saving me my taxi fare – and we met up with Peter. In fairness, he accepted full responsibility for landing on the course and later flew me back to the North.

I thought nothing more of the incident until five months later when I saw some huge headlines in the newspaper about a pilot in trouble. Peter had appeared before the magistrates at Wolverhampton and been fined £50 for flying low without permission and endangering the race crowd. A short time after this he rang me to say that an air traffic disciplinary committee had had him suspended for six months and that he was short of money. He wanted a loan. I told him it was impossible, and that I'd paid him enough over the years.

Still not satisfied, he drove down to Lambourn to see me and stayed overnight, but I wouldn't budge. Grumbling and despondent, he eventually left, and I never saw him again.

During the early part of 1972 I became friendly with Raymond Peacock and his wife, Carmen. Raymond, who suffered terribly with ulcers, was a hard trainer but very generous. He enjoyed having me to stay with him overnight on my way to the races. Like most men, Raymond enjoyed his brandies-and-American, but in no way would he play about and go off with women.

From the start, it was clear things weren't going too well between Raymond and Carmen. She was a lot younger than him and appeared to take a fancy to me. Yet Raymond and I were such good friends I would never take advantage of the girl.

Carmen would come to my room early in the morning and wake me with a cup of tea. I always played the innocent and told her to 'stop the nonsense'. When she teased me, sometimes suggesting that I should go to bed with her, it got beyond a joke and in the end I didn't look forward to visiting Raymond.

The first sign of a bust-up came in the kitchen one morning when Raymond casually mentioned he was having a little domestic trouble. He suggested I should go with him in the car to Chester where he had some business to do.

On the way Raymond revealed he was very worried about

Carmen. He was beginning to distrust her. There was 'something going on, and she might have to go'.

On returning from Chester the atmosphere was so embarrassing that I packed my bags and moved into an hotel down the road.

One thing I couldn't avoid was riding out for Raymond. Next morning when I arrived for work he tactfully took me aside and told me Carmen had told him she was madly in love with me and wanted to run away and marry me. I was absolutely dumbfounded.

Raymond was clearly confused, and chose to believe her rather than me. He was convinced I was having an affair with her. His reasoning puzzled me, at least until I remembered that Carmen was a tremendous worker in the yard, and probably saved Raymond employing extra stable staff. He had a very good reason for keeping her with him.

Raymond and I parted there and then. I brought an end to my riding for him, and to all the marvellous times we enjoyed while buying and selling horses together.

It was sad we had to split up on such a sour note, and we haven't spoken to each other since.

I took our break-up badly. For several days I just drifted on, drinking and gambling. I ended up in a Chinese restaurant in Worcester where I ate a huge meal and drank various bottles of wine, and then found I didn't have the money to pay the bill.

Terry Biddlecombe lived nearby, and he was the only person I knew who could come along and bale me out. So I rang Terry, and he drove over and settled my account.

Terry then took me home with him, and he called in Doc Wilson who prescribed a box of drying-out tablets. I remained in bed for six days, the dreadful result of all the pressure I had been put under by Carmen Peacock.

Raymond was a non-gambling trainer and turned out a lot of big-price winners.

At one time, when still friendly with Raymond, I lived in a flat near Ballsbridge, and I invited him over to look at some horses at Christy Kinane's stable near Cashel. It turned out to be an insane weekend.

We set off from Dublin on the Friday evening and picked up two girls who were hitching their way to a dance in Kilrush.

Raymond and I were both parched, so we pulled up at a roadside pub. Raymond drank Guinness, which he thought fabulous, and I knocked back the vodka. The girls sipped Babycham, and looked at us in amazement as we got tighter and tighter. On reaching Limerick I generously treated them all to a meal at the Brazen Head before we continued on our way. We just drank and ate, and ate and drank. By the time we reached Kilrush it was three in the morning. The dance had long finished, and the hall was in darkness. The girls leapt from the car, thanked us with a smile, and fled down the road.

I was paralytic and flopping all over the dashboard. I couldn't drive another yard, so we swopped seats and Raymond did the driving. We travelled through the night, reaching Roscrea at half-past eight, and pulled into an hotel for breakfast. Being an alcoholic, the last thing I wanted was something to eat. They could keep their cornflakes and bacon and eggs.

Suddenly I had a brainwave: I'd book in as a resident. Such a ruse would enable me to snatch a few drinks, I thought. And it did!

We were both knackered, so we crawled into bed and slept until mid-day. Feeling refreshed, we brazenly checked out and drove on to Naas.

I was still insatiably thirsty, so we stopped at Portlhoise, and I was so wretchedly drunk when we reached Naas that I couldn't leave the car to enter the racecourse. Raymond was just as boozed, but he had arranged to meet a dealer to talk business, and staggered through the gates mumbling to himself and swaying from side to side.

With his talking done, Raymond returned to the car and we went back to Dublin, where I pulled myself together and drove down to Cashel. I bought Act the Creek from Timmy Hyde for Raymond, who passed it on to his owner, Des McLoughlin.

Towards the end of our association I tended to let Raymond down badly. My drinking was out of control. He'd book me for rides and I'd never turn up. I was a real nuisance in this respect and hope that he will accept my apologies for all the ulcers and headaches I caused him.

How much simpler it would have been if I had attended AA meetings, latched on to a programme and stayed away from the drink a day at a time. I could have shared my experiences, my guilt and inhibitions, with other alcoholics, purging myself through the open therapy system that has made Alcoholics Anonymous so strong and so internationally successful.

Fulke Walwyn wasn't easily fooled. He realized I wasn't at all fit to ride and as the 1972–3 season was almost over he suggested I went on holiday so that I could return refreshed when the new term came round. I still had a job with Mr Walwyn, but I had let him and his owners down and I felt ashamed. Reluctantly, I agreed to his advice, and made plans for a holiday in the sun.

Typically enough I didn't fulfil my promise. I continued to ride at exercise for Mr Walwyn, went to the occasional race-meeting and rode out for Alan Jarvis at Wolvey, near Coventry.

Then one morning, completely out of the blue, Jarvis offered me a few rides at Ludlow, and I couldn't refuse. Right through my life I've never been able to say no.

I had told Mr Walwyn I wouldn't ride again that season, and he had told his owners. He had also arranged for Ron Barry to ride Charlie Potheen, and Aly Branford, second jockey to me in the yard, to ride his other horses. I didn't have the guts to ring Mr Walwyn and mention my mounts with Jarvis. Instead, he found out and telephoned me, saying he wanted to talk to me straight away.

So Fulke Walwyn and Barry Brogan split up. I'd broken yet another promise to him. I had given him my word that I wouldn't ride again that season, he had retained me for the following year, and I had kicked him in the face. He was an extremely fair man. If I were in his position I'd have done the same; I deserved all I got.

Without the slightest trace of malice, Mr Walwyn said, 'This isn't good enough, Barry. This can't go on. We have to terminate our agreement.'

I agreed. I had to go my own way, and he had to find a new jockey for the following season.

Ironically, as the season drew to a close, I continued to ride winners for Jarvis and other trainers. I finished a good run by landing the TWW Champion Novice Chase at Chepstow on The Benign Bishop – beating one of Mr Walwyn's horses, Barnard, ridden by Aly Branford!

My last ride in that dramatic 1972–3 season came on Becoz at Bangor-on-Dee. That same evening I drove down to Heathrow and boarded a plane to Paris for a weekend with Brian Lenehan. We arrived late on Saturday evening, and we were due to fly back on Sunday shortly after the Prix Ganay at Longchamp.

We signed in at the Inter-Continental Hotel and I got the best bonus of my life. I found a large fridge in my room crammed tight with miniature bottles of alcohol. Brandy, gin, vodka, the lot. It was Aladdin's cave, a dream come true. I settled down and made myself at home. ...

By midnight I was deeply inebriated, and Lenehan and I left the hotel and took a taxi to a club where we drank champagne and were offered a hostess to share our table for £100. There were several beautiful girls lurking around, but I noticed one in particular. A voluptuous Persian half-caste, and I plumped for her.

I paid the £100 and she joined us for drinks. Then she invited me across the road to a posh hotel where they charged forty-five francs an hour for a room. Again I paid.

My Persian friend was a beauty, and a real professional. But no matter how hard she tried she just couldn't turn me on. I was so terribly drunk I couldn't answer the call. I was limp and useless.

She peeled off her clothes and rubbed up against me, but it made no difference. It wouldn't budge. So I put on my trousers and staggered back to my hotel. On returning to my room, I went straight to the fridge and drank and drank until I collapsed on the bed.

I sank into a deep, deep sleep, and when I awoke I had an insatiable thirst. To satisfy it, I drank lager and vodka, and every miniature I could lay my hands on.

I had no idea of the time, so I went down to reception and telephoned Lenehan's room. There was no reply. He had checked out. I panicked.

'How long have I slept?' I kept asking myself.

I thought it was Sunday morning. In fact, it was late Monday afternoon – I had slept a whole day. And the more I panicked, the more I became confused. I suddenly remembered I should be at Nottingham to ride Atanic for Alan Jarvis, but the race had finished four hours ago.

It was Tuesday morning before I finally arrived back in England, and I didn't need to be told my condition was chronic. I dodged my doctor in London and flew instead to Malta where I knew I could buy the Heminevrin drying-out tablets across the counter without a prescription at Potter's Chemist in St Julians. After collecting the tablets I returned to London and booked in at the Hilton, staying there for four days while drying myself out.

Knowing that the Heminevrin tablets were so readily available in Malta, I had become a regular traveller there. I visited the country seventeen times in five years, usually arriving for supper and leaving after breakfast with a packetful of pills to dry myself out with secretly in England on the few occasions I could summon enough willpower.

# 15
# A Tank with Banks

TO SUFFER TWO DIFFERENT FORMS OF DISQUALIFICATION within five hours on the same day must go down as some bizarre sort of record. That's why 21 February 1973 went into my diary. I was disqualified from driving in the morning, disqualified from riding in the afternoon!

Magistrates at Whitminster in Gloucestershire fined me £60 and banned me a month for crossing the central reservation on the M5 after a 100 mph police chase.

After hearing the verdict I was driven to Windsor, where I was booked to ride The Dikler in the Fairlawne Chase, a warm-up event for the Gold Cup a month later.

Only Spanish Steps (Bob Davies) and Fortune Bay II (George Sloan) bothered to take us on. Three weeks earlier The Dikler and I had trotted up by eight lengths at Wincanton, so he was entitled to be 8–15 favourite.

Frankly, he was only three-parts ready – which was two parts more than me! I had slipped again a week before the race. I had been drinking heavily and chronic withdrawal symptoms were keeping me awake at night.

Before going to court I roasted in a sauna to sweat away the alcohol, and gulped pee-pills to wash out all the excess fluid. Still not satisfied, and in a fit of panic, I swallowed two tranquillizers before I left the racecourse car-park. I thought they'd sedate me, and keep me alert for the race.

The Dikler was in fine fettle and jumped better than ever. We led at most stages of the three-mile race, and were still in front while leaping the last. But Bob Davies was biding his time on Spanish Steps and he came with a rush to join me on the run in.

Without me to help him, The Dikler continued to hang away from the stands. Bob Davies had plenty of room to go around me, but the more we kept edging to the left the more he kept sticking to us and following us off line.

The Dikler and I eventually finished up on the far rails, having drifted the full width of the track. An inquiry was inevitable, and Bob objected for good measure.

I tried desperately hard to keep the race, but not even my persuasive tongue could sway the stewards this time. They disqualified me without compunction and awarded the race to Bob. I blamed myself entirely for that defeat, and until now no one has ever known the exact reason for The Dikler's extraordinary reverse.

I knew that if I had not been drinking I would have kept The Dikler on a straight course and we would have won without stretching a muscle. It was yet another costly example of the way I suffered through alcoholism.

Traumatic experiences and blackouts tormented me almost daily. I was rarely free of the blinding mental torture that impelled me to drink and left me a pitiful wreck.

I experienced one of my worst blackouts on Saturday, 31 May 1975. It was the last day of the jumping season and I arranged to attend a party at Macer Gifford's home in Huntingdon after riding in the final race at Market Rasen.

I travelled to the races with a friend from London, and after finishing second in the nine o'clock event we hurried off to Lincoln to catch a few drinks before the pubs closed.

We crammed a load of stuff inside us, and I bought a bottle of brandy before we set off for Macer's. No alcoholic can leave a pub without a drink in his pocket!

Speeding down the M1 at 100 mph, my friend and I got stuck into the brandy and we emptied the bottle. By the time we neared Macer's house I had become quite heady. I vaguely remembered that I had to turn right at a roundabout. But it was a tricky stretch of road and I was so drunk I blundered.

Instead of turning right, I went left ... and crashed through a large red-and-white barrier. I was oblivious of everything. I had no idea I had smashed my way on to the vast American air base at Alconbury and that I was cruising merrily down the runway.

Lights went on, tanks came out, squad cars zoomed around me and the top brass poured from everywhere. A nuclear raid couldn't have caused more panic.

Outside the air base, and studying every manoeuvre, was a police officer with a book in his hand.

Half-way up the runway, I was eventually ambushed by a phalanx of American officers and most of their military ground units. Three large American cars and a tank escorted me to the gate and I was handed over with full military mumbo-jumbo to the gloating policeman. Without delay, he yanked me out of the car and whisked me off to Huntingdon police station, where I refused to provide blood and urine samples.

I was supposed to be off the drink, and I didn't want people to know that I was back on it again. I was very drunk, and it took me three hours to sober up in a private room in the station.

I later bailed myself out for £50 and went and knocked on Macer's door. It was now five o'clock on Sunday morning. The party was long over and the house in darkness. Macer was tired and in bed, but it was not unusual for him to see me in such a wretched condition. He let me in, left me some drink and went back to bed. I was just a nuisance to him.

By now I had learnt enough from all my hospital sessions to dry myself out without having to be medically supervised. I knew where to put my hands on the vital Heminevrin tablets. Of course, it is an exceedingly dangerous way of treating oneself and shouldn't be attempted by anyone who doesn't know what he is doing.

My friend and I arrived back in London at midday and I went straight on the drying-out tablets; I was soon all right again.

I told no one of the air base incident and nipped back to Ireland to ride a few horses for Liam Brennan. Then, completely out of the blue, I received a summons to appear at Huntingdon magistrates' court. As their date was not convenient for me to attend, I obtained a doctor's certificate to say I had been hurt in a fall at Wexford and they swallowed it.

Obviously I couldn't stall them for long, and they suggested a new date three weeks later. This again didn't suit me, so I collected another doctor's note saying I had been hurt while schooling.

I received a third letter, categorically stating that if I failed to appear in court on that date a warrant would be issued for my arrest without bail. I tore the letter up and ignored it completely.

I didn't wish to lose my driving licence for any real length of time, and I certainly didn't want people to know that I had been drinking again.

During this time I was still slipping over to England from Ireland for the occasional ride, and one Saturday I accepted the ride on Saucy Belle at Bangor-on-Dee. I decided to stay at the Golden Valley Hotel in Cheltenham. I had just finished drying myself out, and my pockets were bulging with Heminevrin tablets. I was living on them.

I was barely fit enough to ride, but I did my best and Saucy Belle finished second to Red Wolf. I had just sat down in the weighing-room when two strapping fellows came in and stood over me. I didn't know who they were because only jockeys, valets and officials were usually allowed in during racing.

One of them flashed a card under my nose and said, 'We're CID officers. We'd like to speak with you in private.'

They told me a warrant had been issued for my arrest, without bail, for failing to appear at Huntingdon magistrates court on a driving offence.

On arriving at Bangor I had collected a spare ride in a novices chase on Manor House for John Edwards and I explained this to them and, in all fairness, they allowed me to ride the horse. They could have arrested me there and then, but they must have thought I was a reasonable guy and that I would keep my promise to meet them after the race.

Riding Manor House was the worst four minutes of my life. I knew that when I got back I would be taken away and locked up for the weekend. I prayed and prayed as we approached each fence that Manor House would come tumbling down and that I would have a bad fall and be taken off to hospital. I had no such luck. Manor House was foot-perfect. He led to the seventh, tired rapidly and we finished last.

The CID men had instructions to drive me to Wrexham police station where I would be formally arrested and taken on to Huntingdon and kept behind bars until Monday morning.

'You can't do that,' I said. 'I have my car with me, and I'm booked into the Golden Valley Hotel.'

Naturally they ignored me. One officer sat alongside me, while the other breathed down my neck, and I drove my car to Wrexham police station where I was arrested and had all my possessions taken from me. An hour later a police car came up from Huntingdon and I was detained in custody to appear on Monday.

I had four booked rides at Hexham on the Monday and I wondered, how the hell can I get there?

I was allowed just one telephone call from Huntingdon police station, so I rang my girlfriend, Sue Barrott. I asked her to arrange with Air-Swift Charter to pick me up after the court hearing and fly me to Newcastle where a taxi could be standing by to rush me the twenty miles to Hexham.

I also needed a solicitor. So Sue rang John Biggs for whom I had ridden many winners. Without a question he sent a qualified person down to represent me. Because of my Hexham engagements he said he'd apply for my case to be heard first. I also had to find a guarantor in case of a heavy fine, and Mr and Mrs Biggs kindly came to court to do this for me.

Once again I was embarrassed and humiliated. It was another example of the insanity of my life.

I wasn't completely honest with my solicitor. I told him I was earning £10,000 a year, when it actually was more like £2,000. Through misleading him this way, I was fined a hefty £300, and ordered to pay a further £3.64 for the damages I caused to the barrier.

Yet it wasn't all misfortune. A shaft of light shone through the gloom. My driving licence was back at my flat in Dublin, so when they asked me if I had been disqualified in the preceding ten years, I looked the three magistrates straight in the eye and told them, 'No, your worships.'

It was a blatant lie. I had lost count of my endorsements and disqualifications. If they had known the details of my appalling driving record they would have banned me for three years at least.

Thank God the magistrates believed what I told them, although the Clerk of the Court almost ruined everything when he stood up and said, 'I think Mr Brogan should take the oath to assure us he has not lost his licence in the past ten years as we have no record of this. . . .'

I trembled at this suggestion. I knew I could never tell a lie in the witness-box and commit perjury.

I could hear my heart pounding. But the Chairman of the Bench shook his head, and said, 'No! No! There is no need for that.'

I lost my licence for a year, and on leaving the court I slipped £10 to a reporter to keep the case out of the newspapers.

It was now mid-morning, and I dashed to a nearby disused airfield and flew to Newcastle where a taxi driver kept his foot hard to the boards and miraculously got me to Hexham in time to ride Blue Baker for Deryk Bastiman in the 2.15 ... and we finished last.

Throughout the day I took care not to mention the case to anyone, and after racing I flew back to Sue Barrott's home in Sussex congratulating myself on keeping my name out of the media.

Then bang! I picked up Sue's paper next morning, and my name was splashed all over the page. 'Brogan Arrested at Bangor Races, Loses Driving Licence'.

I had got myself in another mess, and my career was hurtling downhill. I knew I was existing on borrowed time.

Sue was a super friend. One of the best I've ever had, and I felt a right rotter when I let her down so shamefully in the summer of 1974. She was the widow of Doug Barrott, so wastefully killed in a fall from French Colonist in the Whitbread Gold Cup Chase at Newcastle in April 1973.

I was desperately short of money, and I borrowed £6,000 from a close friend of hers to buy a horse called King Ross in Ireland, although I had no owner for it.

I put the horse in training with Ray Peacock, and after five months I sent him to Doncaster Sales, but he failed to reach his reserve.

At this stage, I telephoned my brother Peter who was working in the Scottish stables of Susan Chesmore, whose main patron was millionaire Sir Hugh Fraser, a racing fanatic and a self-confessed gambler.

Peter had seen the horse at exercise, and he recommended it to Mrs Chesmore who, in turn, bought it on behalf of Sir Hugh. In the end I received £10,000 for King Ross, and I passed £1,000 to Peter as a perk for getting the deal.

At this time I was spending most of my life with Sue and her lovely children Michael and Andy, and her warm and generous parents. They were a wonderful family.

I was frantic for cash, so rather than honour my obligations and send a cheque for £6,000 to Sue's friend, I had a brainwave. I told Peter to transfer the money from his bank to a branch of Lloyds near Ascot racecourse.

It was Royal Ascot week, and I arranged to meet him at the course early on Friday. Peter did as I asked, and I drew the £9,000 from the bank on Friday morning. There was so much loose cash I couldn't squeeze it in my pockets. In the end I put £4,000 in my jacket, and left the remaining £5,000 in plastic bags under the seat of my car.

It became a lucky Friday all round. All my bets were winners and I left the course with a profit of £1,000. I could afford to stay at the Excelsior Hotel near Heathrow Airport. It was a favourite haunt of mine. I lived there, on and off, for long spells.

While up in my room, I counted the notes on the bed and realized it was stupid to be carrying such large sums of money around with me, particularly to the racecourse.

So I rang my bookmaker friend John Banks and arranged to leave £9,000 with him at his home in Sunningdale before racing next day. We agreed it would serve as a betting tank for me.

My first bet at Ascot that Saturday was an even £1,000 on Carlton House, one of the Queen's fillies, trained by Dick Hern and ridden by Joe Mercer. Carlton House won by four lengths, so I was now winning £2,000 in two days. I was in great form and flying high.

My next bet was £6,000 to win £4,000 on Raffindale, ridden by Tony Murray. Roussalka, ridden by Lester Piggott, was the main danger, but I could feel magic in my bones. Raffindale won by a neck, and I nearly died. I retired for the day, with John Banks holding £15,000 for me.

I left the course and played it cool, buying some presents for the children and Sue. Nothing extravagant or Sue would have wondered where all the money had come from. I was cute enough for that, and she never pressed me. She was too soft with me. I definitely would have married her if I could have sorted myself out. She was a terrific girl.

Meanwhile my cunning mind was already working overtime on

the prospect of a huge gambling spree at Newcastle's three-day meeting during the coming week.

I intended having a lot of money on Peter O'Sullevan's tremendous stayer Attivo in the Northumberland Plate. I had a great admiration for the horse, and it was my nap of the three days.

I flew up from Heathrow and stayed at the New International Hotel in Newcastle. I was all alone. I wanted to concentrate on the card without interruption. Only Sue and John Banks knew where I was. I was virtually in hiding.

John Banks and I had arranged to meet secretly before each race to discuss my bet. I wanted to keep away from the weighing-room and other places where owners and trainers were likely to see me.

My first bet on the Thursday was £200 to win £700 on Dawn Review, ridded by Edward Hide. Again, the gods were good to me. It won by a short head. So I immediately put £500 to win £1,500 on Man Alive, ridden by Steve Perks. It obliged by two lengths. I felt supernatural. Everything I touched was turning to gold, but how long could it last?

I dodged the next race, and waited for David Robinson's good thing, Carlogie, in the last. John Banks was immensely keen on Carlogie and tried his hardest to get me to put every penny I possessed on it. He reckoned only an elephant-gun could stop it from winning.

He was right, of course.

I staked £1,000 to win £1,000, and it romped in by four lengths.

So I had three bets, and they all won. I was studying form until my eyes hung out, and collecting valuable snippets of information from those in the know, and chiefly John Banks. A vast amount of money was being turned over, but John and I took absolute care not to carve each other up. Anyway, he had numerous outlets to hedge his bets and spread his liabilities.

All in all, I now had £20,000 in my Banks tank, and I boosted it by a further £9,750 next day, backing four winners and no losers at the same Newcastle meeting.

I kicked off with £2,000 on Intrenched, ridden by Willie Carson, and they won at 5–4. I side-stepped the next race and then put £400 on Dutch Gold at 4–1, and he trotted up by a length and a half. A steering job for Edward Hide.

The fourth race didn't appeal to me, so I calmly recoiled and sprung back in the last two events, with £6,000 to win £4,000 on Cawston's Prince and £1,000 to win £1,250 on Solid Silver.

It was a great, great day. I was floating!

Then I got careless. It was inevitable. I didn't have the discipline to cope with such success. It kept carrying me away. ... Back at the hotel that Friday night I started on the booze. I was still alone, drinking and watching television. Living in a world of luxury, feeling, and dressing, like a millionaire.

When the television closed down I should have gone to my room and studied form or slept. Instead, I took a taxi around Newcastle's night haunts, and quickly blew £600 on roulette at Gray's Casino.

I didn't blink. I mean, what was a mere £600 out of £30,000?

Before starting on the booze I had marked three horses to bet next day: Himawari at Lingfield, and Attivo and All Hallows at Newcastle.

I had decided I would watch racing on television, and make sure I wasn't seen on the racecourse. I planned to put £1,000 to win on each horse, and to link them up in a £500 treble.

More important, I had made up my mind that this would be my last big plunge. No matter how much money was left, this would be the end. I would collect the money from John Banks and return every penny owed to Sue's friend. I was oozing with good intentions.

Then early next morning, and still hazy from vodka, I rang my mother in Dublin and worked myself into a monstrous state. We argued and fought for hours on the telephone.

I intended ringing John Banks with my bets, but by the time I had broken off with my mother John had left for the races. In a mad rush, and in a thick hangover, I left the hotel, took a taxi to the track and surreptitiously met him.

Only three runners lined up for the second race and, although I never originally intended to bet, I couldn't resist having an interest. It was an absolutely uncontrollable compulsion. I put £1,000 on Tom Noddy and watched in horror as it lost by a neck to Willie Carson on Happy Hunter.

The Northumberland Plate came next – and my red-hot nap Attivo. I was so confident it would win I talked of having £10,000 with Banks but, after the defeat of Tom Noddy, my composure took a knock and I settled for £1,000, and put a further £500 on Imperial Prince in the Irish Derby.

Attivo won at 7–4, but Imperial Prince was thrashed a length and a half by Peter Walwyn's colt English Prince, and I cursed myself. I was now down £500 on the day, but the tank was still pretty high.

Lord Derby's Florestan was all the rage for the next race. Not a good-looking colt, but reports suggested he was ultra-fast. He had run second to Auction Ring at Newbury, and pundits regarded this as impressive form. Willie Carson had the mount, and was seeking a treble. The horse's credentials had been enhanced the night before when Intrenched won for the same stable, and Florestan was reputed to be faster. I also heard that van Cutsem had gone berserk and placed £400 on Florestan. This, for him, was a fortune.

Despite the gossip and pointers, I still held my own views about the race, and I fancied The Hobman, ridden by Sandy Barclay. He was a smashing colt, and I was impressed with his debut at York two weeks earlier. Common sense told me I'd do better to put £200 on him each-way at 8–1, rather than go for the odds-on Florestan at 4–6.

But John Banks gave me maximum encouragement for Florestan. He kept talking and talking about it. He mesmerized me. I couldn't think rationally any more. He totally undermined my confidence. So instead of betting The Hobman I stuck a colossal £12,000 to win £8,000 on Florestan, and lived to regret it.

The Hobman won by half a length, but just a stride past the post I watched him stumble, lurch around like a car with a puncture, and hobble to a halt. He had split a pastern, and was put down on the spot. I was furious, and missed the next race in order to fill myself up with drink.

Then came a race for women riders. On form, there were only two runners worth looking at – Cargo (Susan Hogan) and Coignafearn (Margaret Bell). I had a burning fancy for Coignafearn, but for some stupid reason I again opposed my better judgment and put £4,500 to win £3,000 on the 8–11 chance Cargo ... and Coignafearn ambled up by three lengths.

I was desperate to retrieve the money and panicked.

All Hallows, the horse I made a banker in my plans the night before, came next, but in my fury I put £2,000 on Balimar to beat him, and I blundered again. All Hallows won by three-quarters of a length.

My John Banks account had dived from £30,000 to £4,000, and I found a quiet corner and drank myself stupid. John then came along and handed me £500 in notes, promising to let me have the rest when we next met.

What infuriated me was that the three horses I had selected – Himawari, Attivo and All Hallows – had all won, but instead of celebrating a glorious day I was drowning my sorrows for one of the biggest financial cock-ups of my life.

It was imperative that I was not seen in the plush bars frequented by owners and trainers in this appalling condition, so I sneaked into the middle-class bars and hid among the punters. I hated being recognized when I was so drunk and so depressed.

But the drink solved nothing. Once I sobered up, the problem would still be there. How the hell could I tell a lovely, innocent girl like Sue that I had lied to her and lost every penny that her trusting friend had lent me?

Sue was never a girl to explode, so when I told her the cash had gone, she simply kept her cool and treated me with silent contempt.

I felt like jumping under a train. I was ashamed. I was mad at myself for being so utterly incapable of controlling my crazy desire to bet, bet, bet.

Squandering that girl's money has been on my conscience to this day, and as soon as I find a way of saving some money I shall make it a priority that she is paid back in regular monthly instalments.

That was the first time I went deviously wrong. But after winning £30,000, impulse took over; I became confident of lifting it to £80,000, and having enough money to buy a respectable property and be able to pay off my debts which were topping £50,000 at the time.

Throughout those years it was generally frowned upon that I was living with Sue. A lot of malicious gossip went around that I was living off her money. This was nonsense. No matter how desperate things were, I never borrowed off her.

I knew her and grew fond of her long before Doug Barrott died, and there was a standing joke between Doug and me that Sue was my favourite married girlfriend.

After those few years together she finally stood back and looked at the situation objectively; she decided I was a chap she was very much in love with, but I was also a chap who was hopelessly running round in circles. She went through a lot of worry over me, particularly with my drinking and my drying-out. But she stuck by me through my very worst moments.

I remember one horrific night at the Excelsior Hotel at Heathrow when I began drinking while still on Heminevrin tablets. I knew it could be lethal, but again I couldn't control myself.

Within a short time I was suffering from all sorts of pains and palpitations. I was sure I was dying. In desperation, I rang for a doctor and I rang Sue, and she drove up from Sussex to collect me and nursed me for weeks while I dried out.

It was a familiar routine. I often spent five to seven days in bed, drinking gallons and gallons of water to flush out my system, and Sue would nurse me and cheer me up. In many cases my stomach would be so rotten from drink I couldn't digest anything but tasteless baby-food. I caused Sue a lot of bother. But she never ditched me, and for that I shall always be grateful.

# 16
# Going for the Wages

IRREPRESSIBLE BOOKMAKERS WERE STILL CONTINUING TO regard me as a cinch for fixing races, and on the eve of the 1975 Black & White Whisky Gold Cup Chase, I was relaxing in my Ascot hotel when one of them rang my room and offered me £1,200 to make sure my mount, Flashy Boy, didn't win the four-horse race.

The sound of £1,200 being ruffled under my nose was like a lifebelt to a drowning man. I was skint, and the bookmaker knew it. I was vulnerable, and he tried his best to exploit my position. The line-up was: Flashy Boy (me), Easby Abbey (Ron Barry), Santon Brig (Michael Dickinson) and Flickity Prince (Ken Bosley). The bookmaker fancied a substantial bet on Easby Abbey, with a saver on Santon Brig. As for Flickity Prince, he couldn't have won if he set off the night before.

Oh, yes, £1,200 was tempting but, thank God, I rejected it. I dearly wanted to win the Black & White. I even turned down a ride in the Colonial Cup in America on the same weekend to try to achieve it. On hearing I wouldn't co-operate the bookmaker's tone changed dramatically. He swore at me, and slammed down the telephone.

Besides the bribe, that Black & White contest was an event I shall never forget for all the excruciating pain I suffered. In fact, I'm reminded of it every time I make contact with the ground.

A week earlier I had fallen from Flashy Boy at Naas and fractured the main bone in my right foot. The pain was unbearable, and I worried frantically that I wouldn't be fit to ride at Ascot.

I took particular care not to mention the injury to trainer Archie Watson or he'd have collapsed in a frenzy. The slightest disturbance got him worked up. For the next few days I deliberately selected the easiest rides, and I dropped no hint to anyone of the pain I was in.

With the Black & White getting closer, I rang my friend, Dr Paddy Morrissey, and pleaded with him to let me have a painkiller an hour before the race.

Fellow-jockey Jeff King suggested I put some lead in my boot, but the foot still hurt. In this condition I knew I couldn't hope to do the horse justice. I knew it was vitally important for me to win a race of this size to re-establish myself after a miserable spell in the wilderness.

I telephoned Paddy on the Friday afternoon, just twenty-four hours before the race. He agreed to help, but a list of Saturday appointments prevented him from coming out to Ascot to give me the injection personally.

Paddy, who loves horse-racing and was one of the three men who put top Irish trainer Mick O'Toole on his feet, therefore arranged for another doctor to attend in his place, and I agreed to meet him inside the ambulance-room about half an hour before the race. Paddy stressed that the injection would kill the pain for forty minutes only, and that this could pose a problem if the race were delayed.

I arranged with Archie Watson to weigh-out fifty minutes before the race, which would allow me time to sneak off for the jab. So, having weighed-out, I slipped into my overcoat and nipped into the ambulance-room.

To my horror, Paddy's friend hadn't arrived. So I sat on the bench and waited for him. Then, suddenly, the door swung open, and the racecourse doctor burst in, eyeing me curiously.

'Are you Brogan?' he snapped.

'Yes. What's up?'

'I'm told you have something wrong with your foot.'

'Nonsense! Not me, doctor. There's nothing wrong with me. I'm fine. I only came in here to meet someone.'

But he was no fool. He told me to take off my boots as he wanted to examine me.

Showing no concern, I did as he asked, making certain, of course, to remove the left one first.

He grabbed the foot, twisted it, pressed it, and watched my expression. I smiled....

Then he seized my right foot. Wrapped both hands around it, and gripped it like a vice. The pain shot up my leg and I felt like screaming the roof off. But I didn't flinch.

Just one slight twinge, and he'd have spotted the act. The truth would have been out, and Archie would have been seeking a substitute.

It was sheer torture, and I felt groggy and sick. But, most important, he was satisfied. He told me to replace my boots and return to the bench.

Just at that moment, Paddy's friend finally pushed his head round the door and walked in carrying a little black bag. I just hoped he'd see what was happening. I winked, and he got the message.

The racecourse doctor then noticed him in the doorway, and asked him why he was there.

Thinking swiftly, he said he was a doctor, and that he'd heard I'd been hurt in the previous race. I didn't even have a ride in the previous race! But the course doctor believed him, and I was off the hook.

I couldn't leave the room fast enough. There were now barely twenty-five minutes left to the race. I hobbled to the car-park, flung myself on the back seat and the doctor pumped three injections into my throbbing foot.

The Ascot car-park is a full 150 yards from the weighing-room, and when I returned to the course the other jockeys were filing out, so I begged them to slow down and wait for me.

When I reached the paddock the foot was perfect. Totally numb. Archie Watson stood a stride away from me, chatting happily, without the slightest idea of what had gone on behind his back.

Flashy wasn't a brilliant jumper, but he always found a 'fifth leg' in an emergency, and always treated English fences with greater respect than the Irish ones.

Having ridden Easby Abbey before at Ascot, I knew he was a natural front-runner. So, as I expected, Ron Barry sent him off at the head of the party, and I went with them. Michael Dickinson tucked Santon Brig in behind us and, having jumped the first, Flickity Prince was no longer a genuine contender and soon lost touch.

Racing past the stands, and preparing to face the three stiff fences down the hill, I called to Ron and pleaded, 'For God's sake, take a hold. Ease up. We're going too fast.'

It was a bit of gamesmanship. I wanted to stay as close as possible, and feared I was about to be left behind.

Approaching the first fence down the back end, I could see my ruse was about to work. Easby crumpled badly on landing and shot poor Ron a long way from the saddle.

With my only danger out of the race, I put the brakes on, and eased Flashy to a sensible gallop. I wanted him settled. I couldn't afford a mistake. My horse had plenty of speed, but he didn't jump with Easby Abbey's precision and fluency.

In the meantime, Santon Brig had continued to get further and further behind, and Flashy went on to provide a superb exhibition of decisive jumping; we won in a canter by ten lengths.

To win the Black & White Chase gave me enormous pleasure. To receive the trophy from the Queen Mother was a marvellous bonus. We chatted for several minutes, and I completely forgot about the break in my foot.

It was only when I returned to the weighing-room and began to change that the injection wore off. Within seconds I was in such violent pain I couldn't put the foot on the floor. Because of my determination to ride I caused irreparable damage to the foot. I put far too much pressure on the bone and widened the crack. It has never recovered and doctors tell me it never will.

It was during 1975 that I became friendly with Michael Hoare, and we formed an association that led to several successful coups which I planned and executed personally.

Michael was keen to own a share in a racehorse and he introduced me to four tremendous Irish fellows – Nick Sinnott, Sean McHale, Pat Cafferty and Gerry Regan.

They made no secret that they wanted a horse to gamble on. Luckily for us all, I had the ready-made certainty. A powerful, bay horse called Agree, bred by the prolific No Argument, and standing an impressive 16.3 hands. From the moment we shook hands as a syndicate we lined him up for a mighty 'touch'.

They paid a packet for him, but a little discontent came into the camp after a while, and Michael dropped out and sold his share to the others.

Agree's first run was at Limerick Junction in March. He finished sixth of sixteen. The stewards weren't satisfied with my performance and cautioned me for riding an injudicious race. In layman's language, they thought I hadn't tried hard enough. Unknown to them, I was suffering badly from cramp, although I must confess when I saw the video replay I certainly looked a non-trier.

We were building Agree up for a huge killing, and a fortnight later took him to Fairyhouse. He started at 10–1 and was completely unfancied. I finished tenth of nineteen on him without being severe.

By now I had decided we should go for the wages in an amateur riders' event at Punchestown. The weights and distances were perfect. Our hopes were zooming. Then on the very morning of the race a monsoon-like cloudburst broke over the course and the ground turned soft; my heart sank.

Sinnott, Cafferty and Regan all flew over from London with their wives and, although they were keyed up for the biggest gamble of their lives, I considered the ground too loose for Agree, and they sensibly consented to pulling him out at the last minute.

The cash was put in cold storage until May 19, when I took the horse to Mallow and rode him in the Kerry Maiden Hurdle. Again the boys flew over, and they backed him furiously from 5–2 to 11–10 favourite.

The ground was good, and the opposition poor. I was on top form and rode one of my best races to win by a length.

The boys were speechless. They had never seen so much money. They had pooled their cash and put £14,000 on Agree, and they thanked me with a welcome present of £1,000.

With spirits high, and the champagne bubbling, I soon talked Nick and Sean into buying another horse. I picked out Omagh for them, ironically once owned by the famous Curley.

Nick and Sean backed it hard to 5–2 favourite at Galway, but it let them down by a length and a half. Ted Walsh rode it, and I thought he should have won. However, I suppose there were times when I should have won but rode a bad race, so who was I to criticize?

I was now convinced Omagh needed something further than two miles, and we eventually chose an event at Dundalk, over two-and-a-half miles, in late August.

Liam Brennan was training Omagh and, true to form, he gave nothing away. To be sure everything went to plan he saddled two horses in the race. Michael Furlong rode Omagh and Ted Walsh rode Taken On. I suggested the best way to ride Omagh was to let him bowl along in front. Michael agreed. Another coup was nicely organized.

Michael followed my instructions perfectly. Omagh was never headed and hacked up by eight lengths at a splendid 3–1. We battered the bookies, virtually swam in champagne, and I treated myself to another box of the biggest and best Havana cigars. I had become hooked on them and they cost me a fortune. I bought them from J.J. Fox in Dublin and London, and up to 1977 I was smoking eight Havanas a day, at £80 a week!

In the end, when cash ran short, cigars became my last luxury, and I still owe J.J. Fox in Dublin about £400. They used to send me a box of twenty-five every week.

I smoked Bolivar, Monte Christo, Romeo and Juliet, Churchill, Punch Nectars No. 2, and several other exquisite brands of Havana. And they had to be hand-rolled! I wouldn't be seen dead with a machine-rolled cigar. Oliver Hill, managing director of J.J. Fox, once asked me how much I thought I had spent on cigars over a ten-year period, and I was staggered when he told me it was £30,000! Taking into account all the other cigars I bought elsewhere, I must have spent £50,000 on them.

I took pride in my cigar-smoking. I had my own personal pouch, smartly embossed with my initials. I had my own expensive cigar-cutter. I even bought a humidor – an expensive teak box to keep the cigars crisp and fresh and at the right temperature. There is an art to smoking cigars, and I did my best to cultivate it.

Obviously no normal person would spend so much on them. Not even Lester Piggott, and he loves them.

But drink was always my main indulgence. I remember one ferocious binge in London in February 1976 when I drank so much in twenty-four hours I couldn't fulfil my riding engagements at Newbury or Haydock. The stewards at both racecourses reported me to the Jockey Club and I was suspended for three weeks.

One of the Newbury rides I missed was on the brilliant Irish Fashion. I had the agony of sitting in front of a television watching him win the £10,000 Schweppes Gold Trophy by ten lengths with Ron Barry riding in my place.

Irish Fashion was a beautiful bay gelding, and trainer Michael

Cunningham didn't seriously think of running him in the race until I convinced him the horse had a great chance. Michael thought Irish Fashion was out of his class, but I had followed his progress with meticulous attention. I was adamant that he possessed exceptional talent, particularly after I had ridden him at work on The Curragh.

Having persuaded Michael to run the horse, and then having to miss the ride on him through my alcoholic insanity, grieved me intensely. There has never been an easier winner in the history of the race, and in the end he was backed from 33–1 to 16–1.

Everyone filled his pockets, except the befuddled Barry Brogan – the man who set it up!

I was now drinking hour by hour, bottle by bottle. I rang my good friend Father Lawler in Hammersmith and he instantly realized how bad I was. He booked a bed for me in a London hospital where they dried me out over the next two days. It was a nuthouse. I hated the place and eventually put on my suit and walked out. I was shattered. The booze and the suspension had cost me the ride on High Ken in the Grand National, and I didn't know where to turn.

Right down the line, from my first hospitalization, I became more and more dependent on Valium. Few days went by when I didn't swallow one or even two just an hour before I went out to ride in the meeting's first race.

I could lay my hands on vast supplies from many doctor friends. Often up to two hundred pills at a time. I always carried three or four hundred Valium tablets in my bag or in my car so that I would never run short. I was a pill maniac. If anyone handed me a pill and said, 'That will make you better,' I would swallow it right there on the spot. Thank goodness, I never hit the hard stuff.

I then returned to Dublin and stayed with a friend called Gerry McGee, an accountant. During this time I had gone eleven days and eleven nights without sleep. I had become obsessed with Valium. I was taking forty to fifty tablets a day. I was like a zombie. I was also knocking back four or five Mogadon tablets a night to try to sleep. But I kept fighting against it. I was afraid to sleep because I was sure that if I did I would never wake up again.

No matter where I stayed, I was always last to bed. I would

watch television until the tiny dot disappeared into the back of the set, and I would sit alone, in a dream, puffing on my cigars.

On the eleventh night, a Saturday, I dragged myself out of my room and into the deafening streets of Dublin. My aching head couldn't stand the noise, my legs couldn't stand the walking, and I gasped, frantically for air.

By half-past two on Sunday morning I couldn't struggle any further. I stopped at a telephone-box and rang a friend in Alcoholics Anonymous. I was at the end of my tether. There was no knowing what I might do. Despite my fear of dying, suicide had crossed my mind, and on occasions I actually set myself up for it.

My friend and I talked for hours. I entered the kiosk with a pocketful of change and used the lot. It was close on seven o'clock, and a new day, when I finally stepped back into the street. We had talked and talked on how I could get off the pills.

In the end he arranged for an early meeting for me with a Dr Stephenson, a psychiatrist at St Brendan's Hospital in Dublin. I went to him with great hope and stressed that I wanted to see the back of Valium and all other tablets like them.

He was at the peak of his profession, an expert. At last I had found someone who could understand my panic. For the first time in my life I was instilled with the confidence I so desperately needed. He assured me the panics could not kill me, and this was just the type of psychological support that could help me.

He then transferred me to a new drug called Parstelin, an antidepressant, and from the moment I took the first pill I wasn't allowed to eat cheese, yoghurt, broad beans or Marmite, or drink any type of alcohol. If I did, I'd be dead in two hours. Parstelin increases the flow of adrenalin, so all forms of rich food and drink that contain a high-risk level have to be avoided or you're wheeled away with a brain haemorrhage.

Dr Stephenson also prescribed a mild tranquillizer called Norbrium. I was captivated by him. I went through my pockets, the boot of my car, every drawer in my room and grabbed every bottle of Valium and destroyed them all. He assured me that I could not die from lack of sleep and I momentarily took a sensible grip on myself.

I had just finished seeing Dr Stephenson when trainer Archie

Watson offered me the ride on Flashy Boy in the 1976 Irish Grand National at Fairyhouse. I thought, oh God, I haven't slept for eleven days and nights, but I'm in a marvellous frame of mind and I'm on new tablets. I also had to shed a lot of weight to ride the horse at 10 st 8 lbs.

So could I pull myself together quickly enough? That was the six-million dollar question. Archie actually wanted me down at his yard next day to school the horse and get the feel of him. It was a golden chance, and I decided to take it.

In the National itself, Flashy Boy produced some of his best form and, although unfancied at 12–1, we finished a close-up fourth, with victory going to the 7–2 favourite Brown Lad, ridden by Tommy Carberry for Jim Dreaper. But I was delighted with my own performance, and that meant more to me than the way the horse had run.

I was swallowing one Norbrium and one Parstelin three times a day. I continued to ride while I took them, although they were technically two powerful drugs. It wasn't until late 1978 that I was down to two tablets every second day, and could at last look forward to coming off tablets altogether for the first time in years.

# 17
# Bogus Bank Accounts

SOON AFTER RETURNING TO ENGLAND IN 1976, I LIVED AT THE Golden Valley Hotel in Cheltenham for five months. My room cost me £80 a week, but it was cosy and warm, and I enjoyed the luxury it offered.

Later on, I moved into a large, modern maisonette in Clevelands Drive, just 150 yards from the racecourse. It was a smart, residential area, and it cost me £100 a month.

Having virtually ended my association with Sue Barrott, and having no other girlfriends, I found it a lonely and depressing existence. I tried to kill time by riding work for Ted Fisher at Chewton Mendip and building a few contacts for the coming season.

The preparatory work paid off right away when I landed Ted's chaser Dolly Boy, a winner in the first week of the new season at Newton Abbot.

My social life also perked up when I met John and Jean Adams, who lived near Terry Biddlecombe at Tirley. Jean drove over three times a week to clean my rooms, and I developed a super friendship with her and John, and their two smashing children, Anthony and Diane.

For a change I was settled and rational. Yet, inwardly, I knew it couldn't last for long. One day soon I was bound to crack. I sat in my car for an hour behind the Queen's Hotel in Cheltenham, discussing with myself whether to go back on the booze. Finally I walked across the road and straight into the Doubles Bar of a Berni Inn and started on the vodka. I drank all day and all night, but I tried not to let myself get too bad because I'd promised to ride work for Ron Mason fifty miles away at Guilsborough next morning.

To be safe, I put in a 'time' call and arrived punctually at half-past eight, having sunk a full bottle of vodka in a lay-by on the way. I schooled Wagon Master and another horse, and I sat and drank coffee until eleven o'clock. I couldn't leave fast enough to find more alcohol.

I eventually arrived at the Pytchley Arms near Guilsborough and ordered a pint of lager and a large vodka, and drank a few with a crazy guy I'd never met before. We threw ourselves into a non-stop booze-up and this ended with my spending the night with him at his home in Northampton.

On our way back, too drunk to tell the time, we drove off the road into a woodland and tried a few stunts. He was a right fool, and rammed his car into the back of my Lancia, causing £250 worth of damage. I insisted he paid and his insurance company eventually coughed up.

When I awoke in his house next morning I was still desperate for a drink. I took a half-bottle of brandy from my bag and devoured it before breakfast.

The rest of the day developed into one prodigious drinking session and, shortly before midnight, I blacked out and had to stay the night with Ron Mason's head-lad at the lodge.

Then at eight o'clock next morning I flashed through the door like a greyhound from a trap, rushed into the road and hitched a lift to the Pytchley Arms where I'd left my car.

I pleaded with the landlord, Jim Demetri, to pour me a pint of lager, and when he left the room, I reached up to the shelf and pinched two bottles of Remy-Martin. So typical of the alcoholic. I was insane.

I put the brandy in the boot, but drank the lot before I'd travelled twenty miles. Even then my metabolism kept bubbling and squeaking, and I was so chronically dehydrated I again stopped the car and literally got down on my knees and drank the dirty water from the gutter.

Through some miracle I managed to drive back to Clevelands Drive; I locked the car in the garage, stumbled into the house and gulped every drop of liquor I had in the place, pints and pints of it.

I was supposed to be riding at Newton Abbot in the next two days, but both meetings slipped by unnoticed. I was unconscious on the floor in the lounge in a drunken coma.

I've said before that I believe the 'man upstairs' is looking down on me. After that morning I was left in no doubt. By some amazing freak, John and Jean Adams sensed that something was wrong because they had not seen me for three days. So they drove over to Clevelands Drive, and on failing to get an answer smashed their way into the house, found me on the floor and saved my life.

When the doctor arrived, he said that if John and Jean had not called I'd have been dead in twenty-four hours.

I spent sixteen weeks recovering from that holocaust. I spent night and day on a couch in front of the fire, trembling and parched, with John and Jean nursing me.

After pulling myself together I had no zest to return to racing. I knew people were absolutely sick of me, my drinking, my gambling and my unreliability. Many times I promised to ride for people and never turned up because I was round the bend with alcoholism.

John and Jean Adams were a wonderful source of encouragement. They were adamant that if I really worked hard I would get back again. So I took rides for trainers like Tony Brassey, Bob Clay and Ted Fisher, and I'm eternally grateful to them for retaining a vestige of faith in me when no one else wanted me, and when I was nothing more than a public outcast. It was only through their support that I earned enough money to eat and survive.

Like most people, John and Jean encountered a variety of problems with me. One Christmas, I went to Harrods and spent £220 on presents for them. I used a credit card, but I had no money to meet the bill. So the police called at John's house and arrested me, and I was fined £50. Shortly before this incident I had suffered another blackout, walked into Cavendish House in Cheltenham and filled a bag with all sorts of clothes, including items of women's underwear, and walked out without paying. I was stopped by security staff and eventually fined £50 for shoplifting.

As this was my first criminal offence, my solicitor, Matthew McCloy, advised me to plead guilty, and I paid back £4 a week, which was all I could afford.

For long spells while living with the Adams family I had very few mounts. A lot of time was filled by going to the dogs at Perry Barr. At other spare moments, I visited the Golden Gloves Boxing Club, owned by Brendan Joyce, and I sometimes sparred with champions Danny McAlinden and Bunny Johnson. Brendan is a fearless gambler and he begged me to buy him a racehorse. Money was no object, so I bought him Majestic Touch for £12,000. I was pleased with my purchase. The horse won a three-mile handicap chase at Ludlow and I understand Brendan more than covered his outlay.

I also bought Low Profile for him. I paid £5,000 to a Mr Scott in Mullingar. The horse had won two races in Ireland, so I knew he could do a job for us. He was bought with the sole purpose of pulling off a coup in England. Which he did – twice!

John Hurley trained him at Kings Norton near Birmingham. At first, I rode him in handicap hurdles on the bottom weight of 10 st. But the horse was never fit and we eventually put him in sellers, carrying the maximum of 12 st 7 lbs. We were all very patient. We knew his weight would drop in time. Low Profile always did his best, but there were times when we knew he couldn't win because he hated soft ground, and he wouldn't finish in the first four.

Thankfully, as the ground improved, so did his weight. He ran in one appalling seller in Devon carrying a mere 10 st 4 lbs and finished fourth. Jimmy Bourke rode him because I couldn't do the weight. Six days later Jimmy rode him again at Teesside, carrying 10 st 7 lbs and he obliged at 20-1!

Brendan was ecstatic. He staked £7,000 to win £140,000 with Ladbrokes, and gave me a handsome present of £3,000.

By early 1980 Low Profile had won twenty-two races for Brendan but in May he broke his leg at Ludlow and had to be destroyed.

Brendan also runs the popular Garryowen Club in Birmingham where huge T-bone steaks are the speciality and serve as a juicy bait for the large Irish contingent in the city who are constantly on the lookout for a gastronomical bargain.

John Adams had a thriving business in buying and selling vintage cars and I often went with him and Jean to exhibitions and shows but, overall, I must have disappointed them with my conduct and on 12 May 1977 I moved out.

The next day I was arrested in Dublin on charges of opening bogus bank accounts in the names of Tommy Stack and John Burke, two super chaps, and fellow Irish jump jockeys.

The story behind this incident had begun in London a year or so before when I met two ruthless thugs in a gaming club in Soho.

They knew I enjoyed a bet, and also that I was down on my luck, so they suggested telephoning me each day at Clevelands Drive to see whether I wanted them to place an investment for me. They were a violent pair, and my fear of them is still so great that I simply dare not mention their names, even to the police.

I considered their proposition and thought it might be an easy way of gathering a few pounds from betting. But my form was abominable and within a fortnight I had lost £8,000. I never dreamed of paying it back because, as they knew full well, I didn't have a penny to my name.

A year elapsed, and then one day I received a telephone call from these guys saying that unless I produced the cash right away they would report me to Tattersalls and the Jockey Club and send the heavies down to sort me out.

I was literally trembling. I went up to London and handed them two post-dated cheques, one for £4,000 and the other for £3,500. They were post-dated for six months and I hoped I might find the cash from somewhere and pay them off.

They held on to the cheques and after six months rang me again. I was petrified. There was no way in which I could find the money for them. But they wouldn't go away, and back they came with an incredible scheme.

They quizzed me carefully about the way Weatherbys pay the jockeys and I explained to them that most top riders arrange for their money to go direct into a bank account every month. The crooks then asked if Weatherbys would send this money elsewhere. I told them yes, because I had often been short of cash and they had posted it to various places where I had been staying.

I knew I was dealing with a mob that would stop at nothing. I feared for my life, and I didn't know where to turn.

A few days later they telephoned me again and told me to go to the Rutland Arms in Newmarket and to pick up an envelope addressed to Tommy Stack. I duly set off immediately and collected the envelope. It contained a cheque for £2,000, made out to Tommy Stack.

On returning to Cheltenham, they rang me up again and ordered me to open an account in the name of Stack many miles from where I lived.

I remembered that Anne Jarvis, wife of the Coventry trainer, had an account in the Midland Bank in Rugby, so I drove up and opened an account there, pretending to be Stack, and used her name as a reference. Without any bother, I deposited the £2,000 cheque and next day went back and collected the £2,000 in cash, still claiming to be Stack.

Tommy had enjoyed an excellent month, having just won the Grand National on Red Rum, and the crooks knew all about it.

They then instructed me to leave the money in a parcel in the Dorchester Hotel in London where they would collect it. Later that night they confirmed they had picked up the money, and now wanted me to return to the Rutland Arms in Newmarket and collect yet another envelope addressed to Tommy Stack.

This time it contained a cheque for £3,000, and I was told to follow the same routine as I had with the last one. To take it to Rugby, deposit it in the name of Stack, and collect the money next day.

They also told me to visit the Queen's Hotel in Cheltenham, collect an envelope addressed to John Burke and to open an account in his name at the town's Barclays Bank.

Again I had no alternative but to obey their demands, and I used the name of a Maltese friend, George Cutajar, of the Golden Valley Hotel, as my reference.

John Burke's cheque came to £2,347, and I deposited it as instructed, this time claiming to be Burke. The pressure was unbearable. I was a bag of nerves. But I pressed on, and next morning I went back to Barclays and drew the £2,347, posing as Burke, and then drove up the motorway and collected the £3,000, pretending to be Stack.

With the cash in my pocket, I rushed to the Dorchester and left it in a parcel for the thugs to collect.

They were ingeniously cunning. They realized John Burke had just won the Whitbread Chase on Andy Pandy, and had netted a handsome ten per cent of the prize-money.

While all this was happening I was still going to the races every day, riding alongside Stack and Burke and chatting with them in the weighing-room as though nothing had happened.

Ever since college times, Tommy and I were the best of friends, and the whole sickening episode was playing on my conscience. I found it increasingly difficult to live with.

A week or so later these thugs telephoned me again and asked me to nip over to Ireland to collect another envelope, this time in the name of flat jockey Gabriel Curran, who had just won the English Two Thousand Guineas on Nebbiolo. They assured me this would be the last job. There would be no further demands on me to screw my mates.

I was being blackmailed, but there was nothing I could do to stop it. So I left John and Jean Adams, drove my Lancia to Liverpool and crossed to Dublin and booked into the Holiday Inn at Bray, owned by my long-standing friend Seamus Bohan.

It stands in a beautiful position right on the promenade and I chose a room that looked straight out to sea, with a glorious view. A delightful place for a holiday – only I wasn't there for one!

Without delay, I telephoned the Keadeen Hotel in Newbridge, where a letter addressed to Gabriel Curran was supposed to be waiting for me. The manager confirmed the letter was there, so I took a taxi to collect it.

By now, it was deep into the second week of May, and I knew Tommy Stack and John Burke would be wondering what had happened to their money, and that the bubble had to burst any moment.

On Friday, 13 May, I confidently walked into the Keadeen Hotel and asked for the letter. The clerk at the reception desk smiled and told me the manager was keeping it safely in his office for me.

It was a trap. I had been rumbled. Within seconds, a strapping detective appeared and told me to hold up my hands, and he frisked me. The police had somehow latched on to the plot and suspected me. In many ways I was glad the whole wretched business was over.

I was taken into a room and peppered with questions. I was speechless. Then I was driven under escort to Newbridge Police Station where I was again questioned for several hours about the missing money. I made no comment, and demanded to see my solicitor.

The police quickly obtained a warrant to keep me in custody and drove me in a black van to Mountjoy Prison, where they locked me in a cell until Sunday morning.

While I was in there Seamus Bohan engaged a solicitor for me, and on the Sunday afternoon I was taken to a private room to meet the brilliant Michael Brendan Kelly for the first time.

I was listed to appear at Bridewell Court next day, and on that Sunday evening they transferred me from Mountjoy to Bridewell police station, a stinking place where they throw drunks to sober up overnight.

On 16 May 1977 I appeared before the magistrates at Bridewell and was released on £700 bail, kindly put up for me by Kevin Barry, whom I first met as a patient in St John O'God's.

The inevitable army of photographers and reporters engulfed me as I walked out of the court room, but I refused to speak to them. I retreated to the Holiday Inn, and stayed there in hiding. I was too ashamed to come out and face the world. My rare appearances were confined to secret meetings with my solicitor and my senior and junior counsel, Paddy McEnter and Barry White. My English-based solicitor, Matthew McCloy, also flew over from Newbury for all the vital discussions to prepare for the case.

From what Matthew McCloy could glean from the Jockey Club, and from the police in Cheltenham, my name was rancid in racing. If I had any notion of returning to England I could brace myself for three to five years in prison.

# 18
# A Betting-Office Lunatic

AFTER MY APPEARANCE IN COURT MY PASSPORT WAS WITHHELD and I was virtually a prisoner in Ireland. But there was no way I wanted to be domiciled in Ireland for the rest of my life. It's a tremendous country, with tremendous people, but I love foreign holidays and I enjoy working in England.

Sooner or later I knew I'd be forced to go back and face the music – but this didn't happen until 21 May 1978.

But first, I'd like to recall my horrific ordeal struggling to survive in those appalling twelve months in Ireland.

A week after appearing in court I called on my mother at Rathfeigh and got a roasting. Peter, Ann and Pamela felt the same way about me. They said I'd brought shame on the family, although I couldn't agree that what I had done had affected them in any way.

Ten days later I called on my mother again, and there was another nasty exchange of words. I walked out, and I haven't spoken to her since. I've seen her in Dublin, but not to talk to, and I haven't made the slightest effort to make contact.

She definitely thought I would go to prison, and she said that when I was released I should go back to see her.

Her last words to me were: 'Why did you have to do it to your best friend Tommy Stack?'

I left the Holiday Inn and returned to Dublin. I had nowhere to live, so I wandered the streets. A well-dressed tramp. I was disgusted with myself; I was afraid, and needed comfort and support.

I called on a friend I'd known for years. She insisted I stayed for supper and a week later offered me a room. It was completely platonic. I was too confused and shattered for romance. I simply needed companionship. Someone to talk to. For the next eleven months I was rarely out of her sight.

But I had no money, so I went on the streets and literally begged for it. For a spell, between June and January, I put together just enough to have a car. Then the cash ran out, and I was forced to sell it. A man promised me £50, but he never paid up.

During that summer I became friendly with a doctor in Dublin, and I drove him around, like a chauffeur, to visit his patients. He brainwashed me. He made me a mental wreck. He put me on every available tablet, and I was drugged up to the eyeballs. It transpired later that he had planned a series of daring raids on the homes of rich people and needed an accomplice. I wanted no part of it, and ran away and hid from him.

Cheltenham police sent an officer over to press for my extradition, and I was hauled before the president of the High Court in Dublin.

Amazingly, the application was turned down and later that day the officer approached me and pleaded: 'For God's sake, Barry, come back and get it all over with.'

I refused. I was too frightened. I couldn't face up to reality. Yet I still had enough sense to know that the extradition would be granted one day, and that I'd be forced to return.

Several times during those terrible days I felt like going back on the booze, but my girlfriend always intervened and made me see sense. She was a tremendous, comforting friend, and she still is today. She kept me sane for a whole year. She did her best to make me see the light.

By early 1978 I had crept out of my Dublin den and was beginning to circulate again. I started visiting the Shelbourne Hotel and I met up with those fearless punters Jack McMahon, Jim Delaney, Ted Murray, Paddy Clarke and Willie Lawlor.

I started going to the dogs every night. I started going to Harry Barry's betting-office. Lads in the betting-office would always feel sorry for me and hand me £10 or £20 to play around with. During those three months I had several good wins. I once won £400 and spent a little on food – the rest went on gambling and I ended up penniless again.

Sometimes I went racing with Jack McMahon. But I never had money, so I'd tap people for cash to bet. It was a disgusting way to live. I was skint. So skint that I spent six days living and sleeping in a car in the huge Phoenix Park, and without a bite to eat or a drop to drink. I was too ashamed to show my face.

The only pleasant moment I can remember of those monstrous

days was meeting Brendan Kelly for coffee and a chat at the Clarence Hotel, listening to him talking about my case and recalling all his marvellous experiences with Tommy Burns, Vincent O'Brien and my father, Jimmy. Brendan is semi-retired now and a marvellous raconteur.

However it gradually became clear that I couldn't continue much longer bumming my way around and tapping people for money. I had to think seriously of returning to England and surrendering myself to the English police.

I had met a few friends in Dublin and they trusted me with their money. Sometimes they asked me to lodge the money for them in a bank. Sometimes it was cash, sometimes they were cheques. And eight out of ten times I would be on my way to the bank when I'd notice Harry Barry's betting-office and couldn't drive past without going in.

The first time I used bank money to bet, I won £300. It was very easy that first time! So I put the bank money back, and the £300 in my pocket.

Naturally I didn't always win. People trusted me with lodgement sums that varied from £70 to £400. And almost every time I'd end up losing the lot at Harry Barry's betting-office. Then I'd hare around looking for Jim Delaney and plead with him to lend me money to bale me out.

It was nerve-racking. The chances I took were senseless. And for what? I suppose I was immature. I had an everlasting greed for money. Yet money was no good for me.

I also started going to meetings of Alcoholics Anonymous, and I met a lot of good friends who always dropped me a fiver or two.

At the end of January I met two chaps called Frank O'Donnell and Noel McCormack who arranged with a friend to open a Barry Brogan Fund to help raise the restitution money for me. A kind fellow called Frank Duane immediately donated £1,000 to put it on its feet. How I never dipped into the Fund to have some money to gamble I shall never know. That really was a miracle.

Obviously I found it terribly embarrassing, asking people to fork out for the Fund and help to put right the mess I had made for myself.

The Fund eventually reached £1,600, and £1,000 of this went to pay my counsel, the remaining £600 to settle my account with Matthew McCloy.

Meanwhile, back in England, my good friend John Banks was in the stocks for allegedly receiving information from steeplechasing's distinguished rider John Francome, a former arch-rival of mine.

The story ran for several weeks, and I followed it daily in the national press. It helped to take some pressure off me; at least I wasn't the only guy in trouble.

The big bang went off for Banks and Francome when Peter Smiles, director-general of Racecourse Security Services, the Jockey's Club's detective agency, sent an earth-tremor through the sport by announcing that the passing of information between jockeys and bookmakers was causing him more concern than dope. Shortly after this sensational statement it was disclosed that Francome and Banks had been instructed to appear before the Jockey Club's disciplinary committee.

In general, Peter Smiles was perfectly correct. 'Commercial punting' between jockeys and members of the public is absolutely rampant. However, in the John Banks–John Francome case, the gross irony was that John is a jump jockey, and everyone in the underworld knows and recognizes that it's the flat riders who are the worst offenders by far.

After a ten-hour hearing, the Jockey Club's disciplinary committee found that both men had broken Rule 220 (ii), 'in that Francome supplied confidential information to Banks at his request concerning horses in training'.

The committee also found that Banks had broken Rule 201 (iv) in that he 'surreptitiously obtained information about a trial'.

For their misdemeanour Banks was disqualified from racing for three years and fined £2,500, and Francome was suspended for six weeks and fined £750.

After the hearing Francome was reported as saying, 'I would think what has happened to me goes on with other jockeys.'

You bet it does. Few jockeys, if any, are working without a punter close at hand filling his pockets. A punter can vary from a small-time bookmaker to a multiple organization, and from a small-time backer to a professional gambler. The status is bound to differ, but the principle is always the same – buying and selling information.

The punter likes to know what is 'fancied' and 'unfancied' in as many races as possible. Armed with this privileged information, he then invests large sums of money on the right horse, or, if a bookmaker, he can lengthen or shorten the odds, depending on the information he has received.

Rewards from punters to jockeys can vary from paid holidays on the Mediterranean to expensive cars, colour television sets and substantial sums of money which are always handed over discreetly at an inconspicuous rendezvous in untraceable cash.

Frankly, if some jockeys relied solely on the money they earn from mounts and winners, they could never hope to attain the standard of living they enjoy. They make it possible only by breaking the Rules and supplying an endless stream of confidential information to people who are willing to pay high fees for the goods.

Commercial punting is now so prevalent in Britain that if every jockey who participates were brought before the Jockey Club and banned in the same way as John Francome, I'm in no doubt that the whole racing circus would come to an abrupt and embarrassing halt. When Peter Smiles said punting of this sort was worse than dope, he wasn't exaggerating.

What astounds me is how jockeys can continue to get away with it day after day. Local stewards must be blind. Or do they actually see what is taking place but don't have the courage to take the necessary action for fear of rocking the boat?

Whichever of these is true, the local stewards are clearly not doing their job and, in consequence, the trusting little punter is being ripped off with greater and greater impunity.

By the middle of May 1978 I finally reconciled myself to returning to England to face the music. Life in Ireland was splitting me apart and I couldn't cope with the pressure a minute longer.

My special friend, Noel McCormack, accompanied me on a flight from Dublin and we touched down at Birmingham Airport on 21 May. Matthew McCloy had sent me a letter of authority to explain that I was giving myself up, should anyone recognize me and try to arrest me.

Another friend, Patrick Hennessey, met us off the aeroplane, and he drove us to his home in Harpenden where we stayed the night. The following day Noel and I caught a train to London and then travelled on to Newbury where I presented myself in Matthew McCloy's office.

At long last, the fugitive had stopped running.

McCloy advised me, as a priority, to find two people who would stand bail for me. I hadn't spoken to Terry Biddlecombe for eighteen months, but I rang him up and he said he'd do the job for me. Nick Sinnott said he'd do the same. So with these important preliminaries over, McCloy and I walked down the street and I surrendered myself quietly at Newbury Police Station.

After a flurry of telephone calls and a heap of paperwork, the police escorted me to their headquarters in Cheltenham and detained me for forty-eight hours. I appeared in a special court on Wednesday morning, 24 May, and was released on £700 bail, which Terry stood for me. The magistrates also instructed that I should sign myself in at Tewkesbury Police Station at six o'clock every other evening. With great discomfort, I kept this up until September 22, when I faced the judge at Gloucester Crown Court.

On the Wednesday I was bailed I moved in with Terry Biddlecombe at Tirley. I agreed to work for my keep, and he gave me chores like breaking horses, riding out, painting boxes and gates, creosoting fences and mowing the lawns.

During that time at Terry's my gambling habits escalated out of all proportion again. I was penniless, but friends in Ireland kept dragging me out of the mire by sending me money orders and loose cash, and I kept squandering the lot on horses and dogs. I was a betting-office lunatic.

Jim Delaney was marvellous. He never failed to send me £20 or even £50 every week.

It was wonderful of Terry to go bail for me and to provide a roof over my head, and he came under severe criticism for having so much to do with me. Maybe those critics were right: I don't know, though I certainly didn't have a good word to say for myself.

# 19
# Working with Pigs

LIFE AT BIDDLECOMBE'S WAS LIVELY, TO SAY THE LEAST. SINCE I had last seen him, he and Bridget had part and Terry was exploiting his freedom to the full as a swashbuckling bachelor again. There were plenty of parties and plenty of booze. It was all wine, women and song. But I didn't participate. I never became involved with the women or the wine.

I met many of Terry's friends when they called, but there were a lot I didn't wish to see. I was too ashamed to face them. So I stayed in my room, and hid from them.

One Sunday night I went with Terry to the home of his friend Doug Wellan, who later complained that £20 had been stolen from his lounge, and blamed me. The police were called and I found myself in a lot more trouble. To this day I swear I did not steal it.

When I finished work at lunchtime with Terry I would thumb a lift from Tirley to Tewkesbury and go straight into the Ladbrokes betting-office. Again, I did some disgraceful things while betting there.

A girlfriend of Terry's would lend me her Mini to drive to Tewkesbury to sign in at the police station and she usually left her purse in the car alongside the gear-lever. It always had £10 to £15 in it, and I couldn't resist taking the money and racing into Ladbrokes and gambling it all away.

Obviously I couldn't return to Terry's without putting the money back, so I had to rush around and find someone to tap. The fears, the lies and the panics were terrible.

As time went on I became more and more agitated while waiting for the Crown Court hearing to come along, and I started taking the 50p pieces Terry was saving in a jar. Sometimes I took a fiver's worth, sometimes a tenner's worth. Naturally, I always stole the money to gamble, and if I won I would change the cash into 50p pieces and I put them back as though nothing had happened.

This went on until I'd spent the lot. After a short time Terry noticed they had all gone, and on the very morning I was keyed up to enter the Crown Court he confronted me about taking the money. You could have knocked me down with a mallet. Typically, I denied having anything to do with it.

So on the morning of the most important court case in my life I had been caught pinching 50p pieces from the very man who had gone bail for me. It was an abysmal act, and I was disgusted with myself.

By some curious coincidence, a fortnight before the hearing professional jockey Donal Nolan, who served his time with my father, called to see me at Biddlecombe's house and invited me to visit his brothers in South Wales. While with them they became excited about a Cardiff solicitor called Layton Lougher. They were confident he would get me off. So I took their advice, dropped Matthew McCloy and engaged him instead.

I was on legal aid, and although I went into the witness-box I wasn't asked to speak a word.

The probation officer provided an excellent report, and Des Nolan backed it up with a superb character reference.

Terry Biddlecombe was asked to provide a character reference, but he refused because I had taken his 50p pieces, and I suppose I couldn't blame him.

During the weeks leading up to the case I had prepared myself for a stiff sentence. At least three years in an open prison. So imagine my joy when the judge leaned forward and announced an eighteen-month suspended sentence, and virtually allowed me to walk from the court Scot-free.

At first I didn't believe I deserved such luck. Then, after thinking for a while, I realized the judge was a compassionate man. He knew I had suffered enough mental torture and human embarrassment to last me a lifetime. I felt humble, and lucky, and totally indebted to him.

When I moved from Terry Biddlecombe's, I left a few personal belongings behind so I rang him up and asked him if I could call to collect them.

He was very crude and abrupt. He told me: 'Yes, your stuff will be left outside the door. Collect it, and fuck off! I never want to see you again.'

I was very upset by the way he spoke to me. I had covered up for Terry on many occasions, and this was his way of saying 'thanks'. There are a lot of things I know about Terry, but I've always kept my lips sealed. All the same, I was sorry our association had to end like that.

Following the court case I stayed for a few days with friends in Birmingham, and I went for a meal with Cheshire trainer Reg Hollinshead, who generously handed me some money to pay my fare back to Ireland.

I arrived in Dublin on 29 September and met trainer Dan Sherwin, who promised me a job. But Dan was a suspicious fellow and for some strange reason was afraid of me, and the job never materialized.

Most of all, I didn't want to start dossing around Dublin again. So I looked for work with Homer Scott, Mick O'Toole and a few other trainers. They all turned me down.

The message was loud and clear. I wasn't wanted in racing any more. My name was rotten.

I tried hard, but found it impossible to live a decent, normal life and, true to form, I ended up on the streets of Dublin, gambling, betting and bumming around like a tramp. I still had an unquenchable craving to bet – if only I could lay my hands on the money. Then a friend asked me to put £170 in the bank for her. It presented a terrible temptation. I just couldn't walk past the betting-office without going in. I used her money, and lost £50 in cash.

Still not satisfied, I went off to the dogs and quickly lost the remaining £120.

And that was my lot!

I was sick. Physically and mentally. I finally, and categorically, realized I had an incurable gambling illness, and that it was almost as bad as my drinking.

Somehow I had to be brave enough to return to my friend and tell her I had gambled every penny of her £170. I accepted once and for all there was only one hope for me – Gamblers Anonymous.

I had to join them. I had to take it seriously. Just as I had taken Alcoholics Anonymous seriously. If one could work, so could the other.

Inside a week I was attending a GA meeting one night and an AA meeting on another. I was on the brink of suicide. Life had lost all purpose. I had no job, and no other regular source of income. I just sponged and begged wherever I could. Then right out of the blue, Gay 'Rocky' McKenna, Dublin's most popular greyhound trainer, pulled me out of the pit. He gave me a job at his kennels as a labourer for £25 a week, and I began on 1 November 1978.

I spent £15 on food and £10 on cigarettes. My nerves were in tatters. It was my job to chop the meat for the dogs, fill their bowls and clean the muck from their boxes. Gay also kept pigs, and I fed them, too.

For someone who should have been basking at the peak of his profession it was unmercifully degrading. I often thought, 'If only Fulke Walwyn could see me now ...'

But despite the filth and the smells, I was grateful to Gay. At least he gave me hope and encouragement, and a genuine chance to earn my keep.

I was still terrified of being tempted to bet, and told Gay I didn't want to know when his dogs were expected to win. And I never wanted to go racing.

For the first two weeks it was agony. I felt like signing myself into the nearest lunatic asylum. Suicide was constantly on my mind. What a simple way out, I kept telling myself.

But again I was a coward. I couldn't raise enough courage to go through with it. I thought of flinging myself from a building or lying under a train. Most of the time it was sheer self-pity and remorse; I thought the world owed me a living, and I was wrong. It was I who had to change, to win back the confidence of people, and convince them that I had a wealth of good inside me longing to get out.

After two weeks with Gay, he asked me if I'd like a little job in South Wales, and I was introduced to a man in the Burlington Hotel in Dublin who asked me to buy a horse for him and three other men. They each wanted a twenty-five per cent share.

They were lucky. I knew of a young, unraced five-year-old called Mount Shasta which Liam had for sale. So on 14 November I flew over to Cardiff and met John Williams and his friend Alan Davies. I was frank with them, and told them practically everything about my past.

They agreed to buy the horse, and I returned to Ireland and clinched the deal with Liam for a substantial sum of money. As part of the arrangement, Williams and his associates asked me to return with Mount Shasta and train it in secret in the Vale of Glamorgan to prepare it for a coup. A killing of £200,000 was contemplated.

I started working for Williams and his partners on 1 December. Though Williams had been granted a permit by the Jockey Club, he had no real experience of training a racehorse, and relinquished his licence at the end of the season, shortly after I left. He was a fruit and veg. merchant by trade. Williams knew his onions, all right, but that was about all! His associates in the horse were Alan Davies, another fruit merchant, and bookmaker Peter Murphy. What all three knew about racing could have been written on the back of a betting-slip.

Life with the Williams family was quite strange, no disrespect to John, his wife Emma, or son Jonathan.

I told them my main priority was having transport to GA and AA meetings. I went to GA meetings every Tuesday, and I met a friend called Don who gave me great hope that I could get on my feet again without resorting to gambling.

But I still wasn't free of problems. On 22 February 1978 I appeared in front of the Jockey Club's disciplinary committee under rule 201 (vi). They gathered at Portman Square to decide whether my Crown Court case was in any way related to the racing industry. In other words, had I brought the sport into disrepute?

I braced myself for a ten-year disqualification, but the disciplinary panel of Brook Holliday, Julian Berry and Dick Hollingsworth showed tremendous clemency and banned me for only three years. They clearly took into account my sincere attempts to bury the past and lead a new and trouble-free life. They were wonderfully understanding and underlined their wish to help me by giving permission, under Rule 205(v), to continue to work for Williams and not to interfere with my livelihood.

The Williamses were something I had never experienced before and don't expect to encounter again. One day in March, Mrs Williams practically ordered me to leave the house because she disliked the smell of horses, although her husband was supposed to be a trainer.

I was always spotlessly clean and didn't dare wear working clothes indoors. She had nothing to complain of. She had an extra-sensitive nose, and it got me ejected.

So the wanderer moved on. I joined Peter and Joan Murphy at their home in Barry. Their training set-up was a shambles. It took me four months to get the place organized, and I became friendly with Cowbridge trainer Bryn Palling who helped me enormously.

The only good thing about the job was the pay. I earned £50 a week, and was able to save a few pounds; I could afford to nip across to Ireland to see my girlfriend every four weeks.

But there was a lot of responsibility on me. I was under instructions to line the horse up for a massive 'touch'.

A large part of my pay was 'spent' before I received it. I had rung Terry Biddlecombe to apologize for taking the 50p pieces and for running up a £400 telephone bill. I promised to pay him back at £10 a week, and I never missed a date. I also sent £20 a month to all the banks I defrauded. And I virtually wiped out the £500 restitution fine from the court. At long last, a semblance of sanity seemed to be seeping into my life.

I ran Mount Shasta at Devon & Exeter on 23 March and John Jenkins rode him. There were fifteen runners, and Mount Shasta finished tailed off, last but one. Peter Murphy was furious and accused me of 'stitching him up with a bad horse'; he asked me to leave his home and find new accommodation.

So I packed my bags again. Oh, hell, I thought, all my life is being spent living out of a suitcase. Please God, one day I shall have a place of my own and be able to settle down like a normal human being.

I moved in with Alan Davies, his family, and mother-in-law. I continued to attend GA and AA meetings and became friendly with a chap called Peter at AA. He gave me new hope and put a bright new outlook on life when I became depressed after Williams and his partners had kept me short of money.

All the time I was building Mount Shasta up for the big day. I ran him at Newton Abbot, where he finished tenth of seventeen; at Towcester, ninth of seventeen; and at Bangor, tenth of fifteen.

I worked fourteen hours every day, carefully bringing the horse to its peak. I fed him, rode him at exercise, completed the entries, drove him to the racecourse and always took care not to break the rules by setting foot inside the gates.

I chose the Crediton Opportunity Selling Handicap Hurdle at Devon on Bank Holiday Monday, 28 May, as jackpot day. It was one of the most ambitious coups ever attempted.

Apart from Mount Shasta's first run he was always ridden by Tim Forster's capable apprentice Ken Dorsett, and I saw no reason for a change.

The day began with a large team of money-handlers streaming out of South Wales in a fleet of cars bound mainly for the Midlands, where many substantial bets were eventually struck. Coventry, Birmingham and Leicester were singled out as the principal targets. Other cars went to London, Liverpool, Manchester and Swansea.

Though Mount Shasta had always raced as a 33–1 or 50–1 chance he opened up as short as 4–1, which left me in no doubt that a big dog had barked. Someone close to the plot couldn't keep his mouth shut.

This was a blatant leak and, knowing the people I was dealing with, I can't say I was unduly surprised. Discretion is not a word they've come to know.

By the start of the race, an avalanche of late cash had cut Mount Shasta to a ridiculous even-money chance, and the partners started panicking. Someone called out to the jockey, Ken Dorsett, that he should tell the starter the horse had gone lame, and that he ought to be pulled out. But Dorsett had more sense, and took no notice.

The partners were furious the horse was starting at such a bad price, but they had only themselves to blame.

Being banned from the course, I was forced to sit in my borrowed Rover banger on the forecourt of a nearby garage, crossing my fingers while the race was in progress.

The runners set off in a thick mist and torrential rain, and all went well for Mount Shasta until he approached the fourth flight at the farthest point of the track. There, quite incredibly, and without warning, the horse's brand-new bridle suddenly snapped, and Mount Shasta careered off the course and out of the race.

As expected, the stewards couldn't understand why a horse should shoot off the course in such queer circumstances, particularly one that had been backed so heavily. They weren't satisfied and called for an inquiry.

They sent for Williams and Dorsett and asked them to explain the incident. Both said that a bridle pin had snapped and the horse had gone out of control. It was like trying to steer a car after a wheel's dropped off. The stewards could have accepted this explanation but decided, instead, to record it. This meant if further evidence came to light the case was still open, and more and bigger inquiries could be started.

In fact, a full investigation was launched next day by the Jockey Club's detective branch, Racecourse Security Services. They were interested in the amount of money staked on the horse, and who placed it.

Worse still for Williams, he not only lost his money, he lost his horse as well! Mount Shasta was claimed at the auction and moved on to trainer David Wintle at Gloucester.

I thought the horse was a certainty. Like putting Arkle in a seller. I had become very attached to the horse but accepted that it was in the hands of the good Lord that the bridle should break. And it genuinely did break! There was no villainy, no corruption. Williams and his partners lost their money, and they squealed.

Next day, I told *The Sporting Life*, 'I didn't have a shilling on the horse. It was my job to train it, and to place it. And it was never blatantly stopped. I've finished in the yard, and never want anything to do with those people again. It's the first time in my career that a bridle has snapped with me. The horse was pulling hard, and that can be the only logical explanation.'

I left Cardiff on 1 June to work as a painter in London. I believed, and hoped, it was the last I'd ever see or hear of Williams. But I was wrong. Just three weeks later I heard that he had apparently been robbed overnight, while he slept, and was blaming me for it.

The police in Dublin hunted for me, and the police in London hunted for me. Once I heard what was happening I telephoned them, explained my movements and assured them that I had never taken anything belonging to Messrs Williams, Davies or Murphy. The police were satisfied and I heard no more about the so-called robbery.

At this point I was thinking seriously of leaving the country and joining a kibbutz in Israel for a year. I thought learning how to survive would do me a great deal of good.

# 20
# Behind Bars

I HAD BEEN IN TOUCH WITH FRIENDS IN THE NORTH OF ENGLAND, and after a few weeks of living just outside London I decided to go and live up there. Arrangements were made for me to stay in a one-room flat on the seamier side of Newcastle, and my friends bought me a small car and fitted it up with a radio and a meter so that I could run it as a taxi. The future looked quite secure. Little did I realize, when I boarded the 8.45 pm London to Newcastle express from King's Cross on 21 October 1979, that I was setting off on the most horrific journey of my life. Fate has never dealt me a good hand of aces, and this was to be no exception.

This particular road to disaster began on 23 October when I left Newcastle with three other men to go to the Edinburgh races. I was with a bookmaker, his clerk, and a man they employed to dart round the ring to hedge bets with other layers. Being a disqualified person, I wasn't allowed to enter the racecourse, so, when they left me in the car-park, I suggested filling up the old banger with petrol in order to make a quick get-away after the meeting.

I had every intention of driving to the nearest garage, topping up and returning to the car-park to read a book about life in Saudi, another place that appealed to me as a place to live. But I couldn't relax, and began to rummage through the glove compartment of the car. Within seconds I had laid my hands on a large polythene bag. When I opened it I found a huge wad of five-pound notes.

I counted them quickly, and the whole lot came to £2,000 exactly. Immediately I thought of a betting office, and how I could make some pocket-money for myself. I had no intention of stealing it in a literal sense. I really believed I could borrow it for an hour, find a few winners, make a profit and put the money back.

So I walked into Musselburgh and found a Ladbrokes shop.

I started with £100 each way on Little Loch Broom, the mount of John Reid in the 3.30 race at Edinburgh. It showed on the board at 9–2 joint favourite, but ran atrociously and finished ninth, with only three behind it. Without flinching, I followed up with another £100 each-way on Touch Pirate in the 3.45 at Leicester, but again it disappointed and finished fourth at 4–1.

In just fifteen minutes, I was £400 down, and had only half an hour or so before the lads returned from the racecourse. With all this pressure on me, I began to flap. I couldn't think straight, And I put £600 to win on Joe Mercer's mount Welsh Sonata in the 4 pm at Edinburgh. There were only five runners, and it started 11–8 second favourite. I was certain I could recover the £400 and be back in the car when they arrived. I was wrong. Welsh Sonata finished second, beaten by three-quarters of a length by the odds-on favourite.

I was desperate. I was £1,000 down and I had barely twenty-five minutes to get it all back. There was only one way left. I had to risk the lot. Every penny of the remaining £1,000.

Shaking all over, I put the cash on the counter and wrote out Why Not. The irony of the horse's name didn't strike me at the time. It was marked up on the board as the 5–4 favourite, and it boasted excellent form.

A full commentary on the race came over the blower, and I leaned against a wall too scared to let it sink in. At the two-furlong pole, Why Not was still in front. For a moment or two, I really thought my prayers were answered. I even moved to the counter to be first in the queue. Then, suddenly, there was a new leader. Renovate had taken over. My horse was back in third, and still fading. I couldn't believe it. I was frantic. I knew I couldn't go back to the boys and confess the lot.

I had a quarter of an hour to dream up a story, and it had to be good! They were a tough bunch.

I ran back to the car and I drove it into the middle of Musselburgh. To make sure it wasn't found easily, I parked it among thirty others at the back of a textile factory. I left the key in the ignition, the doors unlocked, and dashed away to the little police room on the Edinburgh racecourse, and reported the car as stolen. I was gasping. Breathless!

The officer said he was sorry, ticked me off for being so careless, and flashed a message to his mobile unit to look out for it.

At this point, the lads came back and the officer stood at my side while I shot them the same cock-and-bull story. Then we all trooped off to the main police station and I made a statement.

Until then nothing had been said about the money, but as soon as the lads arrived at the station, it was the first thing they mentioned.

Again I put on the Brando act and swore that I knew nothing of the cash. I told the officer I had travelled up in the back seat of the car reading *The Sporting Life*. I insisted that all this talk of £2,000 was new to me, and the police seemed convinced.

After signing the statement, all four of us boarded an evening train from Edinburgh to Newcastle. We cracked a lot of jokes, and one lad even gave me £10 to buy food.

By next morning, the tension was tearing me apart, so I came up with another load of bullshit. I told the lads I had to pay an urgent visit to a business contact in Scotland, and I packed three bags and virtually sprinted to the railway station.

With time rushing by, I knew the police would be close to finding the car and that a lot of awkward questions would be coming my way. The guns were being loaded, and I didn't want to be in the firing-line.

I couldn't eat or sleep, and my stomach did somersaults. And all because I was a brainless gambler. An addict. Someone who never knew when to stop.

By Thursday, the Musselburgh police had found the car and, even worse, had collected my betting-slips from Ladbrokes. They wanted to interview me.

When I heard this, I knew I was certain for a stretch if they found me. I was already on an eighteen-month suspended sentence for a similar offence.

My first thoughts were to flee to Ireland as I did before, or to do away with myself. To swallow all my pills in one gulp, and to wash them down with a bottle of vodka. I had £4 left in my pocket, and I went into an off-licence and I bought the booze.

With the bottle in my hand, I entered a telephone kiosk and rang Gamblers Anonymous. A chatty, happy woman answered, and I poured out my problems. I told her I was about to sink the pills and the bottle of vodka.

We chatted on for hours. I was drained and in tears. I was

convinced this was the end. There was no turning back. I had come to the edge of the cliff.

But my friend kept clinging to me. She wouldn't let me go. She urged me to be brave. Implored me to go back to the police and give myself up. She insisted that I faced the music like a man. A totally new experience for me, who had always found it simpler to slip away and hide from truth and reality.

This time I had little option. I either swallowed the pills or surrendered as she suggested. I was probably too much of a coward to take my own life, anyway.

So at 9.30 am on Friday, 26 October, I walked into Musselburgh Police Station and made a full confession. I was charged within minutes and next morning I faced a stern, gruff sheriff in a special court at Haddington in East Lothian.

John Brown, a senior psychologist at Glasgow University, and a tireless worker for Gamblers Anonymous, understood my predicament and kindly came to court to explain my reasons for taking the money. He wanted to tell the sheriff that I was mentally sick, and to recommend that I should be sent to a remedial centre in Kent that specializes in the treatment of compulsive gamblers. But the sheriff refused to let John Brown or anyone else speak on my behalf. Instead, he sentenced me to three months in prison, and brushed me aside like a disobedient puppy.

Three months behind bars were bad enough, but my mind was obsessed with the fear of the eighteen-month suspended sentence being activated. It haunted me – although it was never mentioned in court.

To calm myself, I preferred to think that certain offences committed under English law might not be taken into account in Scotland. A detective at Musselburgh had also told me not to worry about it, and I trusted him. But the fear still continued to nag me.

My first taste of the crude life in Her Majesty's care came in a freezing cell at Saughton, the vast Edinburgh gaol for hardened and long-term criminals, where I was allotted a grimy bed-sit with bare walls, stone floor and a rock-hard bunk. Not a patch on the Golden Valley Hotel in Cheltenham that had been my home for many months!

Being locked up alongside child-killers, rapists and monsters of all sorts was agonizing enough, but when the 'screws' took away my pills it was like sticking me in the electric chair. I had lived on pills for ten years. Red ones, green ones, yellow ones, big ones and small ones, they were my food and my survival kit. Now they were confiscated. The withdrawal symptoms were excruciating. I shook violently. Then they took away my cigarettes. I was drugless. Death seemed the only logical answer. I felt rotten, and I lost a stone in a week.

If punishment is supposed to fit the crime, then this was one occasion when justice had more than its share.

By some miracle, I survived, and with a month's remission to raise my spirits, I looked forward to being released on 27 December, my debt to society paid off and the slate wiped clean.

But I was only kidding myself. To my horror, with just a week or so left to my release, I heard for the first time that someone at Gloucester Court was agitating for my scalp. He was insisting that I stood trial over the suspended sentence. I felt badly let down. Both by the police and the sheriff. If I had to face the judge, then why wasn't I told at the outset?

So, just as I was scrambling to my feet, I had to take another blow, and I was back on the floor again.

My solicitor wrote to say that I would have to appear at Gloucester on 22 December, and that I would be moved to a prison closer to the court.

It was the start of ridiculous expedition. I went everywhere. At first, from Edinburgh to the maximum security gaol at Durham, where they lock up the killers. My cell stank. Urine and other filth stained the floor and smeared the walls. I was alone – except for the muck, the mice and the cockroaches!

Thank God, they kept me only four days. Then on to Pentonville, and finally Gloucester. Four gaols in a fortnight! They also took me into Leeds, Wetherby, Leicester, Northallerton and Wakefield, as we picked up and dropped off other prisoners.

My first appearance in front of Judge Bulger at Gloucester was adjourned until 18 January 1980 for further reports. Then, satisfied that he had enough evidence to consider my case, he activated the full eighteen months and I was led back across the road to my cell behind the high, red-bricked walls.

Because my offence was entirely non-violent, my solicitor assured me that I would be moved to an open prison where the discipline would be less severe, and the inmates far less dangerous.

After a month, I was transferred to Leyhill, two miles fom Wotton-under-Edge, where three hundred inmates outnumbered seventeen prison officers! It was a holiday camp compared with Gloucester. Every prisoner was given at least one permanent, daily job. To beat the boredom, I volunteered for two. I cleaned the church and fed the pigs. There were usually 180 to fatten up, and a truck-load of them went to market every Tuesday.

The general facilities were excellent, like a university. We had a well-stocked library, two colour television sets, a bird club, bee club, cinema, rugby, soccer and cricket pitches, and some beautiful tennis courts. I was also allowed a cassette radio, a daily newspaper, magazines, and a visitor every fortnight.

To keep fit, I joined the rugby team and enjoyed the temporary freedom of going outside to play matches against village sides. I started on the left wing but as I rarely received the ball, I switched to the pack to get more of the action.

To use the time purposefully, and to prepare for my release, I took a year's correspondence course in business management, and spent every evening studying accountancy, retailing and banking.

Because I understood the terrible temptations of betting, and how it was entirely responsible for my being 'inside', I decided to start a branch of Gamblers Anonymous to help other inmates who were badly affected by the same terrible disease.

The public at large is generally unaware that compulsive gambling is a serious illness, progressive by nature and virtually incurable, though it can be arrested. The first bet, no matter how small, is like the first drink to an alcoholic. I was a greedy gambler, never satisfied, always chasing the jackpot and always ending up with disastrous results. I was so successful as a jockey I should never have needed to bet, but it fascinated me. Casinos, racehorses, greyhounds, poker games, betting-offices, they all excited me. Inevitably I started to lose, and the more I lost the harder I tried to recover my losses and the deeper I plunged into debt. Slowly and insidiously it began to dominate my life. All I thought of was money and where to bet.

When I joined Gamblers Anonymous I was totally lacking in moral fibre; my gambling had literally ruined me. GA has a simple programme. It has proved successful and given hope to thousands upon thousands of people all over the world. GA gave me confidence. For the first time I heard of people who had committed acts far worse than mine, yet, by staying away from one bet a day at a time, their lives had become sane and manageable. They recovered their self-respect. They emerged from their dream-worlds and accepted that the big day never comes. They could face reality.

For the past two years I have conscientiously applied myself to the programme and am thrilled to say it's working for me. When I look back on my gambling habits, I can see how insane I was. Although I knew jockeys shouldn't bet, I was so badly hooked it never bothered me. However, there is one thing I've learned from gambling which I can pass on to anyone tempted to bet heavily: I have been in racing for twenty-five years and witnessed gambling and gamblers from every imaginable angle, and can assure you that you *cannot win*! My last gamble at Musselburgh proved this categorically and irrefutably.

As for drinking, it's well over four years since I last drank alcohol. When you recall how I boozed before I think I have every right to consider my abstinence as a huge personal achievement. Conquering drink was like climbing Everest or swimming the Channel. And, like all the best climbers and swimmers, I needed help and encouragement and to be part of a team. Thank God I found Alcoholics Anonymous, a world-wide spiritual organization conceived in America in 1935.

AA was my only hope, the only barrier between life and doom. It must be remembered that alcoholism is a disease sandwiched between cancer and coronary thrombosis as the second most lethal destroyer in the world. Although I believe I may still have another drink in me, I know I don't have another recovery – so it's imperative that I follow the AA programme and read their 'bible'. A small black book entitled *Twenty-Four Hours a Day*, the AA 'bible' is a constant and invigorating source of comfort. It remains with me wherever I go. It helps the alcoholic live one day at a time, with lots of time for private prayer and meditation. It's vital to cling to the simple precepts – keep it simple; first things first; there but for the grace of God; easy does it; one day at a time....

Thanks to AA my life has changed and is still changing. I'm living a sober, steady life that I never knew existed. I'm learning how to discipline myself and build up my character. Problems are of course inevitable but I am learning to meet them rationally, fortified by reciting the AA commandments every morning of every day. The material wealth that dazzled me in my drinking days no longer rules my thoughts. Money was a god to me. My priorities were wrong, and I was too pig-headed to accept advice.

You might wonder whether I'm ever tempted to drink again. Of course I am. But I'm stronger now and able to resist, and if I really feel in danger of cracking up I can dial any number of friends in AA who will listen to my plight and talk some sense into me.

AA has become a positive way of life for me. I attend as many meetings as I can, often two a week, and occasionally three. No matter where you are in the world – Egypt, Alaska, Nigeria – there will always be an AA meeting going on close by.

In writing this book, there are hundreds of people I would like to thank profusely for all their kindnesses – Brian Roxbury and Angus McKechnie in particular. Sadly there isn't space to publish a list that would extend to a dozen pages or more, but one day I hope to have the health and opportunity to meet them all personally and thank them from the bottom of my heart.

Every day, from the time I open my eyelids to the time I go to sleep, there is one special prayer that gives me the strength and confidence to face the world and the people in it. I recite it repeatedly, and it gives me much hope:

God grant me the serenity to accept the things I cannot change; the courage to change the things I can; and the wisdom to know the difference.

# Barry Brogan: A Statistical Breakdown

|  | Mounts | Winners | Seconds | Thirds |
|---|---|---|---|---|
| 1962 | 2 | – | – | – |
| 1963 | 36 | 6 | – | – |
| 1964 | 60 | 10 | 4 | 8 |
| 1965–6 | 106 | 15 | 9 | 6 |
| 1966–7 (first season in England) | 153 | 28 | – | – |
| 1967–8 | 290 | 57 | 41 | 29 |
| 1968–9 (Northern champion) | 270 | 46 | 31 | 27 |
| 1969–70 | 241 | 36 | 29 | 37 |
| 1970–71 (Northern champion) | 444 | 67 | 60 | 58 |
| 1971–2* | 500 | 71 | 68 | 58 |
| 1972–3 | 243 | 48 | 38 | 37 |
| 1973–4 | 54 | 3 | 3 | 6 |
| 1974–5 | 121 | 10 | 13 | 12 |
| 1975–6 | 182 | 16 | 22 | 15 |
| 1976–7 | 68 | 3 | 2 | 6 |

* Five winners Norway, two winners Sweden.

*Big races won*: King George VI Chase, Kempton; Scottish Grand National, Ayr; Benson & Hedges Handicap Chase, Sandown; TWW Champion Novices Chase, Chepstow (twice); Black & White Gold Cup, Ascot; George Duller Handicap Hurdle, Cheltenham; Whitbread Trial, Ascot; Cotswold Cup, Cheltenham.

*Highlights of career*: Riding five winners from five rides, Wolverhampton; Second on Moidore's Token in 1968 Grand National; Northern champion 1968–9, 1970–71.

*Best Horses Ridden*: The Dikler, Even Keel, Billy Bow, Drumikill, Flyingbolt.

*Best Season*: 71 winners in 1971–2.